# The Engaged Business School

# The Engaged Business School

BY

**ANTHONY STURGESS**

*Liverpool Business School, UK*

United Kingdom – North America – Japan – India – Malaysia – China

Emerald Publishing Limited
Howard House, Wagon Lane, Bingley BD16 1WA, UK

First edition 2023

**Reprints and permissions service**
Contact: permissions@emeraldinsight.com

**British Library Cataloguing in Publication Data**
A catalogue record for this book is available from the British Library

ISBN: 978-1-80382-942-5 (Print)
ISBN: 978-1-80382-941-8 (Online)
ISBN: 978-1-80382-943-2 (Epub)

Printed and bound by CPI Group (UK) Ltd, Croydon, CR0 4YY

INVESTOR IN PEOPLE

# Table of Contents

# List of Tables and Figures

# Preface

## Overview of the Engaged Business School: Fulfiling Potential or Thwarted Ambition?

The Engaged Business School is a road map to unlocking the potential between business and business schools at a time when it really matters: responding to a global, economic and social recovery. It is a call for academics and businesses to come together and realise the potential that frustratingly is so often unfulfilled.

This call to act has at its core a simple question, which is where the first chapter begins. It would seem to be self-evident that businesses and business schools should be natural partners, the one benefiting from its engagement with the other. Yet frequently this is not evident in practice. This prompts the questions: Why does something that seems to intuitively make sense end up being so hard to do?

Chapter 1 sets out the rationale and case for the engaged business school from the perspectives of both business and business school. The intent is first to make the argument for why engagement matters, and then in subsequent chapters explore how this might be realised. Business and business school needs, national policy and global crises all combine to make a compelling case for engagement, not only reinforcing that it matters, but that it matters now: there is an urgency to the call.

The road map introduces a new model for the engaged business school supported by a framework and process. The flow of the discussion in the book firstly explores the framework, model and process, setting out what is meant by the Engaged Business School. However, there are long-standing and deep-rooted tensions inherent in the relationships between business and business schools. Understandably, they need to be addressed before progressing to explain the engagement model in detail. Then the focus turns towards action and considers what the engaged business school could look like in practice and explores ways in which it could respond and contribute to recovery from crisis.

## The Model, Framework and Process of Engagement

The book develops the idea of an engaged business school using three descriptive tools: a framework, a model and a process. A framework surfaces different levels and varying depths of engagement and clarifies what is meant by effective engagement. It provides a structure for businesses and business schools to better understand what effective engagement means and how it is defined. Then the model shows how factors for successful engagement are interconnected in order to bring engagement to life. Finally, the process identifies the steps and stages which will need to be considered to translate the model and framework into action.

Engagement is an often used term in higher education with many different interpretations, and as a result is not well understood. The intent of the framework is to provide a common language and structure to build a shared understanding between business and business schools. It helps them to determine the level, depth and degree of engagement possible. The framework reflects four ways in which engagement can be understood. Firstly, engagement as activity is probably the most understood, since activities are tangible. Yet activities can be disconnected and transactional in nature, and of themselves provide a limited view of engagement. Secondly, engagement as relationship is less understood but pervasive for effective engagement. Relationships provide a context for business need to be better understood and to connect activity to that need. Thirdly, engagement as vocation gives energy and motivation to the activities and relationship. Fourthly, engagement as mission stresses the significance and meaning of the activities and relationships, giving direction and focus to the energy of vocation. Not all engagements are created equal, and many do not work very well. The framework provides a way to assess the nature of engagement, helping businesses and business schools to makes sense of their relationship and put in place building blocks towards an effective engagement.

However, there are long-standing tensions associated with business schools and their engagement with business. These tensions provide a difficult context to navigate and need to be explored before a model of engagement can be proposed. Two areas dominate. Firstly the relevance versus rigour debates and secondly, the contrasting views about the legitimacy and identity of business schools. Not surprisingly, addressing these tensions is central to understanding how business schools engage with business. Given that these tensions tend to be deep-rooted, an approach is advocated to re-frame the tensions and to seek different thinking and fresh perspectives. This approach of re-framing tensions then emerges as an important means to address tensions more generally in the discussion of an engaged business school. Consequently, understanding how tensions can be analysed is a necessary step before progressing to explore the model of engagement.

Tensions highlight important areas to consider within the engagement model. The model weaves the factors of successful engagement together. It brings engagement to life capturing the connections between important themes and concepts. The model attempts to represent how the inter-relationship of the themes that reinforce effective engagement are reflected in a dynamic rather than a static model. That said it is acknowledged that all models are simplifications and in that sense, as the British statistician George Box famously said 'all models are wrong' (Box, 1976). But they can be what Box went on to describe as useful approximations of the real world. The hope is that the model simplifies to aid clarity, without erring towards being simplistic. To that end the model, in contrast to static one-dimensional linear approaches, recognises the more nuanced inter-connections which underpin engagement and emphasises circular, cyclical and iterative relationships crucial to the development of an effective relationship. The model helps business and business school alike to chart a path towards effective engagement.

The third tool is a process indicating the steps and stages which will need to be considered for businesses and business schools to engage. Engaging in a single project or intervention is often hard enough to do well. The process indicates the steps that are needed for a single engagement, but whilst these steps are necessary they are not sufficient for an on-going engagement. The hallmark of effective engagement should be a long-term mutually beneficial relationship, and that needs commitment. The engagement process crucially highlights the steps and stages that need to be considered to build for the longer term.

Having explored the three practical tools for engagement the focus moves from ideas into action to illustrate the engaged business school in practice. The engagement framework is used to demonstrate three valuable applications. Firstly, the framework is used to develop a mission for an engaged business school. Secondly, it is used to better understand stakeholders and their differing expectations. Thirdly, it is used to map activity and connections in the business school providing a rich picture of engagement across the four levels of the framework.

The discussion then continues to consider how engaged business schools might differentiate themselves. To do this the engaged business school is considered from the different perspectives of a business, a manager, a student, an academic and their host university, to think about how each group can make the most of their connection. Finally, the argument progresses to explore how business schools can seek to play an important role in supporting recovery from crisis. Two broad strategies are proposed, the first is to use grand challenges to shift the focus towards areas of significance and the second utilises the concept of tensions to identify opportunities for different thinking. Together they show how the engaged business school can, through significance and different thinking, achieve impact.

The conclusion ends with a challenge to answer the call made in the opening chapter. Despite compelling arguments for change from many different perspectives over a prolonged period of time, little impact has been made. This chapter seeks to understand why change seems to be so difficult. Yet there is a real opportunity with the two worlds of business and academia having distinctive things to offer each other. So the potential for change is emphasised by two final challenges which provocatively question our willingness and whether we care enough to make it happen.

It would be remiss for a monograph not to end with an explanation of the research upon which the book is based. Chapter 10 is therefore a short explanation of the study behind the engagement story. Given the focus of the engaged business school, the discussion highlight three areas. Firstly, to explain how the engagement stories, which feature in the development of the engagement model, themselves emerged in the study. Then secondly, to recognise that the central role tensions play in shaping the discussion, is also reflected in the approach to analysis of the research. Finally, and interestingly a perspective is outlined of researchers being story tellers. In that respect, I hope that I have been faithful in telling the stories of those engaged in business and business school relationships, and that in some part this book helps us all to develop our own stories of engagement.

## A First Approximation

With that in mind, the intent of this book is not to prescribe but to describe. It is hoped that business schools will utilise the ideas to make their own assessment of their engagement and develop strategies which bring together their strengths and aspirations to chart their own way forward. Similarly for businesses, they too can assess their needs and learn how to connect more effectively to maximise the potential of the relationship.

From the discussion so far it may appear that the problems all reside with business schools. Whilst there clearly are problems, this is not to suggest that business schools do not engage with businesses. On the contrary, with all the competing priorities at play, admirable and important work is being done, often more than is formally recognised. Rather, the idea of an engaged business school is an attempt not to prescribe but to 'describe with insights', to use Mintzberg's turn of phrase (Mintzberg, 2004). It is also written in the spirit indicated by futurist Alvin Toffler in the introduction to his seminal book, *Future Shock*. He argued that when considering the future, imagination and insight are more important than precision and certainty. At the same time, he provocatively suggested that in this context theories do not 'need to be "right" to be enormously useful, not as a final word but as a first approximation'. (Toffler, 1970). I have tried to put forward a positive argument for an Engaged Business School in the spirit of description, insight and approximation which I hope will be useful.

The book is written for those who care about the relationship between business and business schools; they have more than a passing interest. It is for managers, academics and students alike, with the hope of bringing business and academia closer together. It is an audience with some involvement, interest, knowledge and indeed experience of the issues. With that in mind, I hope to explore the issues and themes of an engaged business school, asking readers to make their own connections and consider the extent to which the perspectives argued resonate with their own experience. Readers are therefore encouraged to engage in their own sensemaking and to make up their own minds (Elliot, 2005) as they reflect on their experience. This represents an approach which Tsoukas (2009) suggests is particularly relevant for a practitioner audience, those who are involved, knowledgeable and hopefully engaged.

The book is grounded in my experience of the potential and frustration inherent in business to business school relationships, experience which I suspect many from business and academia share. This book captures the lessons from practice, listening to the voices of those directly involved in making the relationship work. Too often I have spoken to businesses, who don't see the need, or aren't able to connect effectively with a business school. Similarly, I have worked in business schools, who have not realised how they could be so much better connected if only they knew how, or were willing to do so, or perhaps would do so if it mattered more?

# Chapter 1

# A Call to Action*

The engaged business school is a call to action, both for business schools and for businesses to engage and reap the mutual benefits from their relationship. At the heart of the call to action is a question: why does something that seems to be so obviously advantageous appear so difficult to do?

The frustration implicit in the question is captured in two interesting conversations with business leaders. Their stories serve to set the scene, but they do more; they provide an indication of where to begin to look for answers to the question. The first story is a provocative challenge; the second is a troubling reality check. Both stories should be wake up calls for business and for business schools, but they also offer hope and opportunity.

## Untapped Strengths and Well-Kept Secrets

An executive once asked me a rhetorical two part question: 'what is a business schools greatest strength?' and secondly, 'what is a business's greatest need?'. There are, of course, many possible answers to the two questions. The view of this senior leader in relation to business school to business relationships was instructive. For this executive, a business school's greatest strength was latest thinking, something the leader provocatively argued was too often not evident in the programmes and courses offered. It was an uncomfortable answer, with more than a ring of truth about it. I was expecting to have to provide a response, when fortunately, the leader turned to answering the second question. What about business? Interestingly, the executives' answer to this question was the same, a business's greatest need was also latest thinking. The executive then argued that managers and leaders in business were too busy 'doing their job' to find out what the latest thinking might be, never mind to apply that to their businesses.

This first story raises concerns about the relevance and quality of what business schools do, but as concerning is what emerged from a conversation with another business leader. The second conversation was with a non-executive director

---

*This book was developed from the thesis submitted to The University of Manchester, Sturgess, M. A. (2016). 'Developing a Theory of Employer and Higher Education Provider Engagement'.

The Engaged Business School, 1–14
Copyright © 2023 Anthony Sturgess
Published under exclusive licence by Emerald Publishing Limited
doi:10.1108/978-1-80382-941-820231002

(NED) of a potential client. The NED made an interesting observation after listening to a presentation of the range of possibilities that the business school could offer. The talk had highlighted the kind of relationship and insight that is possible when a business school works together with a business. Following the presentation, the business leader commented that the business school was a 'well-kept secret'. The NED had been unaware of what the business school could do to support business. The complement, which expressed the pleasant surprise of the NED, betrays a significant concern, that businesses are often unaware of how business schools can help them.

The first story questions not just the relevance of what is taught in business schools but also the extent to which thought leadership and research-informed teaching are shared. However, the story also suggests that there should be a real opportunity for a business school to connect (what should be) a core strength with an important need (and apparent weakness) of business, and there should be a significant benefit for businesses to do this.

The second story suggests a more fundamental issue: that many businesses simply do not know the potential that exists within business schools. Without doubt, business schools are more engaged than they might appear, yet not as engaged as they could or should be, too often appearing as a well-kept secret to businesses. Therefore, surfacing and connecting the strengths of business schools to the business communities they serve begins with making visible what is already there. And it is not just businesses that have this problem. Business schools themselves can often be 'unaware' of some of their connections with business, typically when carried out at an individual level. This, of course, is not a new challenge; many organisations struggle with how knowledge is shared, as a former CEO of Hewlett Packard (HP) lamented, 'If only HP knew what HP knows' (Nonaka & Teece, 2001). As a result, it may be that some of the building blocks for engagement are already there, but are hidden in plain view.

The two stories express concerns, but they also hold out hope that the strengths of a business school can meet the needs of a business, and that this rich potential is something that is worth finding and should be made visible. The two conversations provide a helpful introduction to some of the challenges with engagement highlighting the importance of relevance and visibility or more provocatively the risk of being irrelevant and invisible to business.

Though anecdotal, the stories resonate with a broader evidence base. There are problems with connectivity and visibility, with how knowledge is produced, exchanged and disseminated and with what is taught and how it is taught. There is, of course, a considerable amount of good work that is done by business schools with business. But there is much that can be improved, and that is where this discussion will begin, starting with considering the situation from a business point of view. Businesses find business schools difficult to do business with, they often are not aware of what is available, find them problematic to access and navigate, and relationships hard to establish (Thomas, Lee, Thomas, & Wilson, 2014; Thorpe & Rawlinson, 2013). What is taught too often is not what is needed, more focused on the interest of academics than on the needs of business (Thorpe & Rawlinson, 2013). The way staff teach is also not appropriate for an audience of managers and business people, with academics applying the same approaches they use with students who have no or little practical experience (Mintzberg, 2004). Too few academics have the skill or the inclination to engage in this kind of executive/practitioner teaching (Kewin et al., 2011). Consequently, there are calls for staff who are able to integrate 'intellectual rigour with practice relevance' (Peter, Smith, & Howard, 2018, p. 145). This position was summarised poignantly by Pfeffer and Fong's now well-known conclusion that businesses schools are teaching 'the wrong things in the wrong ways' (Pfeffer & Fong, 2002, p. 80).

Not only are there issues with teaching but the notion of integrating rigour with practice applies just as persuasively to research as it does to teaching. Here too there has been a long-standing debate, with concerns about the relevance and helpfulness to practice of the research that business schools can provide to businesses. Narratives about gaps, the need to bridge between two sides or issues of translation all point towards tensions about relevance, helpfulness and visibility. The issues with research were helpfully characterised by Shapiro, Kirkman and Courtney (2007) as two kinds of translation problems. The first is a knowledge transfer problem, which demands better presentation of research in terms that practitioners understand with, for example, frameworks and tools that managers can use. The second is a knowledge production problem and is associated with researchers not collaborating with business to identify the relevant areas/topics within which to conduct research. The former problem is described as 'lost in translation', whereas the latter is seen as a gap due to lack of relevance and therefore 'lost before translation' (Shapiro et al., 2007).

The issues though are not all with business schools. Karl Weick suggests that the issue, rather than being on the supply side of knowledge, may be more to do with the nature of the demand. He argues that the relevance problem is not just about academics being wedded to their ways, it is also 'that practitioners will not set aside their fads and begin to work with fundamentals' (Weick, 2001, p. S72). In addition, there are issues that are the responsibility of both business and business schools. A recent report on university and business engagement revealed that businesses often didn't have the capacity to find out what would help from universities, and similarly universities did not provide the relevant information about how they can support business. The authors argued that business schools should play an important part in making this happen (Hughes, Kitson, Salter, Angenendt, & Hughes, 2022).

The problems introduced so far illustrate some of the difficulties that need to be overcome for engagement to work. Teaching and research are two fundamental pillars of a business school and clearly are also problematic. Therefore, in Chapter 4, the inherent tensions behind teaching and research will be explored since the level of engagement possible is always likely to be limited whilst fundamental issues remain in these two areas. There is, of course, a wide range of contrasting evidence associated with engagement and relevance, with many examples of good practice. Nevertheless, there is a deeper sense that potential is not being realised and a recognition that more could be and should be done. In the midst of these wide ranging concerns and frustrations, it is worth being reminded of why it might be important to get this right for those who could gain most from an engaged business school.

## A Call to Action for Managers, Students and Academics

The engaged business school is a call to action both for business schools and for businesses to engage and reap the mutual benefits from their relationship. There is obvious potential to be found when they work together, yet there is a frustration that so much of that promise seems unfulfilled. On the one hand, business schools with competing demands of teaching and research and stretched resources understandably can be reluctant partners, often lukewarm in their efforts and struggling to engage effectively with business. On the other hand, businesses seem unaware of the support available, unable to connect meaningfully with business schools and unconvinced of the merits of doing so. Business schools can benefit from better understanding how to engage with business, and businesses need to know how to unlock that unfilled potential. But it is more than just a call to businesses and to business schools; other relationships matter too. Knowing how to make the most of a business school, what to look out for and how to tap into the possibilities is crucial for business, managers, students and academics alike.

It matters for today's managers and leaders, whether they are currently unaware of the possibilities, or hoping to make the most of their experience whilst studying an MBA or an executive education programme, so too for alumni wishing to unlock the continued benefit of their relationship. A connection with the business school should not be just for the duration of a programme. A longer term relationship that is mutually beneficial is needed. An MBA/executive education student, and subsequently a member of the alumni, should gain from a life time relationship with the business school, and be able to continually develop and engage in learning. In so doing they develop themselves, their organisation, and crucially can contribute to shaping and building the business school. A long-term relationship with managers and leaders such as this starts to change the emphasis from the conventional focus on individual programmes towards a continuing engagement in different ways over time. From this perspective, managers and leaders don't join a programme they join a learning community.

Similarly for current undergraduates, these students are tomorrow's managers and leaders, and for them experiencing an engaged business school is invaluable for their early development and career prospects. It is an environment where their education and experience is integrated with supporting the business community, where they can engage with academic staff who are pursuing research which impacts on the communities they serve and points to a future which these students will be shaping. Engagement creates conditions where learning and practice come together, where the workplace becomes more like a learning place and learning spaces in business schools become more like the emerging ideas about a new work place/space. Engagement results in a 'low walled' business school where young people make an early contribution to organisations whilst they study.

And it also matters for the academic community, providing a rich context within which to teach, research and consult. For academics, the opportunity is to pursue an engaged scholarship, and challenge the tendency to separate relevant applied research from more dispassionate and fundamental research. There is also the potential to re-invigorate the nature of scholarly teaching and engaged learning, working closely with organisations and with those who work in them. Engagement should provide the opportunities for career development and academic fulfilment.

Such aspirations are not without their difficulties. The massification of higher education has skewed the focus within universities with so much attention placed on undergraduate recruitment and the subsequent delivery of mass-education. In the context of finite resources, delivering to multiple stakeholders with a wide range of programmes and services becomes problematic. It is worth noting that business schools are actually relatively small businesses with staff numbers typically in the hundreds. It, therefore, becomes difficult to offer a breadth of provision often resulting in being 'under resourced and under-scaled' (Peter, Smith, & Howard, 2018, p. 9). The issues associated with multiple stakeholders and their competing demands on limited resource is a clear tension that will be explored when the meaning of engagement and its interpretation by different stakeholders is discussed in Chapter 3.

Issues about being able to personalise mass-education hold an inherent tension, the one seemingly making the other impossible. It prompts the question as to whether the business school's relationships with businesses can help. Is it possible to re-dress this tension and provide ways for mass-education to harness the business capability in a region to support the learning and development of undergraduate students? The sentiment of the African proverb that suggests it takes a village to bring up a child could perhaps be adapted here, to recognise that it takes a business school and the business/workplace communities to educate and develop the next generation of leaders and managers. There is of course a long tradition of placements, and of apprenticeships, with the latter being revived more recently. Could these areas be further developed to provide a much stronger two way relationship for business students? Can the relationships a business school has with businesses significantly help to develop undergraduate students? To do this, implies that aspects of work based learning will need to be developed, resulting in the blurring of workplaces and learning places into a more comprehensive integrated learning process.

Bringing working and learning closer together extends the boundaries of a business school. Similarly, the idea of students joining a learning community rather than simply a programme expands the relationships with students and alumni. The continuity of learning implied introduces interesting possibilities. Such a view of a lifelong relationship can lead to different thinking about appropriate business models. For example, Schlegelmilch (2020) provocatively proposed changing from a single purchase of a qualification (currently the norm) to an access model. What is particularly interesting in relation to the discussion of an engaged business school is his argument that the intention of doing this should be to create 'deeper and more long term relationships' (Schegelmilch, 2020, p. 101). Much of the current education system is front-loaded both in terms of time and payment (AACSB, 2022). Education predominantly happens before or at the beginning of careers and similarly payment is typically up front and for specific programmes. There is comparatively little in place to update, extend, refresh and renew learning. Is it time to consider how business schools can more purposefully extend the relationship with their students for the long term?

There is a sense in which all interested parties have a stake in the future of business schools. The engaged business school is an opportunity for all those who are engaged to be a part of shaping that future. Stewardship and legacy should be priorities for which all those invested in business schools have some responsibility.

## A Success Story

The initial discussion has emphasised the problems and difficulties with business schools and their engagement with business. It gives a somewhat frustrating impression of business schools. The intent was to highlight where things need to improve, but it is only part of the story. Business schools have been one of the success stories in higher education over the last few decades (Thomas, Lorange, & Sheth, 2013). The flagship MBA has achieved a remarkable status. The undergraduate programmes are some of the most popular amongst students with one in six undergraduates studying a business and management subject in 2019/2021 (British Academy, 2021). Hand in hand with this success, business schools make significant financial contributions to the university (British Academy, 2021; Thorpe & Rawlinson, 2014). More widely, they are seen as important in the development of national economies (Lorange, 2019). In times of crisis and recession, they also have demonstrated resilience. This was apparent post the financial crisis of 2007/2008, as the Guardian newspaper reported in 2010, following the financial crisis, demand for MBA courses was soaring (Hoare, 2010). There are signs of a similar response emerging from the pandemic crisis. The Graduate Management Admission Council in their 2020 application survey illustrated this counter-intuitive phenomenon. During recessions business school graduate recruitment tends to be counter-cyclical, and numbers were up (AACSB, 2020; Globenewswire, 2020). The reasons given are that a recession is often a good time to upskill, to improve career prospects. That is not to ignore difficulties with the unpredictable nature of a crisis such as the pandemic, with, for example, international student recruitment being an obvious area of concern.

Despite this success, and perhaps in part because of it, business schools are facing challenges. The achievements of a business school make it difficult to excel in all areas. The high volume of undergraduate students creates significant resource pressure which impacts both on research and on the ability to engage more with businesses.

More broadly, for many institutions, there are mounting funding pressures, for example, in England there is an effective freeze on undergraduate fees. In this climate of diminishing returns other sources of income streams become attractive. Ironically, business schools would be well placed to explore different income stream possibilities if they weren't so resource constrained with the volume of undergraduate teaching. For example, business schools could lead on areas that expand on their expertise developed with executive education and continuing professional development (CPD). The increasing need for keeping current and up to date is creating interest in upskilling, reskilling and lifelong learning. These are all areas that resonate with executive education and are more closely linked to business. However, for business schools to explore such possibilities will need both strategic support at a university level, alongside creative solutions at an operational level. Whilst this context is challenging, business schools often start from a position of advantage.

Business schools and universities are in a privileged position; they already have widespread acceptance within the communities they serve. They are trusted and seen as authoritative (AACSB, 2022). As a result, with many businesses the door is already open for conversations to be had, a position which private sector training providers and consultancies could only dream about. There are often alumni from the respective university employed in businesses in the region who have a positive disposition to the university. The conditions and ingredients for building strong relationships are often already in place, yet frequently not realised, or worse they lie dormant. Informally there may be many links and connections, and formally too, but the sum of the parts most definitely does not equal what could be the sum of the whole, if only they were galvanised and brought together in a purposeful manner. The central ideas behind the engaged business school emerge from the tensions highlighted earlier which suggest business schools have a difficulty with engagement. Yet the potential benefit from effective engagement is evident for business schools, businesses, students and academics. Time then to outline the core themes of what is needed to build an engaged business school.

## The Central Ideas of an Engaged Business School

The idea behind the engaged business school is to unlock the potential between businesses and business schools; an intent borne out of a frustration with what passes for engagement, and optimism about what could be, indeed should be possible. Importantly, it is aimed at the dual audience of business schools and businesses, arguing that there is a need for the academic and business communities to come together and build an engaged business school. Too much of the debate about business school relevance has taken place in academia, so the starting point will be with business needs and only then will the two perspectives be brought together. From this perspective business schools are largely an untapped resource for business with the potential to be an influential source of competitive advantage. What then are businesses looking for when deciding whether to work with a business school? When discussing with businesses the possibilities of working with a business school, two questions repeatedly surface. The first is about why a business and business school should engage and the second explores how they should engage. In short, they want to know: 'why should we work with you?', and 'how will you work with us?'.

The central idea of the engaged business school provides a response to the 'why' question. The challenge and the opportunity for business schools is to develop as both 'demand-led', responsive to the needs of business and 'leading demand' by providing research-led latest thinking. It is also apparent that business schools which are unclear about either view-point risk being neither responsive to the needs of business, nor the source of insightful, fresh thinking to lead and help shape demand in the future. Such a position results in a 'middle of the road' compromise, a lukewarm response that is neither one of the other. The ability to hold the tension between being responsive and needs-led and a source of insight and latest thinking is what will be referred to as distinctive engagement. It is distinctive, as will become clear for a number of reasons, but not least because it is either not done well or not done at all.

Business are not just looking for a distinctive provision, they also want to know how a business school will work with them. To that question there is a very clear answer, businesses are looking for business schools that can partner with them and build a strong relationship. They place considerable value on relational rather than transactional engagement. Yet they are often frustrated and find such relationships difficult to build with business schools. What is needed is a relational model to address this issue.

Consequently, the engaged business school builds on the twin business needs for distinctive and relational engagement. Two further themes will be developed shortly to complement these initial imperatives, but for now the overriding motivation to improve engagement begins with responding to these business needs. This motivation to address the tension between what businesses want and what they too often experience should signal the need for change. But there are wider indicators for change, which not only reinforce the need but also create an urgency, suggesting that developing an engaged business school is timely.

## Why Engagement Matters and Why It Matters Now

A call to action suggests an urgency or timeliness about the circumstances, and often emerges from competing tensions. This is evident in the context of three imperatives, each in themselves could be considered a call to action: crises, policy shifts and rising expectations. Indeed, the need to engage more effectively with businesses becomes more compelling when combined with a sense of urgency, and a financial crisis followed by a global pandemic certainly provide that.

The recovery from and reaction to a global pandemic understandably takes shape over time. Searching and far-reaching questions about the nature of business are being asked in parallel with questions about how to help businesses and the wider economy to recover. All of which in turn prompt questions about the role business schools might play to help the recovery. However, business schools are not facing a response to a single crisis. In many ways business and society are still making sense of the global financial crisis. Two global crises clearly place an urgency upon the call for action. Firstly, the financial crisis of 2007 brought serious questions about ethics in business to the fore, and not for the first time. There had already been significant concerns expressed following collapses of businesses like Enron in the United States. Such concerns echoed warnings about extolling the virtues of 'charismatic' and 'inspirational' leadership at the expense of ethical considerations (Alimo-Metcalfe & Alban-Metcalfe, 2005). The financial crisis added to these claims' allegations of reckless leadership with apparent neglect of wider stakeholders whilst reaping individual rewards (Chambers, Drysdale, & Hughes, 2010). Ethical and moral leadership, social responsibility and governance have been identified as lessons that need to be learnt from the crisis (Machold & Huse, 2010). Furthermore, there are calls for business schools to ask serious questions about the role they may have played (Dyllick, 2015; Haynes, 2010), with some even arguing that the roots of the crisis, from a US perspective, can be found in business schools (Giacalone & Wargo, 2009). There are also concerns that the responses need to be more fundamental than instrumental. For example, whilst incorporating ethics and social responsibility into the curriculum and giving them more prominence is needed, it does not go far or deep enough. Students need equipping with an ability to challenge accepted norms, adopt critical thinking, foster a broader sense of responsibility and crucially to develop their moral character (Giacalone & Wargo, 2009; Haynes, 2010). But a serious response should also recognise that apportioning responsibility is a broader and more complex exercise, with economists, bankers and regulators, representing roles and disciplines with a case to answer (Worrall, 2010), many of whom of course will not have been the products of a business school education.

The second global crisis was the pandemic. This represented a very different situation where relationships have been stretched due to the need to separate and distance ourselves from each other, and in doing so it is our inter-relatedness which has highlighted our vulnerability and our inter-dependency. In turn, this has prompted a re-thinking of what businesses are for, alongside re-interpreting our relationship to our planet, our relationship to each other and our relationship to work. Not forgetting that significant questions of leadership have continued to dominate. Moreover, notions of improvement and a desire not to return to the 'same as usual' are captured in phrases such as building back better. Such thoughts prompt ideas of change that are fairer and sustainable, whilst thinking about what might be meant by the idea of 'good business'. All these themes are areas where business schools can make valuable contributions.

There are many indicators of how business schools could engage in the future which can be drawn from what has taken place as the world responded to the pandemic, both the good and the bad. One of the most striking illustrations of what may be possible is the story behind the emergence of a COVID vaccine in record time from a collaboration between Oxford University and AstraZeneca. What is particularly interesting here is that the manufacturing process and the ability to produce at scale were as important as the immunology (Gilbert, 2021). As a result, terms such as efficiency, reducing lead times, scaling, tackling bottlenecks and distributed production were used to explain the project's success. Such terms are the language of management and operations and very much a part of the expertise within business schools. This achievement was accomplished whilst maintaining the rigour of regulation, but at speed and with an intent to produce at cost price and make a vaccine that would be available and affordable globally (Gilbert, 2021; Pike, 2021). In contrast to the Oxford/AstraZeneca approach of finding ways to speed up important checks and balances, alleged

PPE contract issues saw tender processes resulting in the purchase of high numbers of equipment that turned out to be unsuitable for use (National Audit Office, 2022). This of course happened during an unprecedented crisis, but the difference in approach indicates that what may conventionally be seen as competing demands; rigorous checks and quick supply at scale, can be viewed differently. The expedient approach would be to compromise rigour for speed as appears to be the case with some PPE contracts. However seeking ways where both demands can be met (an important theme of this book) is vital and also is possible to do as exemplified by the Oxford/AstraZeneca collaboration.

The pandemic appears to have renewed respect for academia and recognition of the contribution areas such as health sciences can make was particularly evident. It opens the prospect that this recognition could lead to a wider acknowledgement of the contribution that other areas of a university such as business and social sciences and culture and the arts might bring to society. There is certainly potential for this to happen. Much may depend on how academia responds, and, in particular for business schools, raises the question as to whether this opportunity can be seized. The Oxford/AstraZeneca vaccine and PPE procurement stories provide a rich illustration of the importance of many business subject fields, suggesting there should be potential to contribute.

Two crises of themselves would be sufficient to indicate the timeliness for business schools to revisit what it means to be engaged, but they are not alone. In addition, national policy shifts and rising expectations were already placing an urgency, as if it were needed, upon the role that an engaged business school can play. In the United Kingdom, successive Governments have held up universities as being a key partner to support and renew economic growth and enhance higher level skills in the economy. At the same time, universities are encouraged to diversify their income sources, in an increasingly market-oriented approach to education. The dual pressures of finding other sources of income and contributing to economic recovery place a renewed emphasis on engagement with businesses. Government expectations, and that of the parent university, are for a business school to be a key part of addressing these dual pressures. As a result, business schools are situated right on the fault-line of this policy landscape. It is in this context of policy, crisis and expectation, with pressure to change and motivation to do so, that a call for an engaged business school really matters.

Globally many business schools rely on some form of funding from Government.[1] However, there are pressures to reduce this funding (Hawawini, 2005). There are of course differences. Europe tends to see higher education as a public good and supports funding, whereas in Asia and Latin America it is typically less about public funding and more a private, individual responsibility (Peter et al., 2018). The policy landscape for UK universities means that they are facing considerable challenges but also some potential opportunities. The pressure on universities is emerging from a number of different sources. With respect to the

---

[1]For an excellent overview of funding pressures see Rethinking the Business Models of Business Schools. Peters et al. (2018) Emerald Publishing.

engaged business school two policy areas are of particular interest. Firstly, there is the HE policy agenda itself, within which universities must act,[2] where there has been a sustained emphasis on significant change to university funding arrangements and a focus on how universities contribute to economic recovery. Added to this are a range of national policy drivers aimed at enhancing higher level skills in the economy. Both of these policy areas, HE and skills, gain further significance within the context of responding to global recessions and recovery. Higher education policy has increasingly emphasised funding and economic contribution. Successive reports and policy papers have attempted to re-dress funding and have set the tone for the last decade. The Browne review of funding and students finance and the subsequent white paper, students at the heart of the system, set out to re-dress funding as a consequence of the financial crisis (Browne, 2010; Department for Business Innovation and Skills, 2011). More recently the Government response to the Augar review resulted in student fees in England being frozen, effectively building a diminishing return for a main source of university funding (Lewis & Bolton, 2022).

One significant change heralded in the 2011 Students at the Heart of the System white paper and continued in the 2016 white paper (Department for Business, Innovation and Skills, 2016) was to prepare the way for a more diverse provision of HE education to incorporate non-traditional providers. This change ushered in 'a more market-based approach to higher education' (Hughes, Porter, Jones, & Sheen, 2013, p. 13). It suggests that the scope for broader competition with business schools will only increase and presents a challenge to the privileged position they have held as providers of higher education. Diminishing returns and the prospect of increased competition clearly place increasing pressures on business schools.

It is in this context that Government policy places a focus on economic contribution as exemplified by Sir Tim Wilson's 2011 review which was tasked with making 'the UK the best place in the world for university-industry collaboration' (Department for Business Innovation and Skills, 2011, p. 6). This was closely followed by Sir Andrew Witty's (2013) report on how universities can enable and generate local growth. More recently, the levelling up agenda (Housing and Communities, 2022) and build back better plan (HM Treasury, 2021) reflect Governments recognition of the capacity for universities to contribute to economic growth, and to position skills as an important contributor to growth. Not surprisingly, Government skills policy also places high expectations on universities, but also on skills themselves as a driver of growth. The skills white paper (Department for Education, 2021) together with the levelling up paper place an emphasis on skills development through lifelong learning. The white paper cites the Industrial Strategy Council's research (2019) which states that most of the 2030 workforce are already in the workplace, so improving skills that can make an impact for business will need to be focused on those in the workplace in order to keep pace with needs for upskilling and reskilling. As a

---

[2]HE policy in the UK is a devolved matter.

result, the Government proposes to widen access to funding so that individuals have more support to upskill and reskill over the course of their careers. As will be discussed in Chapter 5, skills policy has been seen by successive Governments as a key driver to enable growth and encourage productivity. However, though clearly necessary it is not sufficient to rely on developing skills alone. New skills need to be utilised by managers and organisations for them to be effective, and that is a more complex matter, and one where business schools can make a contribution.

The chapter began with two stories that captured a business perspective of the opportunity and the frustration for better engagement between business and business schools. That argument was then supported by a wider evidence base which reinforced many of those concerns. Nevertheless, business schools have been a significant success story which in many ways is part of the problem with multiple competing demands calling on constrained resources. The continuing success of business schools may well depend on how they create value for those they serve. Engagement with a business school is not solely about business relationships, other groups matter too. The benefits for managers, students and academics, together with business, illustrate a variety of ways these groups can gain from the relationship. These promising possibilities are further emphasised when the urgency presented by two global crises indicate a timeliness to the argument and a challenge to find ways to contribute. Indeed, the policy landscape reinforces this challenge placing expectations upon HE and business schools in particular, to engage with business. There is, however, a final set of voices that so far have been missing from the various calls for action. They are important voices to be heard because they come from within business schools.

There are a number of influential academics calling for change and questioning the future of business schools. Together they argue that business schools are facing questions about their status, legitimacy and identity. There is a recognition that business schools have been a success story, but point to significant issues and concerns about the future, making a strong case for the need to change. There are calls for business schools to define what they stand for in a new way (Starkey & Tiratsoo, 2007), with the suggestion that they need to be able to transform themselves (Lorange, 2019). Collectively they describe a difficult position for business schools, straddled across a fault line between academia and practice. They argue that business schools struggle with their own identity, need to regain their sense of purpose and propose that new business models are needed for business schools to reinvent themselves. (Peter et al., 2018; Thomas et al., 2013)

The engaged business school builds on a growing sense that something needs to change; it does so by highlighting one key question to focus thinking, that of how business schools engage with the businesses they serve. It is grounded in practice and experience with the ideas and insights discussed in the book developed from listening to the voices of those directly involved in engagement. It is, therefore, a timely contribution to the various arguments and analysis calling for change. It proposes practical ways in which business schools can more effectively engage with business at a time when that engagement might be needed most, as a world recovers from a global crisis. The fundamental tension of identity underpins the theme of the engaged business school and is captured in exploring what engagement means. It is an attempt to describe a way in which individual business schools can forge their own identity. There is an acknowledgment from many of the influential voices within business schools that schools need to respond flexibly by assessing their own position and niche. The engaged business school provides a means for schools to do that and shape their response. Crises have always held risks and opportunities, often speeding the on-set of problems already present, emergent or latent, and similarly surfacing new issues. Equally, crises can accelerate innovation and different thinking, frequently out of necessity. The engaged business school provides a timely way to rise to the dual challenges of facing emerging issues, and harnessing innovation and different thinking.

Business school engagement with business really matters. Governments, crises and voices from academia all contribute to this conclusion. Successive Governments have placed increasing demands and expectations on business schools to play a pivotal role supporting business and economic growth. These demands now have an additional dimension, that of economic recovery, as the calls for engagement have intensified in the wake of the financial crisis of 2007 and the emerging effects of the pandemic crisis. Yet there is concern in the United Kingdom that regionally and nationally such engagement is variable (Thorpe & Rawlinson, 2013). More generally, there is unease that business schools are at a point where they risk 'muddling through' and managing a decline unless new creative models can be found (Howard, Lorange, & Sheth, 2013). Behind such concerns is a deeper unease that there is a need to rebalance what they are doing to ensure that they engage effectively (Peters & Howard, 2020), re-dress how they demonstrate impact (Lejeune, Starkey, Kalika, & Tempest, 2018) and even to re-think business education (Schoemaker, 2008). Inevitably such concerns lead to calls for business schools to re-assess their legitimacy and identity (Peter et al., 2018). Despite such concerns, in the United Kingdom the Chartered Association of Business Schools portrays the contribution business schools could make to economic growth as 'transformational' (Thorpe & Rawlinson, 2013, p. i), and as an 'exceptional opportunity' (Chartered Association of Business Schools, 2016). Such optimism is tempered with realism as they caution that this potential can only be realised if there is 'full' engagement. Conflicting messages about the state of business schools and growing external demands for its services suggest it is timely to take a fresh look at what an engaged business school might look like. The engaged business school can be a vehicle for shaping the legitimacy and identity of a school just as the current context provides the motivation and urgency to do so. However, too much of the debate about business school relevance has taken place within the bounds of the university and from the business school perspective. Therefore, the engagement model will be introduced in the next chapter initially through the lens of three questions asked from a business perspective.

Policy and crisis are large-scale reasons to advocate engagement, but it is also important on a smaller scale for individual businesses to be clear about why it matters to them. Earlier two questions were highlighted as being important to business, here a third is added. Three questions can help a business gain that clarity. Firstly, to know why they should work with the business school, secondly, to understand how the business school works with them, and thirdly to explore how the business school continues to add value. More generally these three questions can be asked for and by businesses, managers, students, alumni and staff.

- Why should a business/student/academic engage with a business school? The response to this questions points towards a distinctive engagement.
- How will a business school work with/support a business/student/academic? To answer this question requires a focus on relational engagement.
- How will a business school continue to add value for and with a business/student/academic? Exploring this question is crucial for a continuing relationship and leads to the notion of sustainable engagement.

Each question points to a theme within the model of engagement.

Chapter 2

# Towards a Model of Engagement

Having suggested there is an urgency and timeliness to the idea of an engaged business school, the case for this argument now needs to be explored in more depth. This will be done using a model to illustrate the factors which need to be brought together, a framework to provide structure and meaning particularly in relation to how engagement is defined and finally, a process to translate the model and framework into action. First though, it is important and helpful to gain an overview of the model. This will create a picture of engagement at a glance indicating the general direction of travel of the discussion, before then considering the ideas in detail. Each theme of the model will be introduced; then the engagement stories that ground the ideas in practice will be explored. They capture the experience of those directly involved in business to business school relationships. In a later chapter each of the concepts will be discussed in detail. The term purposeful engagement is used to indicate the aspiration to develop an approach that is mutually beneficial. This does of course raise the question as to what is understood by engagement, which will be explained in Chapter 3, using the framework of engagement. For now, the stories of some of those directly involved in engagement will be used to bring the ideas to life.

The stories are drawn from my own experience of building an engaged service for businesses in a business school. They emerged from three client engagements and include views from operational and senior managers on both sides, within the business school and in the businesses. The client relationships were sufficiently established to be a rich source of experience, where significant time had elapsed and where a necessary level of trust was present for the required depth of discussion to be possible. The participants were key people, from both the client and the business school, who had been significantly involved in the development of the relationship.

The stories, together with the wider evidence which will be explored later in the book, have helped form an approach that I have subsequently implemented at a second business school, to build an engaged service to business.

The model, framework and process together capture the ideas behind an engaged business school. The essence of the purposeful engagement model is to show how success factors are interconnected in order to bring engagement to life, and provide answers to the three questions posed at the end of the last chapter.

The Engaged Business School, 15–30
Copyright © 2023 Anthony Sturgess
Published under exclusive licence by Emerald Publishing Limited
doi:10.1108/978-1-80382-941-820231004

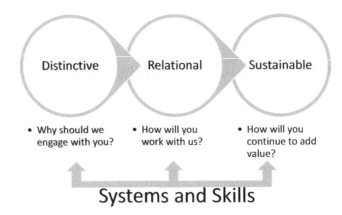

Fig. 1.    Initial Model of Engagement.

Two of these questions have already been introduced. Here they are expanded upon with a third question adding an extra dimension.

The initial model of engagement is illustrated in Fig. 1 and addresses four areas:

1. Distinctive engagement;
2. Relational engagement;
3. Sustainable futures;
4. Skills and systems.

The model proposes that engagement needs to be distinctive, relational and sustainable for it to be effective. The first theme relates to why a business would choose to work with a business school and captures a dual priority: that their needs are met, and that they benefit from latest thinking. The second theme emphasises that businesses value the quality and depth of the relationship with a business school. Then, thirdly, engagement needs to be sustained if it is to be purposeful. A mutually beneficial relationship should lead to an on-going connectedness. Finally, these three themes are underpinned by the right skills and systems being in place, crucial as these are, unfortunately they are often in short supply. Each of these four themes will now be introduced.

## Distinctive Engagement

It is a common adage that organisations seek to differentiate themselves from others in order to adopt a position of advantage. Business schools should be no different. There are of course differences between business schools, but there is also a tendency towards convergence and similarity (Irwin, 2019). Their similarity often is evidenced by a set of typically generic products. There is, therefore, an opportunity to consider what would make engagement with business particularly distinctive. An instructive way to think about this is to seek answers to why a business would want to work with a particular business school. Interestingly, answers to that question suggest that businesses are looking for two approaches which traditionally in business schools have been characterised as opposing positions. They value both the relevance of a 'demand-led' approach and the rigour of 'leading demand'.

This implies that an engaged business school plays two roles:

1. Listening and being responsive to demand (helping clarify demand and then tailoring solutions to fit) and
2. Leading with ideas to shape demand by helping, informing and creating knowledge with new thinking and research.

The first position is characterised by listening and understanding and the second by leading with ideas. However, there is a tension between behaving as a demand-led organisation and/or an organisation which leads demand. This reflects the well-argued and perennial tension and debate between relevance and rigour, the former associated with meeting business needs and the latter with a research-led emphasis. It has been a debate which tends to polarise opinions where the two perspectives are seen as opposing each other. However, if both positions are valued by employers, then perhaps a different perspective is needed. Rather than seeing the positions as being in conflict, it is possible to view them from a position of complementarity: the one enhancing and improving the other. There is clearly both opportunity and cause for business schools to combine listening to business need (a demand-led approach) with application of the latest research, which will lead demand. Indeed, carefully listening to businesses can enable academics to identify crucial areas for further research that is both rigorous and relevant. Given that views about rigour and relevance have been a significant source of difference in the academic community, the issues are explored in more detail later in Chapter 4.

The tension between the two positions turns out to be important in providing insight on the nature of effective engagement. The challenge and the opportunity for business schools will be to develop both 'demand-led' and 'leading demand' approaches. As we discussed earlier, the risk for business schools is to fall between the two positions and end up being neither relevant or rigorous. It is a position that falls short of addressing business needs, and equally lacks meaningful research to challenge and spark different thinking. The middle ground may be a relatively easy place to occupy, but it is not an attractive one, nor is it sustainable. It does not require the discipline and hard work of taking time to listen to needs, nor of pursuing interesting and meaningful research. But it does ask the question as to why a business would come to a business school where this is what they would experience.

## Relational Engagement

As important as answering the question about why a business would work with a business school is to address a second question: how will a business school work with a business? Relationships are absolutely central to effective engagement. The overriding finding from my work with organisations is that employers place a significant value upon relational engagement, yet their experience is that many business schools find this difficult to do. The emphasis on building effective relationships, especially long-term relationships was stressed by employers. This relational focus was enabled through building credibility and reputation. Clearly good relationships are not a substitute for competence and credibility, but they do seem to be important if an engagement with a business is to be long lasting. What also emerged as a critical factor was the need to continually nurture relationships in order to build for the longer term. Yet too often employers experience trans-actional rather than relational engagement with business schools and their parent universities. Even when transactional activities are done well, without the rela-tional commitment, they may remain discrete single interactions without consideration of how they might build or expand to a much wider contribution. Something more is needed for relationships to grow and be sustained, they need to be nurtured. Nurturing is a stronger and deeper concept than rapport building which, although an important part of building relationships and one that is often emphasised, is of itself not sufficient. It would seem that the ability to nurture a relationship makes a difference for a sustainable future to be achieved, which leads us to the third theme of the model.

## Sustainable Futures

The third theme answers the question about how a business school continues to add value to a business. The argument is made that a sustainable future where the relationship continues to grow is more likely to happen if the current engagement generates opportunity and creates value. Such an approach focuses on interven-tions that build capability and capacity both in a business and within a business school. That means there are new opportunities for both parties to explore because of the learning and development that has taken place. Continuing to add value provides a rational basis for working together. It also places an emphasis on designing and delivering interventions with that in mind. An outcome from the relationship should be a growing understanding both within a business and in a business school of what more could be done together, in particular, to explore how to release some of the hidden value within a business school. Sustainable futures are mutually beneficial, continuing to add value and opening up new opportunities for both the business and for the business school.

## Systems and Skills

Underpinning a distinctive, relational and sustainable engagement is the need for new skills and systems. Academic staff with the right attributes, along with the insights and experiences they have accumulated from engagement with the business world (Connor, 2007), all combine to establish the credibility of the business school. Each of the three themes requires a wider range of skills than that of the traditional expertise of academics. They are the skills associated with being an engaged educator or scholar, approaches which will be explored later in relation to the model. The new skills and roles needed, whilst central to the model, can only be effective when supportive systems are in place. Such responsive systems underpin the capacity to build credibility and relationships. Unfortunately, university systems are designed for other priorities with a tendency to be driven by core business needs, which usually means undergraduate provision. However understandable this might be, recognising and supporting such differing relationships with the university is vital. Systems and skills are critical enablers for a business school to engage effectively with business.

The four themes of the purposeful engagement model have been developed from conversations with those directly involved in engagement both from businesses and from business schools. This next section draws upon the stories behind the model. Many colleagues in business schools and businesses will have similar stories; they give meaning to the ideas in the model and root it in experience.

## Stories of Engagement

The engagement stories, shared by those directly involved, shed light on the four themes and ground the ideas in the reality, practice and experience of those telling the stories.

When discussing engagement with those involved, it is striking to note how often a story was used to make a point. In the context of understanding engagement, the stories told by those involved in such relationships are instructive. It is worth noting at this point that the nature of such stories is not necessarily to convey facts but rather that 'they enrich and infuse facts with meaning' (Gabriel & Griffiths, 2004, p. 115). Two aspects of storytelling are of particular interest in relation to understanding engagement. Firstly, organisational stories often have a built-in tension describing situations that are difficult to resolve, or where there are inherent contradictions (Martin, Feldman, Hatch, & Sitkim, 1983, p. 447). Such tensions typically suggest conflict or the need to compromise, but they can also be indicators of the need for different thinking. It is this particular feature of tensions that offers hopeful areas to explore. Secondly, stories are often used for sense making purposes. Sense making is about arriving at 'a sensible, workable interpretation' (Gioia & Chittipeddi, 1991, p. 444), by continually reworking an 'emerging story so that it becomes more comprehensive' (Weick, Sutcliffe, & Obstfeld, 2005, p. 415). It helps to develop a plausible map where information, conversation and action shape meaning and build credibility (Ancona, 2012). From this understanding of sense making, stories gain value in both articulating meaning, and in being a persuasive way to give sense to others. However, it should be noted that through any process of sense making 'people may get better stories, but they will never get the story' (Weick et al., 2005, p. 415). Stories in this context will thus be used as a means of indicating where different thinking may be needed, and to better understand how those involved in engagement make sense of how it works.

There is some evidence to suggest that organisational stories often cover similar themes. For example, Parry and Hansen claim that most of the stories they analysed tended to have a 'general theme of overcoming adversity' (Parry & Hansen, 2007, p. 283). Similarly, Martin et al. suggest that the most common type of story they studied was 'the obstacles story', which made them think that these kind of stories 'may be particularly salient and important' (Martin et al., 1983, p. 445) within an organisational context. The story usually ends with resolution or a solution or provides clarification, though not always. In addition to themes of adversity and obstacles, they can also illustrate the unravelling of a situation (Polkinghorne, 1995), all of which were apparent in the engagement stories.

Therefore, the engagement stories will be outlined in some more detail to better understand how those telling the story are making sense of their situation. To aid this process, the stories will be characterised by the kind of story being told – its type. In addition, where relevant, the kind of ending to the story will also be suggested, namely, whether it ends with a resolution to a tension, an unresolved tension, a moral or final point/punch-line. These ideas will be brought together to help present what can be learnt from the stories by representing them by type, theme, message, tension, moral and purpose, an approach similar to that used by Gabriel and Griffiths (2004).

Reflecting on the stories, it became clear that the story tellers did have differing intentions for telling it, and that these could be summarised as a type of story. Consequently, the engagement stories can be represented as five types. They provide an interesting spectrum of intention from cautionary, problem and provocation stories through to exemplar and opportunity story types. They bridge from a negative emphasis to a more positive outlook. The cautionary story highlights a potential jeopardy and carries a warning, and in a similar vein the problem story focuses on a dilemma pointing out what is not working. The provocation story is a pivot story transitioning from negative to positive. It has a challenge or a provoking question and indicates that with thought the balance can be changed from the undesirable to an optimistic outcome. The final two types are unashamedly positive. The exemplar story draws from what has worked well and points towards best practice, whilst the opportunity story is more expansive, encouraging thinking towards the possibilities and potential for the future.

The stories, therefore, have been chosen for their saliency in providing a rich picture of how engagement develops between business and business schools. The first three stories shed light on the reasons behind a business choosing to work with a business school. The 'selection story' is about why a business chooses a business school and has a note of caution, using a negative example to illustrate what was missing and by implication what the business values. In this case, a past problem is used to stress what is needed when selecting a business school. The second, 'the contrasting provider story', compares good with bad experiences to emphasise what businesses value, it is a cautionary story. The third story is 'the greatest strength story', which was used to introduce the message of this book. It is a provocation story presenting both a challenge and an opportunity. The message is that the strengths of a business school should meet the needs of a business, but unfortunately that is too often not the experience of businesses.

The next two stories focus on the importance of the relationship. 'The relationship story' is an exemplar story which highlights what has worked and why it has worked. It stresses the central role of productive relationships. What was so striking about this story was the critical importance and value of the relationship to the business. Then 'the nurturing story', which is also an exemplar story, emphasises the crucial and continual need to nurture relationships by getting alongside those in a business, finding and creating common experiences. It is about authenticity, rapport and integrity. The first five stories focus on the distinctive and the relational themes, whilst the sixth and seventh stories give meaning to the sustainability and systems and skills themes. 'The skill set story' is a problem story. It stresses the need for the right skills to be in place to work effectively with organisations, and surfaces frustrations that appropriate skills and systems can be in short supply. Finally, 'the springboard story', which is an opportunity story, captures the idea that new opportunities can be created from what has been achieved together. It suggests a mindset that purposefully seeks to ensure that the interventions with the business build capability and act as a springboard forward to creating new value together.

It can be easy to miss the striking amongst the familiar and, therefore, it is valuable to step back and reflect on what is being conveyed in these stories of engagement. Consequently, what appears to be striking and surprising will be emphasised as each story is considered in more detail.

## '*The Selection Story' – A Cautionary Story*

The selection story emerged from a manager in the client[1] organisation who wanted to explain the reasons behind their choice to select a particular business school. This story was important because of past experiences with organisations which had refused to be flexible. The story starts with a previous negative experience and uses that experience to explain the contrast with what the client now wanted (partly as a result of that earlier experience). Credibility was crucial, but so was flexibility and a willingness to adapt, along with reputation, price and the ability to actually listen. The story is one where a problem in the past has resulted in the need for different behaviour in the future. The story highlighted the difficulty that organisations can have in determining whether a potential provider does indeed have the expertise, and whether they have the right approach to meet the client's requirements at the selection stage.

As a result, this story indicates some critical areas which a business school would need to address in order to be considered by a business. Hence, credibility and, importantly, the evidence to support any claims made are viewed by the client as very important. This story proved to be more than an isolated example, as other cases also included elements which questioned provider selection processes because of previous concerns about working with universities. The story

---

[1]Note that from now on the term 'client manager' will be used to mean a manager from the client organisation.

ended with a moral and a cautionary note about potential providers who offered no more than a pretence to listen: 'Some acknowledged (our requirements) and then proceeded to tell us what they thought we wanted'.

### *'The Contrasting Provider Story' – A Cautionary Story of Villains and Heroes*

One of the most powerful and unexpected stories to emerge was the contrasting provider story. It is a cautionary story. This story was emotively and powerfully told. It was also a surprising story, one that was not asked for or sought. Yet a version of this kind of story was also told by others. Other client managers had also had poor experiences at some stage with other university providers. Each used a story about another university to contrast with a successful engagement with a business school. The story is used to paint a stark contrast, and in doing so emphasises what the client organisation sought from the partnership. The client manager explained that another university had begun the selection process with a persuasive speaker, whom (the story teller pointedly said) they never saw again. This clearly seemed to make the point that reality did not match rhetoric. The client felt they had been sold a 'pup', as the university had promised flexibility, and yet proceeded to deliver the opposite. This poor performance was contrasted with the client's experience with another business school, about which the manager commented they 'just knew what the game was'. They felt the experience and track record that could be evidenced was vital. The client manager described the difficulty in getting the other university to deliver in colourful terms: 'we dragged the university along with us kicking and screaming'. The client manager then went on to contrast with a business school where the engagement has worked who were the exact opposite of the other provider, stressing the importance of the key people involved and the quality of the relationship that had been developed. She emphasised the importance of expertise and credibility, and the attitude of a 'can-do approach', which focused on meeting their needs.

### *'The Greatest Strength Story' – A Provocation*

This story set the scene at the beginning of the book and has a dilemma and a provocation at the heart of it. You will remember that the senior executive provocatively suggested that universities have access to the latest thinking yet too often that thinking is not in the courses they offer. Then, as if to balance the argument, the executive recognised that managers in businesses are too busy 'doing' to find the time to think. In essence, the point being made was that universities have what business wants but they don't use it, whilst businesses are too busy to find what they want and then use it. The business leader criticised in explicit and challenging terms what he perceived as business schools providing too much of 'yesterday's skills', when the need was for 'thinking, being creative and decision-making ability'. The story ends with a suggested resolution to this dilemma. The senior leader painted a picture of academic 'experts' sharing their thinking with practitioners. The practitioners then assessing how they can bring that thinking into their business, to determine whether they think it can work in their context. The ideas in this story resonate with what many of the client managers emphasised as a requirement, namely that the content stretched thinking but could also be applied in practice. This story pivots from the frustrations of the first two stories towards the optimism in the next two.

The three stories explained so far point towards a distinctive engagement, and were reinforced by comments made by other business leaders. A common view stressed a desire to work with a provider who would develop a solution tailored to their needs. They also articulated an interesting distinction between knowing they had a demand for an intervention within the organisation, whilst being uncertain of the actual development needs. A difference between knowing and not knowing was drawn: 'We didn't know what we wanted, we knew what the end result had got to be, but we didn't know how to get there'. It was particularly noticeable that many of the client managers highlighted the benefit of in-depth initial discussions and conversations, and stressed its importance in the process because they were aware as one manager put it of 'the needs we didn't even know we'd got'. They required an organisation which would listen to, and work with, them to clarify those needs. In addition, they identified reasons which should favour business schools as a provider. They valued theory when applied to experience and the 'ability to mix the business world with the academic world', whilst recognising the importance of research which informs practice (though also appreciating the importance of practice in turn refreshing research). They also respected ideas that broadened thinking with 'a weight and depth of learning' and 'a level of insight and thinking' but at the same time 'never undervaluing or underestimating the importance of their and their colleagues on the ground day-to-day experience'. The expectation was for latest thinking, not yesterday's skills, and that all too often this seemed to be deficient in the courses offered by some business school providers. It is clear that the qualities of academia were appreciated and valued by clients but, crucially, only when applied and made relevant to the client's operating context. Notably, they valued when ideas informed practice and had an impact, or in other words when the world of academia is effectively blended with the world of business. What was also apparent was the potentially advantageous position occupied by business schools if they are able to harness a demand-led and leading-demand approach.

If the first three stories challenged some of the practice of engagement with caution and provocation, then the next two stories hold up exemplars which explore what is needed to create the conditions for engagement.

### 'The Relationship Story' – An Exemplar of Best Practice

It is perhaps not surprising that a relationship story emerged from one case involving the largest number of interventions, and delivered over the longest period of time of any of the stories. This story had a strong sense of collaboration, centred on the idea that: 'we're in this together'. It seems that this relationship felt like 'everybody was working for the same cause', with a high level of trust conveyed through what the client manager described as a 'very easy relationship' with 'no barriers'. In particular, an ability to have difficult conversations was used to illustrate how the relationship worked to resolve problems 'in the right manner'. The client manager in this case attributed the quality of the organisational collaboration down to the way that individuals built effective relationships. A number of individuals from the business school were praised in examples drawn from the manager's experience. The relationship story actually could have been drawn from any of the other examples, as each client manager was keen to express the importance and the quality of the relationships that developed. This was a story that reinforced what was appreciated and what was considered necessary for success. The client manager provided the key lesson to the story: 'It's all about that relationship. If we didn't have the relationship we wouldn't have been able to achieve what we did. You have got to have that easy flow. To trust somebody, feel comfortable with somebody'. It would be a fair assumption to expect that the quality of relationships is important to employers, but what is striking about this story is just how much the relationship mattered.

### *'The Nurturing Story' – An Exemplar Story With Depth*

This story particularly emphasised the need to work closely with clients to build a relationship, and recognises that trust is a key factor in such activity. The business school senior manager who told the story felt that a potential client 'wanted to know if [the particular university] was the right place for them'. What was particularly interesting in this story was the senior manager's reflection about what 'struck me that caused them to suddenly accept us'. He explained that, knowing the client was a Roman Catholic, he had suggested that 'one thing I do is go to the choral evening song at the Cathedral.' The senior manager commented that the client's eyes 'lit up and his demeanor changed, he said he'd love to'. Later that evening, they then had a convivial meal where the senior manager remembered 'we did talk about business once or twice but we got to know each other'. The result of that evening was significant as the senior manager recounted: 'the next day they couldn't have been happier about the arrangements'. However, the senior manager then cautioned 'You can't do these things disingenuously; the connections have to be real'. He talked about 'finding a chink in the armour' of prospective clients to move towards a deeper relationship than one that is purely functional. 'I'm not suggesting you cosy up to people, but I do think you have to establish a rapport with someone if it's going to work'. Crucially the senior manager explained his motive behind this approach, which effectively is the moral of the story: 'When you get to know people they begin to open up about what the issues are in their business and how you might be able to help'. He then qualified the point of the story insisting that 'this hasn't been just a way of getting an entrée and contract this is about an on-going relationship and I think people really value that'. The story illustrates a skilful approach to client/provider engagement one that includes building rapport, but is deeper and broader in scale, it is about nurturing the relationship.

These two exemplar stories emphasised repeatedly the imperative of adopting a relational approach. Client managers were emphatic: it was all about the quality of the relationship. It would not be unreasonable to assume that relationships would be valued by businesses, but the level of confirmation and affirmation of this theme was surprising. Even when considering the first two cautionary engagement stories, relationship-building is evident as are the consequences of its absence. The process of listening in order to build understanding and clarity about what needed to be done begins to build the trust and confidence upon which a productive client–provider relationship can be developed. The client managers expressed their intent to find 'an organisation that works in partnership with us' and valued that there was 'a shared ownership of the programme, a very wide shared ownership'. Relationships were seen to be of prime value but could not be a substitute for skills and expertise. This combination of relationship and skills was stressed by one manager: 'If you haven't got that partnership and relationship then it is difficult for the programme to work. Don't get me wrong you need the ability and knowledge and experience as well'. Good relationships were clearly qualified with the need for the right skills and knowledge. There needed to be credibility as well as connection. Effective working relationships were evidenced by a sense of shared ownership and responsibility, to the extent that one client manager felt it was like both parties were working in the same organisation. Even when there were issues, it seemed to be the levels of trust in the relationship which provided the client with the confidence that they would be resolved amicably.

Engaging with a client to successfully deliver an intervention/contract is difficult enough but building on and sustaining that relationship requires more than credibility and relationship-building techniques. Sustaining the client/provider relationship requires nurturing behaviours. The 'nurturing story', told by the senior business school manager, offered an understanding of how long-term relationships can be more fully developed. Nurturing was an on-going feature of this story, implying much greater breadth and depth of relationship-building than the more obvious building of rapport or establishment of networks. As illustrated by the senior manager, nurturing requires integrity and a genuine interest and concern for the client, but this intent is always clearly defined by an underpinning aim: to be in a better position to help the client.

The final two stories fittingly comprise a problem and an opportunity story to highlight what needs to be overcome to realise the potential from the engagement. The first story proposes the 'scaffolding' that is needed to build engagement, and the second story envisages a 'springboard' to capitalise upon that engagement.

### 'The Skill Set Story' – A Problem Story

This story began with an assessment of the problems of trying to deliver a client programme within a university context based on inappropriate processes and timescales. It is a story where competing demands and differing perspectives caused tensions. The business school manager went on to tell the story of the difficulties presented in trying to manage the delivery of a client programme, with many staff who were not familiar with the different skills demanded for such engagements. A resolution to one of the tensions was then presented, with the manager explaining how associates were employed with the right mix of complementary skills to address the lack of academic staff with the relevant capabilities. The story was used to make the argument that many organisations didn't want to work with universities because of this lack of skill in engaging with their employees. The manager returned to this story of differing skill requirements, referring to the need for a 'shift of balance', with more recognition of the commercial world within academia. Allied to the problem of needing the right skills in place is the need for the right systems. Here, too the frustrations were evident with systems that did not support client programmes.

### *'The Springboard Story' – A Story of New Beginnings*

This story is about how the client was able to explore and develop other work which, in the view of the manager, would not have been possible without their previous experience of working with the university. It is an opportunity story. It also resulted in further work with the client for the business school. The client manager telling this story was adamant that if it hadn't been for the capacity building that happened through the project, then further new areas of work would not have been secured. It is also worth noting that whilst the university did gain further work, the organisation also pursued other work independent of the university. This story provided evidence supporting the way in which the engagement had created new opportunities for the client. Other client managers also spoke of how they themselves had developed as individuals, how the individuals on the programme had improved and how the organisation had benefited.

## Scaffolding and Springboards

There was clear agreement that business schools needed different skills and different roles if they were to work effectively with clients. There was also consensus from the business school managers that these client-facing skills were in short supply, something which is generally seen as problematic for business schools (Kewin et al., 2011; Thorpe & Rawlinson, 2013). These skills and roles were needed in order to bridge the gap between business and academia. This required skills to help achieve a better balance between the business and academic worlds through use of more appropriate teaching styles that challenge thinking, whilst being contextualised to practitioner's experiences. The broader issue here is worth reiterating: that there are 'too few academic staff with a full balance of understanding of commercial context, and with the skills to effectively conduct executive-education programmes that will satisfy experienced managers' (Thorpe & Rawlinson, 2013, p. 56). The business school managers interviewed had attempted to resolve these issues by identifying associates who did have the skills to address the need. There seems broad agreement that different skills and roles are needed and that they are a priority area of focus if business schools are to engage effectively with employers.

As important as the right skills is the need for universities to have systems in place that facilitate engagement. For a business school to work effectively with an employer, the issue of differing organisational time frames needs to be resolved. It is difficult to build effective client/supplier relationships when systems act in conflict with the requirements of the client engagement. This was typified by systems that 'were all student-focused and [set-up] for the individual student and not for individual clients'. Not only did there need to be a recognition of a different type of 'customer' but as already suggested there are differing require-ments in relation to speed and responsiveness: 'commercial clients want to move fast and expect a response. Universities work in year cycles, so the speed requirements of clients doesn't fit at all'. For one business school manager, there was a sense that client engagement seemed to be working in spite of the university, rather than because of it.

The 'springboard' story provided an interesting perspective on the value of continuing relationships. The main point made in this story was that good rela-tionships result in the partners developing new capabilities, which are mutually beneficial. This closely reflects the benefits that Moss Kanter (1994) argues should be evident in a collaboration: the generation of possibilities and the creation of extra value. In good relationships, value is added to the client along with the development of broader capabilities, whilst learning is shared and transferred in the organisation. Similarly, the HE provider benefits by the learning it gains and by using the enhanced credibility and experience it gets from the relationship (an important aspect for reputation-building) for the generation of new possibilities. These possibilities can be with new clients or in the extension of the existing relationship, often evidenced by a business school gaining new work with the client.

These two final stories have been about scaffolding and springboards. The scaffolding of skills and systems is essential if an engaged business school is to be built; they are critical enablers. If they are missing or limited, then both building and maintaining engagement will prove to be extremely difficult. Then the idea of a springboard establishes and emphasises an important intention of engagement: to generate new possibilities. It creates the image of not only being able to extend what is currently being done together but also to expand what is being done by doing different things with the new capabilities and knowledge gained by the interventions.

The stories represent a lived-experience of engagement and offer insights which may resonate with the experiences of those involved in this field. The overview of the stories is represented in Table 1.

In this chapter, the themes of the engaged business school have emerged from asking questions which attempt to explore what a business might be looking for in a business school. Three themes form the basis of effective engagement, requiring business schools to be distinctive by both listening to need and leading with ideas, relational as opposed to transactional and continuing to add value, and in so doing creating a sustainable future. A fourth theme underpins the other three

Table 1. Overview of Stories.

| Story | Type | Message | Tension | Moral/Punch Line | Purpose |
|---|---|---|---|---|---|
| Selection story | Cautionary story | Justify approach taken, lessons learnt from past experience. | Customised vs standard | 'Some acknowledged (our requirements) and then proceeded to tell us what they thought we wanted'. | Reveals the selection factors that are important to a client |
| The relationship story | Exemplar story | What made the project work so well: a very easy relationship. | Relational vs transactional | 'It's all about that relationship. If we didn't have the relationship we would not have been able to achieve what we did'. | Recognise the central role that an effective relationship had in the success of the contract. Collaborative: We, not us and them. |
| The contrasting universities story | Cautionary story | Reality didn't match rhetoric. | Responsive, listening vs, inflexibility, and failure to listen | Promising flexibility yet delivering the opposite. | Dramatically highlight what is wrong with some university provision. Contrasting with what was right |
| The greatest strength story | A provocation story | Latest thinking is the University's biggest advantage and is business's greatest need. Yet it isn't what universities teach, and businesses are too busy. | Latest thinking vs less of yesterday's skills. | In essence the point being made was that you (the University) have it but you don't use it. We (business) need it but we're too busy to find it and then use it. | A challenge and an opportunity. Proposes a key question: How can academia provide it greatest strength to business? |

Table 1. (*Continued*)

| Story | Type | Message | Tension | Moral/Punch Line | Purpose |
|---|---|---|---|---|---|
| The skill set story | A problem story | Words and actions need to match. | Teaching for business vs teaching academically | The need for a 'shift of balance', with more recognition of the commercial world within academia | Businesses didn't want to work with universities because of this lack of skills to engage with their employees. Recognition of the commercial world within academia is needed. |
| The nurturing story | Exemplar story | Nurturing, getting alongside, finding and creating common ground, authenticity, rapport, integrity. | People with credibility with clients vs skills that not many academic possess | 'You can't do these things dis-ingenuously, the connections have to be real'. | Present the values and behaviours for helping organisations |
| The springboard story | Opportunity story | New opportunities created by the capability built within the organisations. Things they couldn't do before that they are now able to do. | Business and Universities move to the next project and miss potential benefits | If it hadn't been for the capacity building that happened through the project, then further new areas of work would not have been secured | Recognise the value that can be gained from the relationship with new possibilities |

ensuring that the appropriate skills and systems are in place. At this stage in the argument, engagement stories are used to illustrate the themes. They are a valuable way to gain insights both from a business perspective and from a business school viewpoint. The stories whilst offering a rich source of information are also important both as a vehicle for sense making and a means of expressing tensions. Both will be important to understand as subsequently tensions are used as a means of indicating where different thinking may be needed in Chapter 4. Then in Chapter 5, the sense making of those directly involved will inform the model at the centre of the engaged business school, the purposeful engagement model.

The use of engagement stories is only a first step in exploring the engaged business school. In Chapter 5 a wider range of research, evidence and arguments will be drawn upon to assess the stories and determine the extent to which the ideas resonate more widely with that evidence base. Importantly, this then leads to exploring the building blocks for creating an engaged business school. The resulting model brings the factors of effective engagement together and charts a path towards their successful implementation. Before being able to do this, a step back needs to be taken to better understand the term 'engagement'. It would be reminisce of us to continue without defining what is meant by engagement, or perhaps more accurately to frame the various understandings of engagement which form the basis of the use of the word in this model.

Chapter 3

# A Framework for Engagement – The Ladder of Engagement

So far, the case for an engaged business school has been developed through exploring the need, and then gaining a picture of what engagement might look like through the lens of those involved in it. What has been missing from this discussion has been an understanding of what is meant by engagement, and that is not necessarily straightforward. Four ways in which engagement can be understood will be presented as a framework of engagement. Each of the ways to understand engagement are interconnected and effectively can be represented as a ladder of engagement progressing from action through to purpose. Together they represent the understanding of engagement that informs and shapes the engaged business school.

In general terms, engagement is a stronger word than involvement or participation; it suggests commitment. Such a differentiation from the passive to a stronger active language suggests a significant investment of time, energy and resource. That being the case an important aspect of engagement is establishing if it is worth doing. This naturally leads to thinking about who the parties are that are engaging together, and that requires a good understanding of the stakeholders of a business school. Engagement is not something that should be taken on half-heartedly. Not only does engagement suggest commitment, but it also conveys a sense of energy and points towards something that is attractive for the partners to do together. There is an energy, attractiveness and desire about making the relationship work. The term is used widely in universities whether it be civic, public, community, business, economic, employer, student or employee engagement. Most commonly and obviously the kind of engagement carried out by business schools is thought of in terms of business, employer and economic engagement. However, the broader societal perspectives and indeed the employee and student views are important and significant voices not to be minimised.

## Engaging Stakeholders

Given that engagement implies commitment, a good place to start is to explore the relationship business schools have with various stakeholders and the relative

The Engaged Business School, 31–48
Copyright © 2023 Anthony Sturgess
Published under exclusive licence by Emerald Publishing Limited
doi:10.1108/978-1-80382-941-820231006

commitment involved. Two concerns with the current stakeholder relationships are highlighted, followed by a suggestion for two approaches to be adopted to re-dress the stakeholder balance. There are a wide range of stakeholders who have some engagement with or interest in business schools. Here the term stakeholder is used based on its initial intention to move away from the limiting view of shareholders holding supremacy and to broaden the understanding beyond one privileged group identified as being invested in an organisation. The term 'invested in' indicates a more inclusive involvement beyond the financial, recognising different ways groups and individuals may be invested. In principle the term encourages a balanced and equitable approach across a range of stakeholders. To this extent it is helpful for this discussion. The possible breadth of engagement does prompt questions about the stakeholders of a business school. There has been an ongoing debate within business schools about stakeholders and their relative influence. On the one hand, there have been repeated challenges about businesses schools being too wedded to a limited number of stakeholders. On the other hand, there are difficulties with competing priorities with multiple stakeholders.

Firstly, there are arguments which question an economic engagement which has been variously associated with lack of an ethical and societal emphasis. Business schools have been accused of placing too much focus on free market economics, and being a contributor to a business environment where a lack of ethical standards, and irresponsible leadership has been highlighted through major business collapses (especially in the US) and in the 2008 financial crisis (Lejeune, Starkey, Kalika, & Tempest, 2018; Peters & Howard, 2020; Wilson & Thomas, 2012). Many of the criticisms have emerged following significant events with not only a serious economic cost but possibly an even greater societal impact, providing a reminder that economic and societal impact are often closely linked. It is interesting to note that the critique has often come from those who lead business schools or from those who are part of the professoriate (Pettigrew & Starkey, 2016). The extent to which such challenges are recognised as representative of the reality in business schools may be a question of degree, and of course varies from school to school, but it is promising and healthy to see the critique emerging from within. In effect the criticism has questioned the extent to which business school have been too closely aligned to an economic perspective that has supported a pursuit of profit and to a lesser extent broader and perhaps bigger societal questions: a more shareholder and less stakeholder focus. The position is neatly summarised by another business school leader, Professor Chris Mayer, the former Dean of Saïd business school. In his criticism of what he sees as the pervasive free-market doctrine across businesses he acknowledges that 'virtually, every business school course starts with a proposition that the purpose of business is to maximize shareholder value' (Mayer, 2019).

A second area of concern reflects a similarly narrow view of stakeholders and suggests that business schools place too much emphasis on internal stakeholders, particularly the academic community (Aguinis, Shapiro, Antonacopoulougnosis, & Cummings, 2014). Inevitably this focus leads to privileging one set of stakeholders (Lejeune et al., 2018) evidenced with reward and recognition being skewed towards publications in star-rated academic journals and using measurements such as citations. This results in a situation where academics are writing for academics and then are measured by being cited in other academic journals by academics. Such a narrow view of stakeholders results in activity and resource disproportionately invested in a limited number of groups. Business schools of course do have multiple stakeholders but what is at issue is the extent to which they are recognised and valued. A balanced and equitable approach means recognising the multi-stakeholder context that exists and the differing and divergent expectations of those groups (Lejeune et al., 2018). However, balance and equity needs to start with clarity of purpose, a theme to which the discussion will return to shortly.

There have been several attempts to identify the breadth of business school stakeholders which broadly can be summarised as involving academia and students, private and public sector, wider society, government, and non-government organisations, professional organisations and the media (Aguinis et al., 2014; Lejeune et al., 2018; Thomas, Chian, Thomas, & Wilson, 2013). It is an extensive range of diverse stakeholders raising questions about how balance between priorities might be addressed. To make sense of this landscape two areas of focus will be considered: one a response to the narrow view of stakeholders advocating a broader view, whilst the second complements breadth with a sense of depth.

Not surprisingly there have been calls to re-dress the balance with stakeholders. Irwin (2019) has argued for a broader view of stakeholders to raise the ambition towards societal value and public engagement. Similarly, as business schools emerge from the pandemic there are calls for a focus on a broader contribution to society and to sustainable development goals (Howard-Grenville, 2021). This is reinforced with business school accreditation bodies such as the Association to Advance Collegiate Schools of Business (AACSB) who have set guiding principles which emphasise societal impact (AACSB, 2020). Such calls are not unfamiliar, for example the Principles for Responsible Management Education was established in 2007 and many schools have incorporated such initiatives. Yet, the extent to which business schools have really embraced this ambition with action is questionable. This in part may be explained by the multitude of competing demands which make good intentions difficult to translate into action. This complexity is largely due to the fact that a multi-stakeholder perspective is not necessarily straight forward, as Irwin provocatively suggests, 'the contemporary business school emerges as an overloaded assemblage: responsible to multiple audiences and for multiple purpose' (Irwin, 2019, p. 203). A sense of overload and of competing expectations can lead to unsatisfactory but hardly surprising compromises. Before addressing this critical issue of overload a second complementary area of focus for stakeholders will be explored.

The idea of widening ambition with a broader view of stakeholders that raises horizons beyond a business and profit emphasis can be complemented with a locally sensitive approach to stakeholders (Aguinis et al., 2014). In this case the idea of depth is used to emphasise a business school being rooted in a particular place and choosing to build strong and longstanding relationships in that area. Such a local focus reflects a current argument being made about the importance of universities in place-based government policy, which recognises both the economic and social impact of the institutions (UK Research and Innovation, 2021).

Indeed, there is evidence to suggest that a placed-based approach benefits universities, although it does mean responding to challenges presented by the considerable pressure from government for such engagement (Goddard & Kempton, 2016). Interestingly, the civic university commission found that too often good practice in civic engagement happened in spite of, not because of that pressure (UPP Foundation, 2019). Local sensitivity of course is not a new thing for universities, many of whom trace their roots to a civic tradition and continue to maintain strong and strategic regional connections. In Chapter 7, the idea of business schools differentiating themselves by returning to their roots to learn lessons that could inform the future will be explored further. A local perspective roots a business school within its context and its communities. Such a view recognises that differing local stakeholders and their needs encourages business schools to develop differentiated and distinctive provisions shaped by their interaction with a particular place (UPP Foundation, 2019).

Breadth expands horizons, and roots ensure that aspirations are grounded in a business school's sense of place. The idea of place of course may well differ from business school to business school. Here the meaning is primarily about the physical place and locality, although it is recognised that some business schools may choose to define its sense of place differently. The dual approach of breadth and depth is reminiscent of the wings and roots metaphor drawn from a different context by Johann Wolfgang von Goethe, the German writer and poets who observed that 'There are two things children should get from their parents: roots and wings'. Roots here are interpreted as locating and embedding a business school. They provide stability and connection and inform identity and values but they also strengthen the 'ground' around them to be what is often termed as an anchor institution. Wings open up opportunities, spread the possibility of impact more widely both geographically, but also beyond a solely business focus to a business and societal emphasis. Wings overcome boundaries that may have held back, they prevent the idea of roots restricting and constraining. At the risk of overextending the metaphor, there is a further thought to add. There is also a sense that perhaps a business school can encourage a 'roots and wings' approach in businesses, roots that give a strong sense of place and of capability, and wings to grow and explore and to incorporate broader social responsibilities as an integral part of developing their business.

The challenge of a narrow stakeholder perspective has been explored with a broader and deeper narrative proposed, but it still leaves the problem of how to resolve the complexity of a multi-stakeholder context. There is clearly a dilemma between privileging certain audiences and addressing and recognising overload between multiple stakeholders. The one focuses resources and energy on a few, whilst the second spreads resources too thinly for the many. This tension is exacerbated with resource constraints due to the underlying issue (as discussed earlier in this chapter) that business schools are relatively small businesses. The result is under resourced attempts to offer a wide range of services and products to meet differing needs and expectations.

An engaged approach as advocated in this book clearly has risks if engagement means adopting an economic emphasis which at its core is narrow and in that sense is too close to business. It is an important consideration and is discussed more widely as the detail of the engagement model is expanded in Chapter 5. Exploring some of the complexities of those groups and parties who in some way are connected with business schools captures the context within which engagement needs to be understood. If the stakeholder approaches of broadening horizons and being locally sensitive are to be further explored, then there is a need to provide a way to articulate a business school mission and strategic intention. Indeed, there is an argument that this should be the starting place and only when this is done can the relative contribution of different groups, players and parties be considered (Mayer, 2021). Mission and purpose enables an assessment of the key stakeholders which a business school seeks to serve which then allows imbalances to be re-dressed and differing expectations to be synergised rather than competing against each other. Addressing these seemingly overwhelming conflicts returns the focus to the main intention of this chapter, which is to provide a richer understanding of engagement, by developing a framework which indicates ways that the tensions and dilemmas of stakeholders can be addressed.

## Framing Engagement

Clearly engagement has a range of different interpretations, consequently it is not well-understood and as a result is not done well, because critical aspects are missed. To be effective it must be viewed holistically. Therefore, to reflect a rounded view of engagement, a framework is proposed to provide a structure to represent different levels and depths, enabling effective engagement to be built. The framework was introduced in Chapter 1 and consists of four perspectives; activity, relationship, vocation and mission. The tendency is to think of engagement simply as activities which results in a very limited but common expression of engagement. The framework provides a richer view with the pivotal role of relationships connecting activities to the energy and motivation that a sense of vocation brings. Then, crucially mission provides a sense of purpose and direction. Too often engagement starts and stops with activities resulting in a one-dimensional view of engagement. All four levels need to be addressed to build an effective engaged business school. Therefore, engagement has to be understood as activity, relationship, vocation and mission. They also capture an increasing depth through the four levels and therefore it is helpful to consider them as a ladder of engagement. The four different perspectives will now be explored in turn.

### Engagement as Activity

The most tangible way in which engagement is often understood is by the activities that are carried out. There is obvious merit in clarifying the activities around which action is organised to achieve engagement. Activities give structure to what is meant by engagement and help to shape and explain how business schools and businesses connect. The scope and range of activities indicate the breadth of engagement possible for business, students and academics. Therefore, the first step in the framework is to consider what kind of activities are typically associated with engagement. Though activities can often be disconnected, and differ from business school to business school, nevertheless they can usefully be grouped into common types of activity. For example, activities can be grouped as research and development, knowledge exchange, advice and consultancy or as CPD, teaching, executive education and facilitation. In addition, there are business facing activities with wider economic and community development emphasis and finally services associated with students such as placements, internships, business clinic/consultancy and crucially the provision of business-ready graduates (Hogarth et al., 2007). Similarly, the Confederation of Business Industries (CBI) identified activities where they consider higher education might be relevant for the businesses they represent. The CBI highlighted: customised learning; accredited programmes delivered part-time; accreditation of in-house learning and development; and integrated programmes (CBI, 2008). In addition, knowledge exchange has been used as an organising term to describe engagement with business, as is the case with a longitudinal series of studies of university-business interaction. In these studies a wide range of knowledge exchange activities are then grouped into four categories: commercialisation, people-based, problem-solving and community-based (Hughes, Kitson, Slater, Angenendt, & Hughes, 2022).

There is clearly a breadth of interventions attributed to engaged activity. However, there has been a tendency for engagement and knowledge exchange activities to be more closely associated with research and applied research and to science based subject areas (Bolden, Hirsh, Connor, Petrov, & Duquemin, 2010; Hughes & Kitson, 2012). Indeed, Hughes and Kitson argue that this focus largely ignores 'the other reasons why businesses may connect with academia' (Hughes & Kitson, 2012).

This is illustrated by successive Government reports investigating varying aspects of university and business collaboration, which largely focussed on research and innovation, such as the Lambert report (Lambert, 2003) on industry-university interaction through to the Dowling review[1] in 2015. Interestingly, Dowling acknowledges at the start of her review that this theme has proved an 'exceptionally popular target for reviews and studies in recent years' (Dowling, 2015, p. 10). To illustrate her point, Dowling lists 14 reviews with this emphasis which have addressed University-business collaboration, beginning with Lambert's review in 2003.

In sharp contrast, there is an argument that 'employer engagement in educational provision within the University sector is less well understood' (University Alliance, 2015, p. 4). Indeed, there has been relatively little emphasis placed on an appreciation of the role of teaching related activities in supporting engagement, and especially in relation to the provision of higher level skills for those already in the workplace (The Royal Society, 2008). Similarly, the CBI in their survey of business collaboration with universities stress a different balance between research

---

[1]The Dowling review was set up by the coalition government, but which reported to the newly formed Conservative Government.

and teaching activities (CBI, 2008a). They found, of those organisations who said they had developed links with universities, that 45% stated workforce development as the reason for the engagement which interestingly was broadly similar to the number of organisations more interested in engagement for research purposes (CBI, 2008a). According to the CBI, this indicated 'extensive existing practice among employers in using Universities for staff development' (CBI, 2008a, p. 45). Subsequently, the CBI reported that the split between research and other activities including consultancy and training and professional development continued to be broadly the same (CBI, 2015). A remarkably similar balance was indicated by the Chartered Association of Business School. Their members reported that around 5.6% of business school revenue was due to executive education, with income from research activities also generating about the same percentage (Chartered Association of Business Schools, 2017).

More recently, a significant study of business-university interaction over the period 2005–2021 reinforced the argument that there are wider reasons for engagement than research in science based subject areas. The study found that over 50% of the organisations stated that the reason for their interaction with universities relates to business operations and management (Hughes et al., 2022). These interactions were in marketing, sales, human resource management, organisation/strategy and operations (Hughes & Kitson, 2012; Hughes et al., 2022). Quite clearly, these areas of interaction position business schools centre-stage to build on the opportunities.

The significance of emphasising the need to develop skills for those in the workplace also continues to be stressed. The Industrial Strategy Council argue that since 80% of the 2030 workforce are already working (Industrial Strategy Council, 2019) then future skills needs will need to focus on addressing those already in the workplace. This matters because according to the Industrial Strategy Council 2.1 million of the workforce are 'likely to be acutely under-skilled in at least one core management skill (leadership, decision-making or advanced communication)'.

Future skills typically involve upskilling and re-skilling, where upskilling is generally viewed as skills related to an existing role with an emphasis on raising skill levels to improve performance and to keep up to date. In contrast, re-skilling is about new knowledge and skills for different jobs or entirely new jobs (Li, 2022). There are however different terms in use, for example the UK Government uses upskilling in the same way, but then refers to retraining as the term to explain new skills acquisition (Parliament, 2021). These upskilling and re-skilling needs of the economy, business and of individuals, where so many of those likely to need these skills are already in the workplace, do place a focus on workplace development activities and on engagement with business to meet the needs.

One area of business school services which obviously engages with business is executive education. It is an area that the British Academy notes as being distinctive to business schools when compared to many other subject fields in a university (British Academy, 2021). Executive education supports workforce development and can be seen as a form of life-long learning, but is also a dynamic and innovative area with a wide range of interventions supporting individuals and businesses (British Academy, 2021; Lock & Hinxman, 2018). It is instructive to note how activities are grouped for this type of work. Predominantly, these will relate to teaching activities. Indeed, there is a contention about which services and 'products' are included under the banner of executive education. The Chartered Association of Business Schools has previously surveyed member business schools to explore how executive education is defined by the programmes that they run. They found that most included short-courses that are not accredited, with customised programmes usually also a part of the provision. Nearly half of the respondents included their executive MBA with a slightly smaller percentage incorporating other executive masters. Some also recognised their DBA provision, with a growing number including apprenticeships and some 'massive open online courses' (MOOCs) (Chartered Association of Business Schools, 2017). What is apparent is that existing provision does indeed vary considerably.

Before considering how executive education might be changing, it is helpful to think about the ways in which it has been categorised to date. Some provisions appear to focus on one organising category, others combine more than one. An obvious place to start is to group activities based on the customer (based on who pays). In this configuration executive education programmes are grouped together based on the client or in addition an individual who works for an organisation who then pays for the service. Secondly, the type of student has often shaped the provision and is associated with roles in an organisation that are at a certain level, usually managerial and having a certain level of business experience. Alternatively, provision might be organised in relation to the nature of the programmes. Two approaches are often used, firstly where the types of programme are only short courses, CPD or customised programmes that are unaccredited (this categorisation connects with early ways in which executive education was defined). Related to this grouping is to categorise by the level of programmes and often this grouping refers to post-experience master's level equivalent provision. 'Post-experience masters' is a phrase which effectively combines level of programme with type of student. For some business school's executive education provision may be differentiated by location and reflect either a global or local focus. This category emphasises the extent to which international business and students are crucial to executive education, and alternatively whether a local focus on a place-based approach is important.

In reality, executive education provision may adopt a mix of these categories. What is interesting to understand is the context of disruptive changes which are challenging the shape of executive education provision and therefore how it is categorised. Six disruptions will serve to illustrate the pressures at work in this area. First and foremost, the very term executive education is being questioned. There is a challenge about the extent to which the term points to the past when executives meant senior leaders at a particular level, and that this no longer reflects the current situation never mind serving future needs. In reality the term is also not particularly inclusive. Secondly, government policy and related funding influences provision. For example, in the UK degree apprenticeships have skewed the executive education market with many businesses arguing that part of their learning and development budget which previously they might have spent on executive education is now only available through degree apprenticeship funding routes. Raising skills and performance in businesses is another significant area of government policy with initiatives for small businesses such as 'Help to Grow'.

Thirdly, there are trends with online learning and digital platforms that are changing the nature of delivery and opening executive education to a wider range of competition. Fourth, and an area which often goes hand-in-hand with digital platforms, is micro-credentials and lifelong learning which place a different focus and emphasis on executive education. It also connects with government policy with changes to funding mechanisms for lifelong loan Entitlements planned for 2025. Fifthly, there is a very significant re-skilling and upskilling need. Again, these disruptions are interconnected. This area is closely linked to lifelong learning. As pointed out earlier, the Industrial Strategy Council argue that since 80% of the 2030 workforce are already working then future skills needs will need to focus on addressing those already in the workplace (Industrial Strategy Council, 2019). The sixth disruption is internal to business schools and reflects the ability to provide a wider range of interventions. It is about providing a gateway through relationship. The Chartered Association of Business School's executive education impact report (2017) indicated the value of executive education in building client relationships which opened up other opportunities such as knowledge transfer partnerships (KTPs), consultancy, research and connections with and for undergraduate students.

There appears to be little doubt that there is a need to think more widely about who (what we currently call) executive education is for, and that the response to that question may also vary based on the different stakeholders (discussed earlier) with whom a particular business school engages. Whilst this area of business school provision most clearly connects with business it seems that it also is in need of a rethink. Adopting a more stakeholder and relational emphasis encourages business school to ask 'who' before asking 'what' and that in turn changes the focus of executive education from the activities to the relationships, to which our attention will turn next.

The evidence suggests that there is a wide range of interactions with business, which business schools should be well-placed to address. An important area is workforce skills, and the need for those already in the workplace to be developed, and not just those entering as undergraduates. It is also of note that teaching-related activities and broader business interactions seem to account for significant parts of the engagement with business and should be recognised on an equal footing with research activities. Finally, business schools already have well-established activities with business in the form of executive education. However, the indications are that this area is also in need of some different thinking.

### Engagement as Relationship

Viewing engagement as relationship changes how activities are perceived. In terms of the ladder of engagement, this is the lynchpin to connect activities with vocation and mission. It is also a level of engagement that is missed or not acknowledged. The importance of relationships means that an argument needs to be made for a more complex model than the typical customer–supplier relationship. Relational engagement builds trust, connects activities together and links them to vocation and mission.

Up to this point engagement has been discussed as a set of activities carried out by business schools with business and the community. However, engagement can also usefully be thought of as a relationship. Universities build different relationships with employers and therefore an important issue to clarify is 'how to build and maintain these relationships' (Bolden et al., 2010). Indeed, the idea of building a relationship does seem to be problematic as, according to Lambert, 'companies and universities are not natural partners' (Lambert, 2003, p. 13). There seems to be issues due to the two communities not understanding each other (The Royal Society, 2008), resulting even at a business school level in a 'lack of good relationships and networks' (Thorpe & Rawlinson, 2013, p. 10). Disappointingly, businesses find business schools hard to navigate and not particularly responsive (Thorpe & Rawlinson, 2013). Interestingly, Bolden et al. (2010) suggest that a valuable way to develop engagement is by 'holding onto the idea of "engagement" as being about relationships rather than activities' (Bolden et al., 2010, p. 24). In a similar vein the Chartered Associate of Business Schools argue that whilst there are obvious benefits from research and teaching, the more significant benefits derive from the relationships built with businesses (Chartered Association of Business Schools, 2017). It is the relationship that opens up opportunities. It is encouraging to observe this recognition of the value of relational engagement from CABS seems to be reciprocated from business, who recognise that long-term relationships with a partner result in their needs being better understood (Carrington Crisp, 2021).

However, many of the activities associated with engagement are carried out in a transactional manner rather than with the intent of building relationships. Some business schools may have varying relationships represented through different activities, often individual academics or sub-groups may have good relationships and connections with business. Such connections exist hidden in plain view, not really recognised or reinforced by the strategic direction of the business school. In contrast, when the importance of relationships is recognised, the value and significance of the individuals sustaining those relationships comes to prominence. The value of individuals is reinforced by evidence that personal relationships and mutual understanding through shared experiences are critical to any engagement and underpinned by the notion that the relationship should be mutually beneficial (Bolden et al., 2010; CBI, 2015; Hughes et al., 2022).

Relationships are about people, so it is not surprising that personal connections matter. However, to build on this both business and business schools need to consider how they encourage and reinforce individuals with appropriate support (National Centre for Universities and Business, 2022). Business schools therefore need to commit to developing the support necessary to sustain the relationships that enable businesses to connect with their capabilities and resources (Thorpe & Rawlinson, 2013). But this is not just a one-sided responsibility, businesses have also acknowledged that they need to do more in supporting their own capacity to engage with universities (Hughes et al., 2022). The balance between personal engagement and the need for structures that support and extend beyond the individual emerges as an important aspect of the model of engagement which will be explored in more depth in Chapter 5.

A relational perspective facilitates the 'demand-led' approach advocated earlier because of the two-way conversation implied by a relationship (Bolden et al., 2010). Implicit to this approach is a willingness to listen, understand and demonstrate responsiveness to needs (AACSB, 2022). Thinking of engagement as relational rather than simply activities moves away from a tendency to encourage transactional supply-led approaches. By implication this is not a typical customer supplier relationship, with a supply side focus of offering existing programmes or standard interventions. For example, Connor and Hirsh (2008) in their model of employer engagement, focus on collaboration through mutual engagement and argue for a more complex model than a customer–supplier relationship. Their model positions collaboration at the centre of a dialog between an employer and a university. The dialog allows both parties to understand each other's needs and capabilities and to explore how a partnership could work. More recently AACSB suggest that executive education in the future will 'shift away from the supply-led content of yesteryear, to the demand-led, flexible solutions of tomorrow' (AACSB, 2022). This is a view that resonates with much of the discussion to date. Relationships connect and join up activities and bring them to life in the context of shared understanding, trust and mutual respect. However, for relationships to be engaging they also need the energy and motivation of staff and that requires exploring the sense of vocation of academics and of engaged scholarship.

## Engagement as Vocation and the Scholarship of Engagement

Engagement as vocation provides a deeper understanding to the idea of scholarship. This section adapts Boyers seminal work (Boyer, 1990) that explores a richer view of scholarship, connecting more closely to an academics sense of purpose, that is to a sense of vocation. The four perspectives of vocation advocated by Boyer are discussed in the context of engagement, in particular the scholarships of application and integration. The ideas are further developed by building on some of Weick's reflections of a different view of integration (Weick, 1996).

The third approach to thinking about engagement brings the discussion towards the motivations behind the idea and connects with the role of the academic. This is the perspective of engaged scholarship which shares common ground with interpretations of engagement as mission, the fourth element of the framework. Boyer expresses mission as a need to engage in seeking answers to some of the most significant issues across business and society (Boyer, 1996). In a turn of phrase which resonates with one of the key tensions in business schools, Boyer advocates moving beyond what he suggests is the 'tired old "teaching versus research" debate' (Boyer, 1990, p. 16). In an attempt to challenge this kind of tension, which perhaps unsurprisingly reflects the debate about relevance,

Boyer calls for a more embracing view of scholarship. It is a view that rejects defining the work of academics in narrow terms of traditional teaching and research. However, critics such as Fish, author of a provocatively titled book *Save the World on Your Own Time* suggest the opposite (Fish, 2008). For Fish, a university should be just about teaching and research and the academics role is therefore to produce knowledge in a dispassionate, separated and rigorous manner, and to then disseminate that knowledge. Though, from Boyer's perspective, scholarship certainly does mean a primary focus on original research with dispassionate freedom, what he refers to as the scholarship of discovery. However, scholarship also means looking for connections, 'giving meaning to isolated facts, putting them in perspective' (Boyer, 1990, p. 18); or the scholarship of integration. For this to happen Boyer argued for sharing across academic disciplines. Similarly, Weick describes a very interconnected approach towards teaching practitioners, but with an important difference. The expectation that discoveries and ideas will emerge from working together in the classroom context as with Boyer is prominent. Weick (1996) points to the tendency for academics to teach from within their discipline boundaries in an isolated and unconnected manner. In contrast, practitioners are more likely to discuss connections in the world which completely disregard such artificial boundaries. This resonates with Boyer's original work on integration. But what is particularly interesting is that, whereas Boyer discusses academics working together across their disciplines to achieve this integration, Weick introduces the idea that it is the practitioners who are ideally placed to make those connections. Similarly, Gulati (2007) points to classroom engagement with practitioners as a context to test ideas and build theory. The notion of collaborative learning from across academic disciplines and especially through managers and leaders making connections offers a powerful perspective for engaged scholarship and indicates some of the practices that can build a sense of vocation.

These first two of Boyer's interpretations fit with more widely accepted views of scholarly activity, namely investigation and synthesis. But Boyer argues for a broader sense of scholarship with two further categories. The scholarship of application seeks to apply theory to problems of significance, but it is not a one-way process, theory is applied to practice, and practice informs theory, in a quest to ensure knowledge is useful (Boyer, 1996). The last of Boyer's engaged scholarships, recognises that for any academic's work to be of consequence it needs to be understood by others; it needs to be taught. Yet for Boyer, 'teaching, at its best, means not only transmitting knowledge, but transforming and extending it as well' (Boyer, 1990, p. 14). According to Boyer this can be done by listening and learning from students and reflecting on their perspectives and insight. So, in this context academics learn as they teach, and together with students are extending and reinterpreting theory. Boyer sees the four scholarships as complementary, together forming a scholarship of engagement.

The idea of scholarship as vocation, where there is a strong intrinsic motivation to contribute does lead to more fundamental questions. This is captured by Pettigrew's observation: 'if the duty of the intellectual in society is to make a difference, the research community has a long way to go to realise its potential'

(Pettigrew, 2001, p. S67). He points to the limitations of efforts to resolve the theory to practice gap which typically take the form of researchers being asked to improve their dissemination. This is otherwise referred to as a knowledge transfer gap (Van de Ven & Johnson, 2006), where too often research is lost in translation (Shaprio, Kirkman, & Courtney, 2007). Pettigrew argues forcefully that dissemination is 'too late if the wrong questions have been asked' (Pettigrew, 2001, p. S67), a view which resonates with Van de Ven and Johnson's (2006) knowledge production problem, where research is lost before translation (Shaprio et al., 2007). As a consequence, Pettigrew argues that a 'wider and deeper form of engagement between researchers and practitioners is needed in the co-production of knowledge' (Pettigrew, 2001, p. S67). Similarly, Boyer considers there is plenty of evidence that society is 'vitally enriched as scholars and practitioners speak and listen carefully to each other' (Boyer, 1996, p. 15). Boyer has developed an expansive view of how scholarship can engage with practitioners and provides a more integrated language to recognise the contributions possible when academics engage with practitioners to connect ideas, bridge the gap between theory and practice, and create insights with practitioners through teaching.

Whilst the focus of engaged scholarship is mainly with academics within business schools, there is also value in recognising the dual role that managers on academic programmes might play. Professional masters and doctorates where business professionals conduct research and investigations into their own organisation have raised the profile of a dual role. Such roles have variously been referred to as researching professionals (Bourner, Bowden, & Laing, 2001), insider/outsider researcher (Brannick & Coghlan, 2007; Evered & Louis, 1981) and scholar-practitioners (Carton & Ungureanu, 2018; Tenkasi & Hay, 2004). They offer the potential to act as boundary spanners between academia and practice (Smith & Wilkins, 2018).

Finally, returning to where the discussion started, Boyer's articulation of an engaged scholar provides a tangible expression of what practice looks like. As a result there is more clarity for academics who have a sense of vocation which is rooted in a motivation to make a wider contribution (Atta-Owusu & Fitjar, 2022). Such academics, with the right abilities and experience such that they understand the needs of business and know how to work with partners, are central to shaping the nature and scale of engagement (Ulrichsen, 2019). Given the importance of this kind of academic talent to engaged scholarship, it is a significant frustration that too often there is a lack of appreciation of such roles, evidenced by a limited recognition in terms of progression (Atta-Owusu & Fitjar, 2022). This surely needs to change if universities and business schools are serious about engagement being a part of their strategic intention.

### *Engagement as Mission*

Engaged scholarship shares common ground with interpretations of engagement as mission, which is the fourth level in the ladder of engagement. Thinking of engagement as mission brings direction to the energy and motivation of vocation and together they generate a sense of purpose. This section will consider the national and institutional interpretations of engagement as mission in order to position engagement in a strategic context. Later in Chapter 7, consideration will be given to how the framework can be used to develop individual missions for a business school.

Engagement is often expressed in the mission of a University, with the Universities Commonwealth Association advocating engagement with the wider society as a core mission of a University (cited in Gourley, 2004). In this setting the National Co-ordinating Centre for Public Engagement (NCCPE) defines engagement as 'a two-way process, involving interaction and listening, with the goal of generating mutual benefit' (2013). Additionally, the NCCPE have led calls in the UK for universities to sign up to a public engagement manifesto, to recognise their 'major responsibility to contribute to society through their public engagement' (National Co-ordinating Centre for Public Engagement, 2010, p. 1). More recently, the Civic University Commission recommended that Civic University agreements should be developed with a call for place based civic engagement to be explicit in a university's mission (UPP Foundation, 2019). Similarly, UK research funders produced a concordat for engaging the public in research, with a 'vision for a research culture that values, recognises and supports public engagement' (Research Councils UK, 2011, p. 4).

Increasingly, government policy has tended to highlight the contribution universities can make by engaging with business and contributing to economic growth. Whilst there is a broader discourse about public engagement, there is considerable pressure for universities and in particular business schools to engage specifically with business. Such expectations are illustrated in statements such as this, from the Wilson review of university-business collaboration: 'for UK universities to take their place as world leaders in business support and interaction, we need a new covenant between business and universities' (Wilson, 2012).

More specifically, in the context of mission, engagement has often been described as being a third stream of activity, and referred to as knowledge exchange (HEFCE, 2011), alongside the traditional university emphasis placed on teaching and research. The term 'third stream' can be problematic, implying a third, lesser stream, which tends not to be 'an integrated strategy of most HEI's' (Kewin et al., 2011, p. 20). There is evidence that this is changing. Government policy has increasingly stressed the significance of knowledge exchange to support and enable economic recovery and growth (RSM PACEC, 2017) with until 2018 the Higher Education Funding Council (HEFCE) trying to shape the engagement of universities with business and the wider community. The government's view over time has framed its funding of knowledge exchange within wider policies focused on reducing the deficit, promoting economic growth and rebalancing the economy towards the private sector. This results in incentivising the kind of knowledge exchange that demonstrates performance and in aligning the allocation of funding with strategies such as the Industrial Strategy and levelling up (Research England, 2020).

Alongside the economic and social focus being placed on knowledge exchange there has been a drive led by Universities UK to establish principles to better recognise the contribution of knowledge exchange. Mission and engagement are two of the principles they identified for effective knowledge exchange (Universities UK, 2020). The concordat also emphasises building capability and ensuring there is reward and recognition for knowledge exchange. This increasing national activity indicates a desire to affirm knowledge exchange's strategic importance and to ensure that it is properly recognised in the strategy, policies and processes of universities.

It is interesting to note that the evidence suggests that the nature and scale of engagement in knowledge exchange depends upon the motivation and ability of individuals supported by the institution's culture, in order to legitimise and affirm the value of knowledge exchange (Ulrichsen, 2019). In effect bringing together the sense of vocation expressed by individuals with mission.

There is however still much to be done to better understand engagement as mission and its impact and value. For example, when CABS investigated how business schools delivered public good they found some schools did clearly articulate their position. Such business schools, they referred to as 'purpose-driven', suggesting that evidence of mission related to engagement, in this case coalescing around public value, is emerging. However, they noted that the broader relationships in which business schools engage with the private, public and third sectors are not well understood. They state that little is known about the way this is organised or delivered (Chartered Association of Business Schools, 2021).

## The Framework From a Business Perspective

It is clear that there are a wide range of opportunities from which businesses would benefit if they were able to improve their engagement with business schools. The framework can help to do this in two ways, it can clarify what a business should be looking for in a business school, and it can indicate what a business needs to do differently. Part of the difficulty businesses have in accessing resources and capability may well be associated with business schools not making this easy to do, so the framework can help a business to know what to look for in an engaged business school. However, businesses should also use the framework to change their own practices to make themselves better able to realise this potential.

The first part of the framework views engagement as activity. At a very basic level a business can determine if the business school delivers the kind of activities that it needs. Similarly it is also helpful to know if staff in the schools are responding to needs that the business articulates in a flexible manner. A business may want to know that they can access a range of activities should they need them including, for example customised programmes, accredited masters, short CPD interventions, consultancy and research. Engagement as activity highlights the wide range of interventions possible. Many businesses may find that their initial involvement with a business school is actually through CPD, short courses or supporting an individual member of staff on a master's programme. The challenge for a business is to think about how it might then gain more through these initial interactions. One area that holds promise is the future skill needs of the workforce. This is a crucial area for business with the dual focus on upskilling and reskilling the workforce. Future skills are an example of where different interventions and activities can be brought together. Staff need to be updated, they need to develop new skills, and businesses need to access research on emerging skills and consultancy to establish their specific needs. The challenge for business is to identify a business school who can bring these activities together for them.

Making sense of the range of activities available requires a relational approach. Businesses see the benefit in establishing long term relationships, because they recognise the added value gained from a business school knowing and understanding their organisation. It is therefore important for businesses to ensure they have staff who can connect and work effectively with a business school. Businesses may well have individuals who have a good relationship with an individual at a business school. There will also be many staff familiar with business schools and universities having studied in one at some point. Therefore there are usually many touch points which can be developed further. It is as much a business's responsibility as it is for a business school to have staff who can see the potential and are able to build relationships to connect and combine activities to make a more coherent whole.

The third perspective of the framework is to view engagement as vocation. This view seems to be more of a business school priority, however there is a part for business to play if they are to realise the benefits this perspective can bring. In 'the greatest strength story' the value of latest thinking for business was highlighted alongside the frustration that the executive's managers were too busy to keep up to date. Business can contribute to this area by calling for the latest thinking, and by being a part of creating that emerging thought leadership. New knowledge is often created in the business context, but not always developed further, indicating that much more could be made of this. If academics are to research in areas of value to business then communication needs to be two way, there is a responsibility placed on businesses to highlight their needs.

The term scholarship is not one that is frequently used in business, yet the idea of developing scholar-practitioners who are able to bridge between academia and practice may be helpful. Many leaders and managers have already been introduced to this approach on executive style masters programmes. The idea encourages managers and leaders to continue a scholarly approach in their practice as managers. Scholarly practitioners value both theory and practice (Tenkasi & Hay, 2004) and are characterised as having a 'foot in both camps' (Carton & Ungureanu, 2018). In addition, there is scope to develop thought leadership within the business by identifying some staff to study a professional doctorate with the intention to develop thought leadership in a field/sector. Such initiatives raise the capability within the organisation and blur the boundaries between a business school and business. More significantly, there is also the possibility of creating posts which bridge between business and academia as a strategic intent to make the most of the relationship.

The importance of strategic intent leads to the final perspective of the framework: mission. Businesses as stakeholders have a contribution to make to a business schools mission, they have influence in shaping how a business schools serves it various communities. There is also a sense that business should also consider their purpose in engaging with business schools, and the extent to which strategic intentions might come together. Where there are good relationships and high trust, then it becomes much easier for the honest conversations to be had about potential competing expectations (an area highlighted earlier in this chapter with competing stakeholders). It encourages business to be a part of finding solutions together with a business school.

## A Language and Structure for Engagement

This chapter has explored the engagement framework where mission provides direction to the energy and motivation of vocation, it provides intention to the relationships which in turn bring to life, connect and shape activities. What is apparent is that the activities that variously are associated with engagement are extensive, with as much attributed to learning, CPD and knowledge sharing as to research. Notably the interventions are across all areas of business operations and therefore far broader than a narrow STEM or science-based subject focus, a position not always reflected or emphasised in government policy. Activity is an easy way to explain engagement, but it is also a limiting way to do so. Seeing engagement as about relationships changes things. The heart of this framework is the pivotal importance of relationships. It is also an area that universities and business schools have not always done particularly well. Building relationships is the crucial part of the framework which connects to people and businesses. Where it works well it is largely because of individuals making it happen. The challenge for business schools is to value and encourage such individuals, but then to also build beyond towards relationships at an organisational level. This important issue is explored in the model of engagement in Chapter 5.

Whilst relationships bring engagement to life there is still more needed. Businesses do not just want to be listened to and valued, they also want to know that a business school is credible and competent with staff who bring relevant expertise and know how to work with them. The engaged scholar brings together particular skills and an approach to scholarship, together with a sense of motivation. It is a different focus to conventional academic progression and needs to be recognised and fostered if engagement is to be embedded in the mission of a business school. And mission is the overriding perspective which connects significance and crucially direction to the other three. This is about developing an intentional engagement mission. When mission and purpose are clarified the stakeholder questions can be explored. This is not an easy task given the multiple stakeholders associated with a business school and the concerns that a narrow perspective privileges a few at the expense of others. However, a mission begins to identify where to prioritise and to build relationships with particular groups and parties. Whilst understanding engagement as mission is emerging as a part of strategic conversations in Universities; how to organise and make it happen is less clear.

The framework offers a possible way to articulate what engagement looks like. It can be helpful in a number of ways. Primarily it provides a language and structure for translating mission into action, ensuring important aspects of engagement are not missed or ignored. The framework can also be used to map current engagement and also as a tool to develop an engagement mission. Business schools of course, to varying extents, are already involved in engagement. So, the framework can be a way of mapping what is currently in place, and identifying areas that are missing, weak or poorly connected. A mapping exercise at each level of the framework brings together what is currently there in the school. It can be used to identify strengths and surface business-facing elements many of which are often unconnected and lack focus. It also identifies client and partner relationships already present but not necessarily valued. This process surfaces latent potential and begins to integrate engagement. Indeed, it can be helpful to carry out this exercise as a first step before then using the framework to develop and articulate mission and purpose, in so doing bringing together a business school's strengths and aspirations.

Finally, returning to where this discussion began, there are still questions to resolve with the issue of stakeholders. So far, an approach has been suggested to clarify the strategic intention and frame the engagement with stakeholders. Using the engagement framework helps a business school firstly to identify stakeholders which relate to its mission and purpose and then secondly to think through how it connects with stakeholders. The use of the framework to assess stakeholders will be considered in more detail in Chapter 7 when applications of the engagement framework will be explored as part of the discussion of an engaged business school in practice.

The issue of addressing competing expectations of stakeholders is improved by a mission which provides more clarity about the choice of relationships and groups with whom to engage. However, the nature of a business school means that it will still have multi-stakeholders with the subsequent risk of overload and inevitably there will be tensions and apparent conflicts. Some important areas of tension have already been highlighted, for example between narrow perspectives such as reinforcing a particular economic focus contrasted with a broader societal emphasis, or the narrow in-ward looking focus on academics at the expense of other stakeholders. Similarly, the broader societal theme could also conflict with a deeper local sensitivity. As in the tension just mentioned priorities can often be good in themselves but compete for finite resource. It is apparent that alongside the fact that a clear mission helps with the clarification of stakeholders, something further is needed. A means of addressing and reframing tensions and conflicts is needed. The usual response to a tension is to choose one or the other, or to compromise between the two positions. Of course, making a choice or compromising may be appropriate, but so is the opportunity to re-frame and to think differently. It is this third perspective of different thinking that is of interest as a way to resolve what may appear to be competing expectations of different stakeholders. This approach seeks synergies and ways in which expectations can be complementary rather than conflicting. This is the topic of the next chapter.

# Chapter 4

# Resolving Tensions and Stories of Engagement

There are clearly tensions between competing stakeholders, and it is also apparent that there are conflicting views and tensions about the legitimacy and identity of business schools, which were mentioned in Chapter 1, but up to this point without any explanation. Addressing these tensions is central to the argument proposed in this book. There is a necessarily wide-ranging discussion needed to be had in order to position the idea of the engaged business school in a context, with some of the issues such as legitimacy and relevance being longstanding areas of contention. These are significant issues of themselves and have been addressed comprehensively elsewhere.[1] It is not the intention or purpose here to comprehensively address the complexity and range of the debates associated with the issues. Rather the hope is that sufficient justice will be done by discussing areas that are germane to this discussion. Attempting to consider long standing tensions in a short space is problematic, but to not consider the issues would be just as problematic, since they are pervasive in the discussion of an engaged business school. It is hoped that a balance will be struck.

Understanding how tensions are viewed and analysed are therefore particularly helpful to navigating a path through the dilemmas. This chapter will explore different approaches to analysing tensions, from holding tensions through to releasing tensions and re-imagining them. In particular, two areas will be considered:

- Using the idea of tension to rethink the continuing competing perspectives on the legitimacy and identity of business schools
- Analysing tensions inherent in business and business school interaction to develop a model for engagement

---

[1]Two excellent discussions of legitimacy can be found in Pettigrew & Starkey, The Legitimacy and Impact of Business Schools – Key Issues and a Research Agenda, 2016 and Thomas, Lorange, & Sheth, The Business School in the Twenty-First Century: Emergent Challenges and New Business Models, 2013.

**The Engaged Business School, 49–64**
Copyright © 2023 Anthony Sturgess
Published under exclusive licence by Emerald Publishing Limited
doi:10.1108/978-1-80382-941-820231008

## Understanding Tensions

Competing tensions often lead to the need to compromise and settle for less. It can seem too difficult or even impossible to satisfy competing needs. Usually something needs to give, and this may of course be an appropriate action to take. However, tensions can also be an indication of a need for different thinking, suggesting that what Heifetz and Linsky (2002) refer to as a holding environment may be required to enable this to happen. Reframing sets a challenge of trying to find a way for both priorities of a competing tension to be met, instead of an either/or outcome, or favouring more of one and less of the other. This means adopting what Paul Polman, former CEO of Unilever, described as an 'AND Mentality' (Lewis, Andriopoulos, & Smith, 2014). Reframing involves thinking differently about multiple tensions, testing underlying assumptions and seeking synergies.

Tensions are typically understood as conflicting positions, contradictions or inconsistencies which pull in opposite directions (Higson & Sturgess, 2014). They may be visible in dualities and inconsistencies, and are often experienced as competing and contradictory poles that demand a choice of either one or the other (Bartunek & Rynes, 2014). Dualities are polar opposites, with the difference between the opposing positions experienced as a tension. However, they are not necessarily either/or choices, or 'contradictions that are mutually exclusive' (Seo, Putnam, & Bartunek, 2004). In fact, Seo et al. (2004) helpfully suggest that there is a spectrum of ways in which a tension or duality may be viewed, which they express in four possible responses.

These four responses will be explained shortly in relation to the tensions associated with an engaged business school. In particular, the idea of re-framing and transcending the tension will be used to inspire different thinking. Whilst tensions can provide helpful insights, Poole and van de Ven (1989) helpfully caution that in the social world they can be complex and imprecise where opposing positions are relatively vague. Nevertheless, they can assist in identifying relationships and possible resolutions for the competing views. Tensions by their very nature indicate an uncomfortable position, one that it is tempting to try to resolve quickly to release the pressure. However, with the approach advocated here there is a need to hold the tension and provide time and space to think through possibilities and consider the potential for re-framing and different thinking.

## Tensions Between Academia and Business

First though, it is helpful to acknowledge that there are some important differences in the perspectives of practitioners in businesses and academics in business schools on many of the important areas where they engage. The extent to which these differences should be minimised, or whether maintaining the tensions can actually be beneficial illustrates the nature of the discussion to follow. Bartunek and Rynes (2014) helpfully identified a series of tensions related to ways of reasoning, perceptions of timeliness, communication, relevance and rigour and incentives.

Firstly, whilst both parties may value interesting research, they often differ in how they make judgements about what constitutes 'interesting' (Baldridge, Floyd, & Markoczy, 2004). This illustrates how approaches to reasoning between practitioners and academics differs in how they frame problems which then changes how they then seek answers and in the goals they then set (Banks et al., 2016; Bartunek & Rynes, 2014). Views about timing and timeliness are a second area of contention. This is clearly evident in academia's generally lengthy timescales for developing research, which is something that practitioners do not often value. It is also a problem related to understanding of the relevance debate. The challenge here is for a world of practice that may be seeking relevance as 'immediate prescription' (Vermeulen, 2007, p. 754) to be balanced with the time needed to reflect and gain a better understanding. Together they raise questions about the time at which ideas/ insights should be considered to be useful, and the extent to which 'near-term' or longer time periods are important (Augier & March, 2007; Learmouth, Lockett, & Dowd, 2012). Approaches to thought leadership and emerging practices, which accept that theories and ideas are still in early stages and should be treated as such, help in this respect. Similarly, some publishers are now recognising this need to present ideas earlier in the journal acceptance cycle on themes which are new and emerging. For example, the impact pathways series in the International Journal of Operations and Production Management (Emerald Publishing, 2021) is an attempt to do just that.

Difficulties with communication are usually implicit and sometimes explicit in so many of the tensions identified. The earlier discussion has raised well-argued concerns that research is not translated in a way which makes sense to practitioners, who thus do not always recognise the value of such research (Bartunek & Rynes, 2014). Just as concerning, there seem to be few common communication channels available where someone in business would be able to access research (Banks, Barnes, & Jiang, 2021). Both the language and medium of communications are issues, prompting calls for explanations in plain English and a more persuasive means of communication (Kittler, 2018).

The fourth tension highlights the crucial issues of *relevance* and *rigour*, which according to Bartunek and Rynes (2014) has generated the bulk of the literature. Relevance and rigour are also a central theme in the discussion of an engaged business school. It is interesting to note from the communication discussion that if research communication is unclear then even if it has relevance, that relevance will not be recognised by the practitioner. Even worse, is the thought that they would never come across relevant research that could have an impact. The fifth tension stresses differences between *incentives* and points towards differing motivations. Academic incentives for progression and recognition are closely tied to publishing in academic journals and consequently skew activity in this direction. In contrast practitioners may seek solutions which they consider will more easily result in impact. A challenge here is for practitioners to value and be interested beyond the immediate and more broadly to 'gain insight they did not yet have' (Vermeulen, 2007, p. 755). These areas of difference are by no means exhaustive, and for Bartunek and Rynes holding the tensions is valuable and necessary in order to understand them better. When it comes to minimising or maintaining they suggest choosing the difficult path of maintaining tensions. This means that you hold and value difference and revisit the tensions in order to continue to understand where difference can be helpful and where it can hinder.

## Tensions About the Future of Business Schools

Holding and valuing difference is a helpful way to consider how to reframe the difficult tensions associated with the legitimacy and identity of business schools. Instead of seeking the resolution of perennial tensions in the debate, the tensions will be viewed as a necessity and seen as constructive and to be continued. This perspective adopts an insight from Anderson's wider assessment of the debate about the purpose and idea of a University. Anderson argues that rather than attempting to reach a conclusion or fixed resolution, instead there is a need to continue seeing the debate as 'a set of tensions, permanently present, but resolved differently according to time and place' (Anderson, 2009, p. 45).

Three tensions highlighted by Anderson will be explored in the context of business schools. The first is certainly a perennial issue which has fostered extensive debate: the tension between differing approaches to research. This is exemplified on the one hand by those who place more emphasis on research that is applied, such as knowledge transfer, and on the other by those who see it more as the pursuit of dispassionate truth. This tension is characterised by the rigour-relevance debate in business schools (Grey, 2001; Starkey & Madan, 2001). Relevance and rigour are not only pertinent to the research debate, but they also feature in relation to differing approaches to teaching, for example between encouraging open and critical thinking, contrasted with the teaching of skills that are vocationally or economically useful. This contrast is evident in the teaching of business subjects, particularly in approaches in leadership and management education (Thomas, Lorange, & Sheth, 2013). These first two tensions point towards a more fundamental issue: that of creating a balance between teaching and research whilst managing the challenge to move towards a more engaged scholarship (Boyer, 1990). Then crucially, there is another tension around which much of the recent debate seems to have focussed. This is the tension between balancing economic and utilitarian pressures, and the need to maintain a critical, independent distance which inevitably raises conflicting views about autonomy and accountability and legitimacy (Anderson, 2009). The context of the recent crises, have served to amplify the debate around this last tension, focussing it, as already implied, upon a particular part of the University: the business school. This suggests both a relevance and currency for exploring the engaged business school, situated as it is in the relationship between a business school and organisations, where each of the tensions identified by Anderson, may themselves be magnified by the current economic and social pressures.

Applying Anderson's insight requires holding the tensions and thinking through how they might be resolved. To do this we will return to the spectrum of responses proposed by Seo et al., firstly to provide some structure to analyse tensions. Then, secondly they will be applied to better understand the tensions in relation to the engaged business school, notably the three just discussed of research, teaching and legitimacy. Teaching and research have already been highlighted in Chapter 1 as significant concerns, with businesses finding both to be problematic. It is therefore no surprise that underlying the issues are difficult tensions which need resolution. Finally, business school identity and legitimacy is captured in the third tension.

The responses to tensions identified by Seo et al. (2004) provide some helpful insights into how tensions can be analysed. The first of the possible responses is perhaps the most familiar. Selection is the choice of one pole of the tension as opposed to the other; it is when interested parties ignore one pole in preference to the other. The second response is separation, which is when the contrasting positions are separated temporally, analytically or topically. The third response is to integrate the positions. This is more commonly recognised as agreeing a compromise between the two positions. Then the fourth response is what Seo et al. (2004) refer to as transcendence, an approach that seeks synthesis and a reframing through applying different thinking to the situation (Bartunek & Rynes, 2014). It is this fourth response that is of particular interest especially given the intent to hold the tensions in place.

A useful way to explain the four responses to tensions is to apply them to the relevance debate, as a way to then lead into a consideration of the three tensions of research, teaching and legitimacy. The relevance and rigour debate is often reduced to an either/or outcome or a less of one/more of the other balancing act (Gulati, 2007). The former fits the selection response, whilst the latter is more akin to the integration view of compromise. An alternative argument asserts that the relevance gap cannot be bridged because the world of academia and the world of the practitioner are different (Kieser & Leiner, 2009). This perspective resonates with the separation response. Then there is a viewpoint advocating a move towards an 'and' rather than 'or' perspective in the relevance debate, which is an attempt to seek a synergistic way forward and to 'accept that rigour and relevance are not opposites at all' (Gulati, 2007, p. 779). Such an argument indicates a transcending perspective. Similarly, returning to Weick's (2001) insight about the relevance gap introduced in Chapter 1. His proposal to rethink the so called gap between relevance and rigour as a problem with practitioners and not just academics, can also be seen as an attempt to reframe the situation. Thus the four tension responses proposed by Seo et al. (2004) provide a very helpful way to frame the range of tensions expressed in the relevance-rigour debate, and especially to indicate arguments attempting to transcend and synergise the tension, which in turn may point to areas of different thinking that could shape more effective engagement.

## Tensions in Research

The tensions expressed in the relevance-rigour debate show no signs of reducing (Thomas, 2022). But there is also a view that the divide that seems to lie beneath rigour and relevance is no longer fit for purpose (Irwin, 2022). The debate about the relevance gap is important, contentious, and often polarised. Yet it is also central to any attempt to explore engagement. That it matters for academics is evident from the volume and intensity of the debate, but it is also vital for business. Understanding the relevance-rigour issues and finding solutions so that research impact can be realised can make a difference for businesses. Yet, it has been a one-sided debate. There is one important aspect which should underpin the debate, and which to a large extent has been neglected in the majority of the literature. The missing aspect ironically is the perspective of the practitioner; that is the voice of business. Instead of hearing from business, the challenge about relevance to *practice* has become 'an endless debate amongst academicians' (Thorpe, 2011, p. 21). The arguments about research whilst expressing very different contested views, have predominantly focussed on the role of academia (i.e. the supply of knowledge and research), and have taken place in journals aimed at academics. Whilst an extensive literature has developed around the debate, Bartunek and Rynes (2014) also discovered in their review of that literature that there is a noticeable absence of the practitioners view (Bartunek & Rynes, 2014). Allied to this lack of practitioner perspective is a tendency for the debate to be extensively about the producers of knowledge. The following discussion engages with the academic debate, whilst considering a business perspective. Having explored the debate, the engagement stories introduced in Chapter 2 will be used to bring a stronger business focus to the discussion.

Invariably the tensions associated with research are expressed in term of relevance and rigour and especially the so called relevance gap between research and practice. Views about the relevance gap range from those who think it should be bridged, to others who consider it unbridgeable (Kieser & Leiner, 2009), and to those who think it should not be bridged, even if it were possible to do so (Grey, 2001). There have also been interesting attempts to re-frame the debate. These vary from suggestions that the nature of the research questions asked needs to change, to finding areas where interests overlap between academics and practitioners. The first re-framing idea improves the relevance of research by researchers ask the 'right' research questions, and ensuring that they are shaped by insight from practice, through collaboration with business (Gulati, 2007; Vermeulen, 2005). The second re-framing idea recognises that there are valuable areas in which the interests of practitioners and academics overlap, and consequently can lead to more focus on finding common ground rather than any perceived gaps (Baldridge et al., 2004). Asking appropriate questions and finding common ground turns the discussion away from a primary focus on an academic perspective and suggests responsibilities for practitioners. This is emphasised by Weick's (2001) call, discussed earlier, to re-assess the relevance gap, recognising that relevance issues may actually be due to practitioners as much as they are to do with academics. The idea of a shared responsibility leads to a discussion of a better integration of teaching with research. This then provides a bridge into a discussion of relevance and rigour in relation to the second of the tensions: teaching.

However, before progressing to a discussion of the tensions related to teaching it is instructive to return to the core debate of relevance and in particular to some of the challenges that make it a priority. The debate is played out in a context where business schools face challenges to their traditional role of creating and generating knowledge (Ivory et al., 2006). The assertion that a Business school is a privileged site of knowledge creation and generation is increasingly questioned (Starkey, 2006) where other entities (such as consultancies, corporate universities and training organisations) occupy the same 'space' (Ivory et al., 2006). New knowledge production is likely to emerge from a range of different sources outside of a business school, with an emphasis on the co-production of that knowledge (Starkey & Tempest, 2005). Co-production implies a high degree of integration between research and practice, which inevitably is likely to increase the tensions between so called 'applied' and 'pure' research. But there is a second area of tension to be considered here, which is emerging from renewed concerns about academic freedom and control. In particular, there are concerns that the research agenda may be manipulated by pressure to research what businesses and successive Governments are willing to pay for as opposed to what is needed (Gourley, 2004). And perhaps of more concern, is the danger of assuming that business actually knows what knowledge will be useful to it (Grey, 2001).

Such concerns clearly suggest risks associated with the position Business Schools find themselves in, but they may also herald significant opportunities (Starkey & Tempest, 2005). The contrasting perspectives of the relevance debate are captured in an insightful exchange of views from two academic articles in response to a wider study of knowledge production in business schools. Starkey and Madan (2001)[2] set out their argument with a call for a re-focussing of research towards the idea of relevance, which they carefully argue involves building a relationship between academics' keen to listen to the needs of practitioners and practitioners convinced of the value of research. In doing so, they stress the need to balance the important tension between maintaining a distance in order to secure rigour, with getting involved and delivering relevance (Starkey & Madan, 2001). This considered view of engaging with relevance encourages insightful scholarship recognising that there is value for business when academics challenge current practice and provide alternative perspectives.

In a critique prompted by Starkey and Madan's paper, Grey (2001) suggests a sharp contrast to their argument. He argues strongly against a dash to relevance, instead highlighting the need for independent thought and the freedom to experiment without concern for the relevance of the knowledge produced. However, Grey also stresses that he is not simply making an argument for disengagement, rather that he is advocating different *terms* of engagement. For Grey, the ability of a university to offer dispassionate, neutral research, at a critical distance from relevance, is what, often attracts businesses to seek out engagement with universities (Grey, 2001). According to Grey this critical distance, provides a distinctiveness which attracts businesses. Without such

---

[2]The debate in this section refers to several papers produced as an Economic and Social Research Council (ESRC) research grant led by Professor Ken Starkey to investigate the dynamics of knowledge production in the business school.

differentiation, he provocatively asserts, universities 'become entirely irrelevant' (Grey, 2001, p. S31).The argument is indicative of the rigour relevance debate, which seems to stress either the incompatibility of the two positions, emphasising the entirely distinct, unconnectable and unbridgeable worlds of academics and practitioners (Kieser & Leiner, 2009), or reduction to a compromise, where 'to gain one, we must lose some of the other' (Gulati, 2007). Yet Grey's point about achieving relevance by maintaining distance offers an interesting insight. It suggests there may be merits in moderating what is often considered the pervasive argument to reduce the relevance gap (Hughes, Bence, Grisoni, O'Regan, & Wornham, 2011).

So, there is an interesting and complex debate about how business schools should demonstrate their engagement with, and relevance to, the business world. The challenges explored so far also indicate possible grounds for different thinking, whether it be the dilemma of separation and proximity, the pursuit of the 'right' questions or the discovery of common ground. There is also a recognition of the joint responsibility of academia and business in making sense of these tensions. This joint responsibility becomes clearer as the tensions associated with teaching are considered next.

## Tensions in Teaching

As a reminder, this tension is between a critical and theoretical approach and an applied more vocational emphasis, with its obvious resonance with the rigour-relevance debate. This tension emerges from arguments which at their extreme express criticisms of two positions which appear poles apart. A rigour view of relevance in teaching might criticise anecdotal delivery characterised by a lack of depth and a prescriptive style which risks promoting fads without a robust evidence base. As a consequence, teaching lacks challenge and critique, in preference to acceptance and indeed complicity with business agendas and prevailing paradigms. In stark contrast, a relevance perspective of rigour in teaching may take issue with academics teaching their pet research interests irrespective of relevance to those being taught. Too often teaching consists of isolated facts and theory and is disconnected and so distant from practice as to be irrelevant. In addition, a one-way view of knowledge being transmitted from academic to student is questioned. Similarly, there are concerns that knowledge is limited to a discipline/business function rather than addressing the integrated complexity of management. Whilst these views may express more extreme perspectives, nevertheless they serve to illustrate practices on both sides of the argument that regrettably we still to some degree recognise in the classroom.

It is perhaps not surprising that there are calls for approaches which ensure a better integration of theory and practice in teaching (Schoemaker, 2008). In a context where the research-practice debate rarely mentions teaching (Kriz, Nailer, Jansen, & Potocnjak-Oxman, 2021) there is also concern that academics privilege seeking new theories and areas of research in preference to assessing the relevance of known knowledge to practice to then inform teaching. Making sense of what is known to inform teaching therefore is underdeveloped, when it should be an important part of scholarship (Rouseau, 2012). Too often teaching is seen as the poor relation with academics seeking to justify more time researching at the expense of teaching. This argument implies that the dissemination of ideas and research is reduced to a preoccupation with publication routes at the expense of teaching (Kriz et al., 2021). Yet there are other possibilities, for example there is a ready-made context where dissemination could happen through teaching with existing business relationships on executive education programmes (Mitchell & Harvey, 2018).

An alternate way of viewing the differences in approaches to teaching is to recognise that what is taught and the way it is taught should necessarily differ. Mintzberg helpfully explains that business schools often have at least three very different strands to their role. Business schools can be thought of as a starting school, a developing school and a finishing school. What is taught and how it is taught thus will be very different depending on the career and development stage of individuals (Mintzberg, 2004). To some extent many of the issues in teaching are due to not recognising that the three stages described by Mintzberg all require different approaches. To Mintzberg's three roles of a business school it might be appropriate to add a fourth that recognises the need to continue to keep up to date, an updating school.

Coupled with the emphasis on research being integrated and relevant to practice are ideas about a richer exchange with the student or participant. Current students are of course tomorrow's practitioners and those on executive education and post-experience programmes are actually todays practitioners (Mitchell & Harvey, 2018). In a move away from being passive recipients of knowledge students can engage in a conversation about issues relevant to them, and in doing so could be considered as translators of research (Tushman, O'Reilly, Feollosa, Kleinbaum, & McGrath, 2007), (Mitchell & Harvey, 2018). The potential for practitioners to be an active part in translating theory into practice is implicit in Weick's approach discussed earlier, but interestingly, Weick goes further.

He builds on Boyers richer and more rounded view of engaged scholarship where teaching extends and expands theory in the light of practice. Interestingly, Weick effectively argues for a scholarship of integration above that of application because in his view 'people do want to know what to do, but even more, they want to know what things mean, how to make sense of events, how their labels may constrain the options they see' (Weick, 1996, p. 257). This focus on integration encourages practitioners and academics to make connections together, to give meaning to facts, to find alternative interpretations and engage with sense making together. Such an approach combines application of theory to practice with integration as new connections and extension of theories and ideas are made. In this sense practitioners are a means of translating ideas into practice in business. They can operate as scholar practitioners offering the potential for business to better engage theory with practice. It is a role which is able to appreciate both research and practice because it straddles both business and academia (Carton & Ungureanu, 2018).

What is also interesting to note is that Weick (1996) often uses vivid stories to move away from superficial simplicities and to help practitioners make connections, thus asking practitioners to set aside their business specific knowledge and enter a different world. Weick's stories have some parallels with Starkey and Tempest's (2005) argument for how they consider business schools can become more relevant. They paint a picture of academics who act as scribes to the manager's storytelling. In the future, they contend that this storytelling relationship will change. It will be shared storytelling, as academics will need to develop the role of sage more than scribe, and perhaps in combining the two as a guide, descriptions that seem to fit well with Weick's interpretation of a scholarship of integration. For Weick there is a need for universities to keep their distinctiveness, but also for them to be engaged by demonstrating a scholarship of integration which uses teaching to make connections and find meaning with practitioners. This is not an either/or position but one that seeks to embrace both nodes of the teaching tension. And being distinctive may be more important than ever. The inter-dependency of research and teaching means that there are not just concerns that business schools are losing their privileged status with research. Starkey and Tempest (2005) also suggest that their privileged position with respect to teaching and disseminating knowledge will also be contested to the extent that its production of knowledge becomes less relevant. There is an uncertainty captured in these concerns which is mirrored in questions about the legitimacy of business schools.

## Legitimacy Tensions

Whilst the tensions so far have been discussed separately, it is clear that teaching and research are interdependent tensions but when turning to the third tension it becomes even more plain to see. Addressing the tension of legitimacy of the business school, inevitably pulls at the tensions with teaching and research. Legitimacy issues were introduced in the opening chapter of the book, but without exploring the reasons behind those uncertainties, now however the underlying issues need to be explained. Issues of legitimacy coalesce around what seems a simple distinction, the extent to which research and teaching in business schools is *for* managers/business or *about* managers/business (Thomas & Wilson, 2011). At one level, the distinction effectively is about where a business school is located within a university, that is, the extent to which it is considered a professional or a social science school (Pettigrew & Starkey, 2016). This in turn has resulted in a paradox, that in seeking wider legitimacy in the university through the pursuit of scientific research from the perspective of academia, it has not resulted in research that is useful to the practice of management (Alajoutsijarvi, Juusola, & Siltaoja, 2015). Unfortunately, the tendency in the language used leans towards a binary understanding of the tensions, suggesting the choice is either one or the other, a position that the discussion so far suggests should be challenged. For example, Starkey, Hatchuel, and Tempest (2004) capture the issues both in terms of the debate of whether business schools are for or about their subject and secondly that the subject itself is broader than management and should encompass society as well. They argue that business schools should encompass knowledge for 'and' about both management 'and' society.

In practice this dilemma is played out in the tensions of research and teaching. Whilst ideas of legitimacy may emerge from a straightforward dilemma, they can be traced back to a much bigger debate. Frequently, this debate evokes the fundamental difference between John Henry Newman's eloquent justification of a liberal education, and John Locke's opposing view (which partly informed Newman's treatise): that the focus of a University education should be on utilitarian skills for a profession (Newman, 1907). Newman's 'idea' of a liberal education has been a continuing influence on educational thinking (Grey & French, 1996), particularly characterising tensions between a 'liberal vs professional education' (Finlay, 2008, p. 17) within the continuing debate about the place of business schools within universities. Indeed, Newman's argument that professional schools should develop separately from universities still resonates, with some questioning of the existence of business schools within universities. Moreover, this tension is not just evident between University and business school. It can also be said to exist within business schools, where there is a recurring argument about the nature of management education, 'which has always been particularly, and brutally, torn between liberal and utilitarian conceptions of education' (Grey & French, 1996). This argument about the nature of management education and the balance between professional skills and more liberal intellectual skills has continued to be prominent. As part of their discussion of business schools regaining a 'new sense of identity and legitimacy' (2013, p. ix) post-financial crisis, Howard, L'Orange and Sheth (2013) stress the importance of incorporating Newton's principles of a liberal education in the management curriculum. They emphasise the value of developing intellectual capacity and freedom of thought which in turn enables individuals 'to become introspective, open-minded, insightful and possess the ability to absorb knowledge critically in framing problems and making decisions' (Howard, Lorange, & Sheth, 2013, p. 94) Given the importance of the context of this emphasis, it could be argued that Newton's idea of a liberal education is still both influential and topical.

Yet there are undoubtedly some key questions about the relevance of Newman's arguments to the current context. For example, Newman did not see research as a core function of a university, emphasising instead the importance of teaching and dissemination of knowledge (Starkey & Tempest, 2005). Understandably, such 'ideas sit rather uncomfortably with the contemporary university' (Anderson, 2009). Indeed, concern has also been expressed about the over-simplification of a debate on polarised views of education as either intellectually worthwhile liberalism, or economically useful vocationalism (Collini, 2012).

Nevertheless it is interesting to note how the title used by Newman for his collection of works: the Idea of a University, is still widely used to frame discussions of purpose within a university and business school setting (Anderson, 2009; Howard et al., 2013; Starkey & Tempest, 2005). Clearly for those advocates of Newman's work, this is a constructive way to 'remember and reflect' (Howard et al., p. 62) on his ideas. Yet there are concerns about whether the debate actually makes any progress, instead resembling a process of 'perennial self-questioning' (Grey, 2001, p. S27), prone to repeating similar arguments every generation (Collini, 2012). Despite this sense that little progress is made, the discussion brings us full circle to Anderson's proposition of repeatedly revisiting ideas about the purpose of a university and in this case of a business school, in the context of tensions that remain and continually encourage resolutions. The premise is therefore to see tensions as ways of identifying areas where different thinking is required to find ways where 'and' solutions are possible.

It would appear that legitimacy for a business school is to be found astride apparently opposing views. Business schools are both for and they are about business and management and they are both for and about not just business but also society. Similarly, they encourage and develop not just professional skills but also liberal intellectual skills. Then returning to the original tension, they respond to economic pressure 'and' maintain a critical independent distance.

Legitimacy conveys a sense of appropriateness, and trustworthiness, along with conveying 'the right to be there'. It connects well with an understanding of the mission and purpose of a business school. Previously, we discussed Pettigrew's call for academics to make a difference in society. Such a mission focus emphasises the need for engaged scholarship which has a more vital and richer relationship between practitioner and researcher. This sense of vocation and mission can build the integrity and legitimacy of the business school. There is of course the possibility that different business schools may find their legitimacy in different ways reflecting the context of the university within which they are situated and their wider stakeholders. Alternatively, there is an argument that seeking legitimacy through accreditations and journal rankings could lead to a lack of differentiation and more conformity (Thomas, Chian, & Cornuel, 2012) in the sector.

There is now, thanks to Boyers work a more integrated language to recognise the contributions possible when academics engage with practitioners to connect ideas, bridge the gap between theory and practice, and create insights with practitioners through teaching. It should not have gone unnoticed that many of the tensions discussed earlier between business and academics are addressed by the argument for mission and academic engagement coming together. Differing reasons for tacking problems are reduced when the right questions are formed collaboratively. When incentives are connected to a mission of making a contribution and a difference, then rigour and relevance should come together to serve that purpose. And all of this engagement is underpinned by a depth of collaboration between practitioner and academic which ensures dialog and communication that is characterised by carefully listening to each other.

Tensions with research, teaching and legitimacy have all been explored, with much of that debate taking place amongst academics. In that respect, it was apparent that the arguments which encouraged different thinking about the tensions were increasingly dependent on practitioner engagement. To introduce more of a practitioner view of tensions we return to the engagement stories.

## Tensions and the Engaged Business School

Tensions can be explored with more of a business perspective by revisiting the engagement stories introduced in Chapter 2. The stories were instructive in shaping the model of engagement based on the three imperatives of being distinctive, relational and sustainable, underpinned by skills and systems. Here the stories will be re-visited to explore the tensions that emerge.

### *Distinctive: A Demand Dilemma*

Two stories predominantly inform this imperative. Firstly, the 'selection story' indicated reasons why the client chose the business school to be its service provider. This story emphasised the requirement for flexibility and the need to listen to the client, which both point to the tension between providing customised or standardised solutions, and the associated dilemma of a client wanting their needs to be met, despite being unclear about what those needs are. A second story also supported the analysis of the demand dilemma theme. The 'greatest strength story' sheds light on the leading demand aspect of the demand dilemma theme. The story highlighted the value placed upon latest thinking by the senior manager, but also cautioned that too often yesterday skills were taught rather than latest thinking. This story began to pose interesting possibilities between approaches that lead demand and those that are demand led, indicating that the thought leadership of a business school is valued by a business. This story suggested strategies to reframe the tension implied by the 'demand dilemma' with the suggestion that a business may well have its needs met by latest thinking. Tensions, as has been demonstrated are not necessarily clear and usually indicate conflict and inconsistencies. For example, the customised versus standardised dilemma is not necessarily straight forward. A business school may have a very good and tested programme or element of a programme which addresses the issues a client has. Similarly, customised programmes hold a risk in terms of the confidence that something untested will actually address the business need.

### *Relational Engagement*

There are three stories which provide the basis for this theme. The 'relationship story' and 'the nurturing story' both provide exemplars, whilst 'the contrasting provider story' highlights the stark difference between a good and bad experience. The 'relationship' and 'contrasting provider' stories together stress the tension between relational and transactional engagement. They underline the importance and value of building relationships.

The third story related to the theme is the 'nurturing' story. The senior university manager told the story to illustrate his approach to working with clients. On initial reading, it suggested that 'building rapport' was important. However, this story pointed towards the need to consider the deeper, more embracing theme of 'nurturing'. This is a more nuanced position which indicates a tension between a cursory view of relationship building and a deeper more involved position.

The story also indicated an issue and tension expressed by the senior manager, namely that he did not think many academics had the skills needed to effectively engage with such relationships. The tension was between finding people with the skills to be credible with clients whilst recognising that not many academics possess those skills.

### Skills and Systems

Clearly the 'nurturing' story and the 'contrasting provider' story raise questions about the skills needed for engagement. Relationship building skills are emphasised and the need for consultative skills. However, the story which proved to be most helpful in this regard was 'the skill set' story, which explored what was needed for a Business School to engage with a client organisation. It was a story that highlighted tensions, both in skills and in systems and processes, which were deemed necessary to meet the client's needs. The tension between teaching for experienced professionals against traditional academic teaching is highlighted. There are then wider support needs for more consultative skills and project management processes. Then there is the tension that conventional university systems struggle to cope with a client. This involves things like timetabling constraints, and fitting non-standard start times into the academic calendar, through to different contracting relationships.

### Sustainable Futures

The final theme, draws upon two stories. The 'greatest strength story' not only supported the demand dilemma theme, but also pointed towards client aspirations in relation to the benefits to be gained from working with the business school, and the idea of creating new opportunities. However, the main story that addressed this final theme was the 'springboard to new opportunities' story. The story suggested the hope that much wider benefits could be realised from the relationship. The story raised the issue of how further benefits could be realised from the relationship and hinted at the tension between a tendency to move onto the next thing, without seeing the new opportunities emerging as a result of the relationship.

### Conclusions

This has been a wide-ranging discussion that has sought to explore the legitimacy of a business school through an engaged business school lens, an argument that is essentially asking business schools to rediscover its sense of mission. As with so much of the arguments associated with business schools, legitimacy is a tension often characterised between identifying with the academic institute as a conventional school or relating to business as a professional school. The message of this chapter has been to think differently about such tensions, adapting Anderson's idea of holding tensions so that they are permanently present.

The rigour and relevance debate plays a central role in this discussion almost as a proxy for the legitimacy question; rigour representing a traditional academic position and relevance corresponding to a business focus. The one typified by research that is 'about' business and management, the other with research which is 'for' business and management. The difference in views is often expressed as the 'relevance gap'. It is a contested debate with some views advocating the need to bridge the gap, whilst others maintain that it is unbridgeable, or that it should not be bridged. In contrast to the either/or debate on relevance and rigour is a view which stresses their complimentary roles. What emerges from this different perspective is the value of asking the right questions. Others have expressed an alternative perspective, with an emphasis on seeking more situations where the interests of academics and practitioners overlap. However, what shouldn't be discarded in the dash to reduce the gap is the potential value in maintaining distance and separation.

In effect different thinking challenges business schools to move on from what Boyer termed the tired research vs teaching argument. Similarly, the underlying arguments behind the relevance gap are being called into question as no longer fit for purpose. There is also a need to challenge the process of disseminating research being reduced to publications in academic journals, whilst neglecting to invest in assessing existing research and its potential to impact practice, through the medium of teaching. As Weick advocated, academia should not lose its distinctiveness and distance from business, but at the same time should embrace engaging with practitioners to extend, adapt and connect ideas with practice.

In essence the uncertainty of legitimacy can be reconciled through a sense of mission, by exploring what it means to be engaged and drawing upon the sense of purpose that it brings. And that might be made possible by holding in tension the two poles of finding legitimacy both in the academic institution and in relevance to the business world. Indeed, perhaps a level of discomfort with both positions indicates that a business school is in its rightful place. Close to business but not too close, with a degree of separation to challenge as well as encourage. Similarly, with the wider university, contributing to the life, vitality and to its financial viability, whilst leading and challenging for a more engaged university.

The tensions have highlighted some important aspects to consider in relation to a model for engagement. Together with the engagement stories drawn from those directly involved in the practice of engagement they provide the basis upon which to build a model.

## A Model of Engagement

The engagement model is about being distinctive, relational and sustainable, and is underpinned by skills and systems. The stories and tensions bring to life the realities, difficulties and possibilities of engagement, so it would be frustrating if a model didn't capture some of these interactions. In the next chapter the detail of a model will be explained. The ideas so far have concentrated on the themes and consequently the information resembles static data which crucially does not capture the interrelationship between themes (Clark, Gioia, Ketchen, & Thomas, 2010). Tensions indicate relationships within themes which need to be captured in the model, but there are also connections and interactions between the themes which need to be explored. Models of course are only ever attempts to represent and describe how things relate and work together. They try to strike a balance between the risk of being too simplistic so that they don't adequately provide a picture of what is happening or too complicated so that it becomes difficult to visualise how it works. More importantly they are also not representing the themes if they are static, and do not capture the dynamic nature of the interactions.

At present the themes might hint and suggest areas where they relate, but there is no clear indication of possible patterns between them and therefore how they might be connected. There is a need to move to a more dynamic representation, one that recognises that some of the relationships between factors are likely to be processual, whilst other are cyclical or may be iterative.

The first thing to acknowledge is that engagement is played out between a business school and businesses, so the model needs to represent this sphere of collaboration and influence. To do this the model draws upon ideas on collaboration developed by Connor and Hirsh's (2008). Their model positions collaboration at the centre of a dialog between an employer and a business school. The dialog allows both parties to understand each other's needs and capabilities and to explore how a partnership could work. This approach resonates with the very strong sense that relationships are critical, gained both from employers and from the literature.

The dynamic conceptual model attempts to position the factors which make up the themes within a collaborative and relational context. So the diagram is framed with the business school represented on one side and the employer on the other. Between them is a sphere of influence and activity represented as a central oval circle of collaborative engagement.

The next chapter works through the interconnections that bring engagement to life and attempts to represent them using the collaborative space between business and business schools as its foundation. The experiences and insights from those directly involved in engagement will be explored by drawing upon insights from relevant fields within the literature to shape and make sense of engagement.

# Chapter 5

# Purposeful Engagement: The Model Explained

This chapter focuses on a model to capture what successful engagement might look like. It is a model that is central to the idea of an engaged business school, but it should be remembered that it combines with two other tools of engagement, a framework and a process. The framework clarifies what a business school intends engagement to mean, and how it connects with purpose. It enables business and business schools to scope the extent of their engagement. The model then weaves the strands together for what should happen to make that engagement work well. Finally, the third tool is a process which provides more practical ideas about how to engage in a way that ensures the model can be applied.

Each theme of the model is now explored in depth particularly emphasising the interactions, connections and their dynamic relationships that combine to enable effective engagement to happen. Firstly, the direction of travel for the model will be outlined by providing an overview of each theme. Then each theme in turn will be explored in detail. The tensions, stories and evidence from wider literature will be used to develop interconnections from the themes to shape the model.

## An Overview of the Purposeful Engagement Model

### A Distinctive Engagement

Distinctive engagement is firstly an expression of intent by a business school because it attempts to describe the way in which it is different. Difference of itself does not necessarily create an advantage, it needs to be coupled with meeting a need or seizing an opportunity. So it is also a recognition that employers are often looking for a distinctive offer from a business school. This section builds upon the tensions and issues described in the 'selection' and the 'greatest strength' stories, to explain the demand-led and leading demand dilemma that business schools face. Analysing the tensions points towards ways to resolve and reimagine them. Three possible approaches to reimagine the tensions will be outlined. The first suggests thinking differently about leading-demand. The second encourages consideration of an alternative perspective of the opposite pole of the demand tension; demand-led. The third suggests that, rather than viewing the tension in

The Engaged Business School, 65–93
Copyright © 2023 Anthony Sturgess
Published under exclusive licence by Emerald Publishing Limited
doi:10.1108/978-1-80382-941-820231010

polar opposite terms, it should be re-framed and so viewed from a perspective which sits somewhere between the two extremes. Re-imagining this position leads to the possibility that the tension between demand-led and leading-demand can be mutually beneficial since it keeps the two extremes of the tension 'honest'. In this sense the two extremes need the correcting influence of the other. The demand-led approach carries the risk that academics may be too close to business, in the sense that there may be compliance, compromise, and a tendency to chase fads (Kildruff & Kelemen, 2001), rather than insight, challenge and fresh thinking. Alternatively, the leading demand pole could steer academics towards insignificance, irrelevance and disinterest (Tranfield & Starkey, 1998), rather than a dispassionate scholarly pursuit of fundamental ideas that can shape thinking.

The model envisages a role for business schools that is responsive to demand, but also helps to create and shape that demand. A demand-led approach is needed because businesses are often unsure of their needs (Hogarth & Wilson, 2003), which typically results in solutions that are specific to the individual workplace (Brennan & Little, 2006). This suggests a need for a consultative process to identify needs and an emerging role for academic staff to act as consultants (Nixon, Smith, Stafford, & Camm, 2006), interpreting needs and applying latest thinking to meet them. This brings into play the other pole of the tension because latest thinking requires a leading-demand approach. Research, teaching and consultancy form the critical core expertise of the engaged business school, and their interrelationship is developed at the centre of what is meant by distinctive engagement. With this model, the interplay between the two poles enrich each other, ensuring that the needs of the client are addressed with latest thinking, and that the research agenda is informed by a consultative process interpreting needs and client issues.

### Relational Engagement

The quality and importance of the relationship in the model resonates from the experiences of those involved in engagement and can be seen in the 'relationship' and 'contrasting provider' stories. In order to frame this theme the implied tension between relational and transactional engagement illustrated in the stories is investigated. To do this, insights from the fields of consultancy, professional services, communications and relationship marketing are explored. If the intent is to establish a sustained relationship with longer-term benefits, then clearly relationships need to be built. To gain a better understanding of this important area, the analysis and discussion will be structured by considering relationship building first from a process perspective to determine the steps and stages necessary. Secondly, the implications of time will be considered in forging relationships and deepening them. Third, attention will be paid to the complexity of relationships in organisations in terms of different levels and roles and the nature of the relationships developed. In summary, there is general agreement in the literature that relationship building is a vital part of engagement with a client.

A relational approach though requires more than just relationship building, it is supported and informed by credibility. This is often an important factor in a client's decision to work with a business school. The argument here will position relational engagement as shaped by relationship-building and credibility. In turn, relationship building is informed by: investing time; connecting levels; and progressing through stages of development. Similarly, credibility is developed through reputation, expertise, and building trust and confidence. However, there is another factor to consider, a more nuanced issue, but crucial to the understanding of relational engagement in this model: the idea of nurturing.

This idea helps to capture the breadth, depth and continual vigilance necessary for sustaining relational engagement. Nurturing is more than rapport-building and networking, though (according to this model) both are important. Therefore, nurturing is not a linear activity which happens only at certain stages of the relationship development process. Nurturing is a continuing activity creating the conditions for a sustained relationship (Huxham, 2003). This all-embracing theme is depicted in relation to the other themes through the image of 'nurturing' encircling the collaborative sphere which has already been proposed as the backdrop for the relationship between the business school and a business. Finally, the factors discussed need to be drawn together making clear their interrelations so that the relational engagement process, of establishing credibility, building relationships and sustaining them through nurturing behaviours, is viewed within a wider collaborative context in the model.

### Sustainable Futures

Distinctive and relational engagement should generate opportunity and create value, and in doing so result in a purposeful engagement. Sustainable futures answers the third question posed earlier: how will a business school continue to add value for and with businesses? It is an important question to ask since it begins to build a compelling narrative that engagement doesn't just work for the immediate needs but it holds the potential for far greater benefits in the future.

The 'springboard to new opportunities' story provides an example of how an engagement can result in continuing benefits, and in particular can enable clients to do things they were not able to do before.

The idea of sustainable futures is supported by Kanter's (1994) three principles of effective collaborative relationships: generating possibilities, creating extra value and nurturing. A focus on relational engagement and on meeting the client's needs can then develop towards what is sometimes referred to in consulting as a stage of enrichment (Stumpf & Longman, 2000). Not only does this approach create value for the business, it also enables opportunities to be realised that weren't available before. Achieving benefits for the business is of course critical for effective engagement, but a sustainable approach also needs to generate benefits for the business school. A purposeful engagement should be mutually beneficial, with new possibilities emerging for both partners.

### Skills and Systems

The 'skill set story' presents a dilemma between intent and reality. It captures the tensions between the business world and the world of academia, with the main point of the story arguing for a shift of balance. The story points to an important consideration of both the skills and capabilities needed by business schools to engage with businesses, and of the processes required to manage client programmes and interventions.

According to this story, longer timescales evident in academia contrast with the immediate needs of business. These are wider issues than just the longer timescales typically associated with research processes. They are also reflected in the length of education programmes, and in the time taken to validate a new programme, which typically conflict with a more pressing business expectation. Then there is also a tension between more traditional academic teaching approaches and teaching and learning styles appropriate for business.

Earlier in Chapter 1 some of the problems associated with skills were highlighted. For example, there appear to be too few academics with the skill or the inclination to engage in executive/practitioner teaching, a view that is supported from wider research (Kewin et al., 2011). Different skills are needed by academics to facilitate and work alongside participants. In addition there are unfamiliar roles for academics such as project management, client management and consulting, as well as more familiar roles such as programme management. These roles point to the need to manage not just the programme or course but also the client. Although problems were expressed in relation to finding academics with the right teaching skills, there may be an argument that these skills can be developed (Thorpe & Rawlinson, 2013), whereas it may be expertise in client management that will be the limiting factor (Cockerill, 1994).

With differing roles comes the need for different systems to support the activity. The final aspect of this theme relates to the supporting systems to enable engagement. The issues revolve around a tension of different timeframes between business and academia, but they also reflect that in clients, universities are dealing with a different kind of customer. University systems are set-up around the individual student, not to cope with the needs of an employer organisation.

The discussion of skills and systems draws to a conclusion the initial overview of each theme. It has outlined the areas which will now be considered in much more depth. Now the focus will change to pay much more attention to the inter-relationships and connections between factors in order to create a dynamic model.

## Distinctive Engagement – Addressing the Demand Dilemma

The discussion so far has recognised that the needs of businesses are indeed complex, often unclear, and interestingly that businesses have an expectation that providers will work with them to identify those needs. Indeed, the evidence suggests that businesses are seeking providers who can give that support. But that is not all, they are also searching for the latest thinking. Therefore, it is clear that there is potential for business schools to play a role navigating this landscape. On the one hand, responding to demand but on the other, leading demand. That is, to play two roles: one which is responsive to demand (helping clarify demand) and one which helps to inform, create, and shape demand. Such roles imply business schools are subject to a tension between behaving as a demand-led organisation and an organisation which leads demand. The issues of this demand dilemma will be explored through two initial tensions which emerged in the 'selection' story. Firstly, the tension between customised and standardised provision and secondly, the related tension caused where clients specified bespoke solutions, despite being unclear about what their needs actually were. Analysing these two tensions will help inform a discussion of how to reframe the tension implied in the demand dilemma, between being demand-led or adopting a leading demand approach.

### *Customised or Standardised-Provision Tension*

The 'selection story' is about a past problem or obstacle which the organisation had to address. The story allows the client organisation to make sense of the situation in order to provide a new, workable interpretation of what is needed (Gioia & Chittipeddi, 1991). The purpose of the story is to clearly emphasise the factors which the client considered important when selecting a provider, using an example to underline their importance. Central to this story is the tension which is implied between the offer of a customised, flexible approach or one which is rigid and inflexible. This tension appears to be managed by selection, where one pole or the other is chosen (Seo, Putnam, & Bartunek, 2004). However, there is a second and related tension which is created by the client wanting a bespoke solution to meet their needs, yet at the same time being unclear about what exactly those needs are. This introduces an added complexity to the first tension. It introduces a dilemma, since providers can only offer effective customised solutions to specific client's needs once they are properly understood and expressed. Investigation of these tensions may suggest potential ways in which the issues can be re-framed and thus create possibilities to transcend the dilemma (Seo et al., 2004).

The first tension is clearly illustrated where the other university in the story claimed it had listened to the client, but then proceeded to provide a standardised solution. In terms of tension analysis, the other university managed the tension by selection (Seo et al., 2004), selecting one pole, in this case the supply-led pole. They implied that they understood the organisation's needs but then proceeded to provide a solution based on their existing programmes, apparently managing the tension in a misleading way. Unfortunately, this approach seems to be more widespread evidenced by a HEFCE report evaluating employer engagement interventions, which noted that some universities 'dress up' existing provision, pretending it is as a result of a consultancy process (Kewin et al., 2011). This of itself is concerning, but leaving aside the misleading behaviour, it should not lead to automatically discounting situations where a standardised solution may be appropriate. It could be argued that the dilemma described above echoes the competing demands faced by consultancies: that of offering clients a bespoke solution, incorporating novel innovations or of using standardised but tried and tested solutions, which might be as effective but less costly (Whittle, 2006). If standardised solutions can be seen as appropriate under certain conditions, then it could be argued that the tension between customisation and standardisation is a fact of life. This would suggest that the provider and client must come together to make a judgement as to whether a bespoke or a standardised solution is most appropriate. There may be a need to think through a mix of provision, some of which already exists, and other elements which need to be designed specifically for the situation. However, such a judgement implies an open and honest consultation between the client and provider, to clarify the client's situation needs. This leads to the second tension in the selection story.

The second tension is evident with the client requiring a bespoke solution to meet their needs, yet at the same time stating that they are unclear about those needs. This seems to be a common request, suggesting that it may well be an important consideration. Alongside this unclear understanding or expression of 'need', client managers also stated an associated requirement for a provider to be flexible. The first point to note about this position is that it confirms Brennan and Little's (2006) argument that organisations are often unclear about their needs, and as a consequence those needs tend to be specific to that organisation (King, 2007). To address this need in the selection story involved spending a considerable amount of time in conversation, in order to build mutual understanding. This clearly had a number of benefits in building the relationship, but it especially helped in terms of identifying and clarifying needs. In effect, the tension is resolved through effective need exploration by both the business school and the client although, as will be discussed shortly, even this approach may hold some hidden complexity. Such a process effectively reflects the consultative activity of diagnosis (Kubr, 2002), and is increasingly recognised as a priority area in employer engagement where business schools need staff 'effectively diagnosing employer needs', working as 'consultants' (Nixon et al., p. 44). It is not unusual for a client to be unclear about their actual needs, reflecting a wider issue that seems to be present with a significant number of organisations. This is a perspective recognised by Schein who argues that clients 'often seek help when they do not know exactly what their problem is. They know something is wrong but the help they really need is in figuring our exactly what that is' (Schein, 1990).

Although progression to a consulting solution may seem a straightforward approach, resolving the tension of unclear needs may be more complex than it seems. One possible hidden complication emerges when recognising the importance of making connections at different levels in the client organisation, which also suggests that needs and expectations may be interpreted differently at each of these levels. Therefore, adoption of a consultancy approach to help to diagnose a client needs may not resolve the tension if they are expressed differently at different levels of the organisation. In this situation, analysis of the tension can enable implicit assumptions to be identified (Seo et al., 2004), such as a more complex understanding of the 'client'. Seo et al. (2004) suggest one approach to managing this tension is by separation of the poles by levels of analysis, or what Poole and van de Ven refer to as level of 'reference and connection' (Poole & van de Ven, 1989, p. 567) in the social world. To separate by level, a means to categorise by type of client or position of client can be adopted (Alvesson, Karreman, Sturdy, & Handley, 2009). Schein recognises that the notion of client can be 'ambiguous and problematical' (Schein, 1997, p. 202), because of the tendency to think of the client as one organisation or as one person representing the organisation with a single, common view (Alvesson et al., 2009). To counter this problem, Schein (1997) prefers to use the term 'client system' recognising that providers are 'always dealing with more than one part of the client system, and some parts may not have the same needs or expectations as do others' (Schein, 1997, p. 203). He proposes a helpful distinction between 'initial contact' clients who first bring the provider into the organisation, 'primary clients' who ultimately 'own' the issue being resolved, and between 'ultimate clients' who experience the benefit of the interventions directly. Separation by level, using the level or position of different clients in the organisation, enables the second tension to be resolved by ensuring the different needs of the various types of client are each addressed. This also enables the provider to recognise the relative positions of different 'clients', usually associated with levels of authority, but may also indicate the type and degree of involvement in the interventions (Alvesson et al., 2009). Such a separation can prevent the assumption that a need identified at one level, or with one type of 'client', means the second tension is resolved.

In the engagement stories, business school managers emphasised the importance of relationship-building and of understanding issues at different levels in the organisation. And, as one business school manager argued, they recognised that the presenting problem 'may well not be the real issue at all'. This led to a considerable amount of time spent talking with the client to assist in understanding the organisation and its issues. All the client managers confirmed the need for this level of conversation, and one client manager also appreciated that 'the university had fantastic relationships with key managers in the organization', demonstrating the commitment to build relationships and a shared understanding with different stakeholders, many of whom were part of the client system.

The 'customised or standardised' tension poses an interesting question about understanding the conditions in which a standardised solution may be beneficial for the client. The evidence from the engagement stories also supports the idea that businesses often do not know what their actual needs are, and significantly that the needs may actually differ within the organisation. This suggests that a consulting process is appropriate to determine the needs of the organisation. However, the resolution of the 'unclear needs/bespoke solution' tension means there is a need to recognise the importance of gaining clarity and building relationships at different levels of the organisation. Consequently, the use of Schein's 'types of client' framework can help to identify explicit and potential differences in needs and expectations throughout the organisation. The argument also provides support for the rationale of developing relationships at all levels in the organisation.

### Re-framing the Demand Dilemma

The tensions discussed so far form part of the broader dilemma caused by perceptions of business schools as being either demand-led or leading-demand.

As part of the exploration of this tension, the 'greatest strength' story will be used to help inform the discussion. The significance of this story is that it indicates the frustration seen by some in the unfulfilled potential of academia to work more effectively with the business world. Interestingly, the story also implies that one business need may be to gain access to the latest thinking, and is perceived by the business in this case to be something which business schools can help them to do.

Critics may suggest that an emphasis on latest thinking tends towards the promotion of fads and fashions (Grey, 2001). However, latest thinking can also be interpreted in the way the senior executive seems to indicate: as academics bringing their latest ideas to business. Whilst the phrase 'latest thinking' may limit the breadth of ideas, it does suggest a direction to explore. Of course, there is much value to be found in ideas that have stood the test of time or in consideration of fundamental principles, although the principles relevant to an unpredictable and complex business environment may need to be clarified (Weick, 2001). It is perhaps in this sense that even 'old' ideas, when applied or interpreted in a new context, may become latest thinking. These aspects of the 'greatest strength' story will be incorporated into the subsequent discussion.

It is hard not to notice similarities between the demand dilemma and the relevance-rigour debate, since each reflects a balance between responsiveness to clients and meeting their demands (which relates to relevance), and provision of ideas and insights which they may not have thought about (which has similarities with rigour). Yet as we discovered in Chapter 4 that debate has tended to be one-sided, with little attention given to employer perspectives of the rigour-relevance debate (Bartunek & Rynes, 2014). It is therefore particularly informative at this point to reflect on the views of the various managers from the client organisations represented in the stories. What is immediately noticeable is that the clients valued both poles of this tension, appreciating the 'weight and depth of learning' offered by a business school and also being assured that the intervention would 'meet our explicit needs and the needs we didn't know [we had]'. Their views imply that it may be possible to re-frame the tension between demand-led and leading-demand. Such a perspective indicates opportunities where business schools could differentiate themselves via a dual approach that both meets demand and leads demand. However, before thinking through how this might be achieved, it is useful to consider some other ways of managing the tension.

One mechanism for managing this tension could be a conscious movement towards one pole or the other (selection). If the provider focussed on the request for bespoke solutions, then the demand-led pole would be selected. On the other hand, a choice to lead with latest thinking might prompt a provider to choose the leading-demand pole. Alternatively, another strategy to manage the tension might lead to an adoption of a compromise solution situated somewhere between the two poles of the spectrum. These strategies were evident in the relevance-rigour debate which was discussed earlier. However, such approaches can often result in an unsatisfactory solution or 'a middle of the road approach' (Seo et al., 2004, p. 76), which is neither demand-led nor leading-demand. Just as concerning, as we have discussed previously, are the persistent claims that business schools deliver programmes which lack relevance and practical application, or that they are based on narrow research interest of academics rather than what is actually needed (Thorpe & Rawlinson, 2013, p. 10). There is also the concern voiced in the 'greatest strength story' about programmes and courses that do not include latest thinking but instead focus on 'yesterday's skills'. There seem to be genuine concerns that business schools often fail to address this tension effectively, resulting in compromise, irrelevance, self-interest or out-of-date ideas. Yet the views of those in business from the engagement stories imply that both poles of this tension are indeed valued, which warrants consideration of how a dual approach might be effective.

To explore a dual approach to this tension we will return to the fourth way to analyse tensions proposed by Seo et al. (2004). They suggest that one way to transcend a tension is through thinking differently, that is by reframing the situation or what they call 'connection'. A connection strategy 'seeks ways to embrace, to draw energy from, and to give equal voice to bipolar positions' (Seo et al., 2004, p. 101). Instead of thinking of the two poles as opposite and mutually exclusive, this strategy searches for ways in which two poles can both be valued, and are mutually beneficial. So, the next section will explore three possible methods to enable this tension to be transcended. The first suggests thinking differently about the leading-demand pole. The second encourages consideration of an alternative perspective of the opposite (demand-led) pole. The third method suggests that, rather than viewing the tension in polar terms, it should be re-framed and so viewed from a perspective which sits somewhere between the two extremes.

In proposing that academics should bring and present their latest thinking to business, the senior executive in the 'greatest strength story' implicitly suggested a promising strategy for consideration. He introduced the possibility of transcending the duality by creating a demand that businesses need. The implication is that a business school, by adopting a 'leading-demand' approach, can effectively shape and create demand with businesses, effectively offering something businesses hadn't realised they needed until they see it. What is also interesting to notice is the senior manager's perception that, what he called latest thinking, is both a strength of business schools and also something that business needs. In this interpretation of the context, if a business school's research incorporates latest thinking and ideas that businesses need, then a business school begins to create and shape demand. This would represent a situation where the ideas that business schools research are indeed what organisations need. However, as discussed earlier when analysing the 'greatest strength' story, there is a frustration conveyed by the senior manager that businesses are too busy to find out about the latest thinking, and business schools do not incorporate enough of that latest thinking into their teaching. Hughes, Bence, Grisoni, O'Regan, and Wornham (2011) express a similar frustration. They characterise academics as not being close enough to practice, whilst at the same time those in business don't 'make the most of management academics as a source of knowledge' (Hughes et al., p. 40). In the 'greatest strength story', the senior manager proposed addressing this tension by suggesting that academics should present their research to practitioners who could then determine what is relevant to their business. This requires the practitioners to apply the theory and ideas to their business context, identifying need and matching ideas to their situation. In other words, in such situations practitioners would carry out the activities, such as identifying need, which were expected on the demand-led side of the tension. This scenario also implies that academics are able to effectively translate their ideas and communicate them to practitioners.

A second approach to transcending the tension focuses on the demand-led side of the tension. In order to be able to lead-demand there is an assumption that business schools have identified areas of research that are relevant and significant for business. To do so implies close connection to, and understanding of, the organisation and its issues. This discussion so far has indicated both the value and the importance that clients attach to finding a provider who can help them identify their needs and provide bespoke solutions. To do this business schools need to adopt a consultative approach. The resulting close proximity to the client, and focus on trying to understand their needs, can enable the business school to identify crucial questions and areas for further research that are relevant and interesting to practitioners. The executive stressed the importance of a consultative approach by emphasising the need for the business school to 'keep watching, looking out for ways to improve, things to change, introducing new ideas or seeking out new ideas as needs arise.' To effectively identify and respond to client needs means combining access to an existing body of knowledge and generation of new knowledge, then applying both or either one to the business context. Therefore, this approach to demand-led consulting is enhanced through the ability to apply latest thinking to the needs identified. Interestingly, what has just been described is effectively the attributes of good scholarship: staying up to date with the latest knowledge, contributing new knowledge (Pearce & Huang, 2012) and then sharing the latest thinking (Burke & Rau, 2010). So again, the benefits that are associated with one pole in the tension continuum can enrich the other; they are mutually beneficial. This discussion therefore points to a way in which business schools can lead demand by having a consultative dialog with business, in order to define problems, questions and approaches that would facilitate knowledge generation (Starkey & Tempest, 2005).

A third way to resolve the tension between being demand-led and leading demand draws upon Weick's reframing of Boyer's scholarship of engagement, designed to see the scholarship of integration as central to teaching practitioners. This perspective is situated somewhere between the leading-demand and demand-led poles. At one extreme, leading-demand suggests a research focus, while at the other demand-led implies a consultative approach. Therefore, it could be said that the teaching perspective lies somewhere between the two poles. This is not a compromise position between the two, but rather a case of applying different thinking. According to Weick's interpretation, the classroom becomes a context for both application and integration. The scholarship of teaching, as envisaged by Boyer, has the potential to be transformational, combining as it does, the application and extension of research ideas. This resonates with ideas from business school managers involved in the engagement stories who pointed to teaching delivery with a client that focussed more on the facilitation and learning process than on specific content. The rationale behind this approach, as the academic explained was 'because a lot of its power is in its delivery, in the discussion that goes on and not particularly in the curriculum'.

These three ways to reframe the tension between a demand-led approach and a leading-demand perspective build on the two traditional, core activities of academics (teaching and research) but also adds a third: consulting. Consulting might be seen as a familiar activity within academia, however the model proposes a more central role for this activity, within the context of engagement. This differing role of consulting and its relationship to teaching and research is an important part of the model and consequently needs investigating.

There is a well-recognised triangle of relationships between research, teaching and practice with two-way connections between each of these activities (Kaplan, 1989). However, there has been an ongoing criticism that the connections to practice are underdeveloped resulting in a gap between theory and practice. It is a gap which continues to frustrate and is even described as dysfunctional (Burke-Smalley, Rau, Neely, & Evans, 2017; Hordósy & McLean, 2022). According to Burke and Rau, the gap is too often discussed in terms of research needing to be better connected with practice, yet they suggest there is a 'glaring omission' of how teaching and research interplay to proactively narrow the gap (Burke & Rau, 2010, p. 132). The discussion to date both supports and extends their conclusion.

The three reframing strategies explored here address the issues Burke and Rau raised. Firstly the 'omission' to which Burke and Rau refer is explored in the particular application of the scholarship of integration, advocated by Weick. Integration combines both the teaching-research link where academics bring theories and ideas to practitioners and the teaching-practice relationships where those ideas are applied, connections and theories extending by the interplay with practice. Secondly, the research and practice relationship is demonstrated through the practice of academics presenting latest thinking to practitioners (the approach recommended by the senior manager). This is a dissemination of latest thinking, which is then shaped by managers assessing and discussing the relevance of ideas with academics. These events are effectively two-way dissemination activities. They differ from teaching activity because they are not a part of a programme, they are intended to explore ideas in two way conversations. What is missing from both Kaplan's and Burke and Rau's analysis is the consultancy relationship. There should be a fourth activity incorporated into the research-teaching-practice relationships. Consulting forms an important bridge with practice, both informing and shaping the interactions with research and teaching to practice. In the third strategy introduced above, a consultancy–practice relationship ensures that latest thinking addresses important questions, issues and practitioner needs. The consultancy-teaching relationship also helps to shape teaching to meet and address those needs.

The consultancy – research – teaching combination encourages both the development of approaches which connect the three strands, and it also offers the potential for a business to benefit from all three. Clearly consultancy is the least understood of three. It is helpful because it can be seen as an intermediary position in the relevance gap where consultants act as translators and brokers of

knowledge, activities which can be carried out both by academics and by practitioners such as management consultants and/or those in an organisation
(Bouwmeester, Heusinkveld, & Tjemkes, 2022). Academic consultancy is an
advisory role bringing the expertise, knowledge and investigative skills of scholarship to advising, problem solving, and developing new ideas (Kinnunen, Holm,
Nordman, & Roschier, 2018). This is often thought to be about drawing upon
existing knowledge in order to help an organisation address a particular situation
(Fudickar, Hottenrott, & Lawson, 2018). It is not surprising that there is also
some blurring between research and consultancy (Perkmann & Walsh, 2008),
although there is potential for broader research themes to be informed and
influenced by what emerges from specific consultancy. In this respect, research
and consultancy can be complimentary.

The interplay between research, consultancy and teaching in order to impact
practice is a helpful way to think about the tensions of demand-led and leading
demand approaches. The value of a three-pronged approach is illustrated next in
an application which of itself is an important aspect of engaging with business,
and at the same time provides a context where the value of separation and
proximity can be evidenced.

Many business interventions are related to the development of skills in order to
address specific needs. Primarily, developing skills is a teaching-led intervention.
However, skills in themselves do not necessarily guarantee better performance in
a business, much more is needed. The problem is captured in the concept of skills
utilisation. In many ways it is a straight forward concept expressed well by the
UK commission for employment and skills (UKCES) who recognised that 'there
is little value to an organisation having a skilled workforce if the skills are not
used well' (UKCES, 2009, p. 12). Although the idea sounds like a statement of the
obvious, making it happen is a much more complex and nuanced issue, where
several factors impact on skills utilisation. For example, creation of
high-performance workplaces, improvements in leadership and management, and
Government provision of wider incentives in the economy for firms and managers
to change their behaviours are all important to successful utilisation (Payne &
Keep, 2011). Indeed, UKCES (2009) identify similar issues associated with both
raising skills levels and making use of them more effectively. Foremost is the need
for better work practices which encourage high performance. Then there is the
need for more businesses to focus on producing high quality products and, by
implication, moving to a high skill, high value proposition.[1] However, UKCES
point out that in the UK there are neither enough high performing workplaces,
nor (again by implication) enough organisations with high value strategies. The
issue of skills utilisation thus becomes a complex and integrated problem,
involving work practices, business strategy and wider incentives and environmental factors.

---

[1]High skill, high value propositions or high value business strategies draw upon Porter and
Ketels's (2003) argument that the UK is in transition from a low skill, low economic value
economy to a high skill, unique value economy, competing on unique value.

The inherent complexity of not only developing skills but ensuring that they then have an impact points to more fundamental issues. Warhurst and Findlay (2012) argue that the use of skills, especially those deemed higher level, is closely associated with business strategy. So it can be inferred that higher level skills are dependent on the extent to which an organisation pursues a move to higher value products and services. The contention here is that skills are a derived demand, dependent on other factors which tend to be more important to an organisation (Keep, 2022). For example Hogarth and Wilson (2003) refer to skills as a third or fourth order priority. To explain the relationship between priorities they begin with the wider context and only then turn to priorities in the organisation. They firstly highlight that skills are dependent (derived from) the product/service marketing strategies. Then, as a second order of importance, they are dependent on the way the organisation is structured to enable the strategy. Only then, at a third order of importance, come the people management practices within which skills are situated (Hogarth & Wilson, 2003). This all suggests a more complex landscape. To navigate this landscape implies that there is a need for a breadth of interventions to address the different 'order' of priorities. Of even more concern are the dissenting voices that doubt the extent to which demand anticipated by Government really exists. This is especially important, given that skills are a derived demand. If a business does not see the need to progress to a higher value product/service strategy then neither will they see the need to move towards a higher level skills strategy. Demand for skills is derived from a business need. Consequently, at a more fundamental level, if businesses are not convinced of the need then little will change (Hogarth & Wilson, 2003; Keep, 2022; UKCES, 2009).

What is clear is that managers play an important role in the midst of this complexity. They develop strategy, create work conditions and practices, and they are central to encouraging individuals to use their skills productively (Warhurst & Luchinskaya, 2019). Given the importance of managers, the UK fairs worse than its European counterparts with many more businesses in a long tail of stagnated productivity, in part due to the low level of management skills (Haldane, 2018).

Two possibilities and responsibilities for business schools emerge from this discussion. Firstly, it is apparent that there is a role for business schools to argue persuasively for businesses to develop strategies and practices which in turn call for new skills. If businesses are unaware of the benefits and don't see the need, then skills will not feature highly on their agendas. Secondly, the complexity and interconnectedness of what is needed to enable skills to be productive and have an impact call for a consultative approach. The organisational issues, management responsibilities, work practices and team performance issues all indicate a role for an academic consultant to combine the factors which enable skills to be utilised.

Now to turn to the part that separation and proximity might play with skills utilisation. The argument so far has established that it is not sufficient for skills to be developed, they need to be utilised by managers and by organisations. In this context a now familiar argument emerges stating that too much of the research into skills utilisation has been focussed on dispassionate critique of the issues and policy agenda, and too little has been engaged with trying to improve practice (Warhurst & Findlay, 2012). This poses the question about how research might be carried out in practice. Three approaches illustrate the possibilities. The first pairs academics with different strengths together. This involves having a research team with some members maintaining a distance and others working closely with the organisation. It will be important for the academic team to respect the different perspectives that they bring to the research, and that they adopt different roles in order to combine the twin approach of distance and proximity. Secondly, the two positions could be adopted by the same academics by cycling between maintaining distance and achieving proximity. This requires periods of engagement followed by stepping back and reflecting. The former approach brings together a more conventional academic colleague with someone who is more of engaged scholar. The latter requires an engaged scholar to develop the discipline of stepping in and stepping out.

A third response adds a very important dimension and recognises the idea of co-production of knowledge. This view pairs an engaged scholar with a scholar practitioner situated in the workplace (Carton & Ungureanu, 2018). This approach can also begin to connect with resource and capability in the organisation, where some staff may have had experience of research and investigative skills gained from post experience masters programmes. The scholar practitioner role, which is often described in terms of stepping in and out, to balance proximity with distance, could proactively operate this way, cycling between the two positions. It may be that stages in projects or programmes lend themselves to stepping back and from such a vantage point assessing what has been emerging in practice. Such a cycling is not unlike the vivid metaphor that Heifetz and Linsky adopt to explain their approach to adaptive leadership: the balcony and the dance floor. They argue that to gain clarity and perspective, distance and a clear view is needed. However, to influence and affect practice you need proximity, you need to be on the dance floor (Heifetz & Linsky, 2002, p. 53). They call for a cycling between the two. Observing at a distance is a safe place to be, but it is unlikely to change reality. That serves as a reminder of Pettigrew's assertion that the purpose of academic research should be to make a difference.

Skills development and utilisation is a teaching-led activity, but a consultative approach is needed with businesses to weave what is required to be in place in the organisation for skills to be used productively. However, there is a need to convince a significant number of UK businesses of the business necessity for skills, and that points towards generating an evidence base through research. Teaching, consultancy and research together provide a more comprehensive way to address important, but often difficult challenges.

This wide ranging discussion has brought us to a conclusion that the demand dilemma can actually be re-framed as a mutually beneficial tension. This tension is resolved by research that *leads* demand, but which by implication then begins to *create and shape* demand from practitioners and clients. The demand-led pole incorporates a consultative style. At its most effective, this consultative approach both draws on latest thinking to inform bespoke solutions, and identifies where research is needed to address key questions relating to business. The leading-demand position is broad and inclusive, recognising the value of fundamental research, which can act as a challenge to business, as well as being inspirational through the exploration of latest ideas. This strategy informs both teaching and consultative approaches. Perhaps Weick's alternative view of the relevance gap, attributing part of the problem to practitioners, does require a gap to be maintained. As Weick suggested, this may be an important challenge, requiring practitioners to learn to think beyond the immediate. It would also appear that employers and practitioners may be more open to the insights and depth of thinking that universities should be able to offer. Perhaps Weick's other concern, that practitioners may need to change their ways as much as academics, is closer to reality than he imagined.

A distinctive engagement provides business with a focus on meeting their needs, and the added value of thought leadership. It provides an answer to the question why a business would work with a particular business school. Being distinctive is a vital element for effective engagement, but it needs to be combined with what was frequently stressed in the engagement stories as a critical factor. Businesses value the quality of the relationship they have with a business school.

## Relational Engagement

The quality and importance of relationships has resonated throughout our discussions to date. In the 'relationship story', the client was emphatic: 'It's all about that relationship. If we didn't have the relationship we wouldn't have been able to achieve what we did'. The argument in this section will build a view of relational engagement as comprising three themes: relationship building, credibility, and nurturing. Each will be considered in turn to help understand how relational engagement works. However, in order to frame these themes the implied tension between relational and transactional engagement will be explored first, as illustrated in the 'relationship' and 'contrasting provider' stories.

In order to explore this tension, the discussion will engage with literature from the fields of consultancy, professional services, communications and relationship marketing, where relevant concepts and theory have emerged which offer the potential to help frame the relational engagement evident in the stories. The rationale for doing so is partly because there are many interesting similarities between professional services (and especially consultancy firms) and universities which provide services to business clients. In fact, Gummesson elaborates on this similarity, suggesting that both academics and consultants are 'in professional services; they are "intellectuals" and "knowledge workers"' (2000, p. 7). And each work in a knowledge economy, where they are both influential contributors to what are sometimes referred to as knowledge intensive firms and organisations (O'Mahoney & Adams, 2011). Yet they also compete for similar work, with academics needing to differentiate themselves from consultants and in so doing maintain a distinctiveness (Ivory et al., 2006), whilst some consultants attempt to add credibility to their consultancy by seeking associations with business schools (O'Mahoney & Adams, 2011). At the same time, the relationship between consultancy and academia can be problematic, with academic research about consulting tending to extremes of critical or positive assessments (Bouwmeester &

Stiekema, 2015). Nevertheless, there does appear to be a range of areas where academia and consultancy interact, not least in relation to how consultancies and professional services engage with their clients.

### *Transactional and Relational Tensions*

The 'relationship story' is a success story which stressed the critical importance of the relationship in order to make the engagement effective. The language and statements in the story indicate the value of high degrees of trust, shared commitment and collaboration. The moral of the story makes the point that the client thought the success of the engagement was 'all about the relationship'. This is a view that resonates with the idea of viewing engagement from the perspective of relationships, as articulated in the engagement framework (Bolden, Hirsh, Connor, Petrov, & Duquemin, 2010). The story also reflects the importance of individual relationships, yet, often engagement is discussed in terms of developing 'institutional relationships with businesses' (Thorpe & Rawlinson, 2013, p. 7); a relationship between organisations. Therefore, it is particularly interesting to note this emphasis on the significance of individual relationships. This point, which is echoed by Bolden et al. who also noticed that one or two relationships, especially at the early stages of an engagement, are the 'nexus of the partnership' (Bolden, Connor, Duquemin, Hirsh, & Petrov, 2009, p. 32).

The 'contrasting provider story' provides something of a balance to the positive message of the relationship story. It uses a powerful contrast between 'good' and 'bad' in order to highlight exactly what was valued by the organisation in the relationship with the Business School. Lessons from this story centre on the importance of providers being flexible, of having a clear track record (which could be evidenced), and of genuinely listening to the client. The quality of the relationship was seen as crucial, demonstrating the expertise and credibility of the university and having a 'can-do' approach that was focussed on helping the client. The story illustrates a tension that was difficult to resolve whereby the client had to overcome adversity (Parry & Hansen, 2007). It was a story of opposites, which provides a very helpful context in which to compare the factors considered important to the client. Together with the 'relationship story', the 'contrasting provider story' informs the relational/transactional tension, which appears to be a tension managed by selection of one pole or the other (Seo et al., 2004). The tension is about the kind of relationship that is developed between client and provider, and whether it should be relational or transactional.

In relationship marketing, transactional relations are depicted on one end of the continuum and contrasted with relationship building at the other extreme (Gronroos, 1991). In this context, there is an argument that relationship building is the best-fit approach for an organisation that provides services (Gronroos, 1991). In fact, Gronroos and Helle argue 'service is inherently relational' (Gronroos & Helle, 2012, p. 345), and consequently advocate a much richer understanding of the relationship. However, there is a tension about the strategy that an organisation may choose to adopt, for example whether to be relational or transactional (Broschak, 2015). From the examples of other universities provided by the client managers (especially in the contrasting provider story) it is apparent that such a tension exists. The two relationship strategies are quite clearly differentiated and recognisable in the descriptions given. For example, the participants in the stories stressed the value and significance of having a good relationship, they emphasised the need for a relationship evolving over time, and for organisations growing together with a high level of contact and engagement. All of which recognises that relational characteristics tend towards long term engagements with wide-ranging activity and connections (Broschak, 2015). The stories provide strong support for Broschak's argument that such relationship strategies tend to be 'founded on attributes such as attraction, trust and commitment' (Broschak, 2015, p. 306). In contrast, transactional relationships are 'short-lived and episodic' (Broschak, 2015, p. 307), and are more arms-length with limited amounts of information shared. A transactional strategy also tends to adopt a standardised provision approach where typically, that provision is considered more as a product than as a service (Gronroos, 1991).

The relational engagement tension captures key differences expressed in the contrasting provider story. The argument suggests that the tension should be managed by selection, by choosing a relational engagement. This view is also supported by Connor and Hirsh (2008) and by Wilson (2012) in his review of Business-University Collaboration. They all argue that a traditional supplier-customer model is inappropriate for HE/employer engagement. Instead, they propose relational approaches in keeping with Bolden et al.'s assessment that 'HE-employer engagement is fundamentally relational' (2009, p. 40). It is therefore a concern when some universities appear to be unaware or unwilling to apply relational strategies to their engagement with employers. There is a suggestion implied in some of the stories that some academic staff do not have the skills and experience to work with employers in a relational manner. This is as a wider issue, with similar concerns highlighted by an evaluation of the HEFCE Higher Education Employer Engagement Initiative. This report identified that many institutions found it both challenging to motivate staff to get involved and crucially, difficult to 'attract and retain the "right" staff with a mix of HE and commercial experience' (Kewin et al., 2011, p. 114). This aspect of skills and experience will be considered in more depth later in this chapter. However, if a business school can successfully adopt a relational strategy then there is considerable potential to differentiate itself from other providers. What also emerges from this overall discussion is one further, important aspect of relational engagement. Namely, that if the intent is to establish a sustained relationship with longer-term benefits, then self-evidently relationships need to be built.

### Relationship Building

To gain a better understanding of this apparent truism, literature associated with a consultative approach in which client relationships feature prominently will be drawn upon. In order to do this, analysis and discussion will be structured by processual (order and process), temporal (time spent on building a relationship and sustaining a relationship), and spatial, (levels in an organisation) considerations. There is general agreement in the literature that relationship building is a vital part of engagement with a client. Pellegrinelli (2002) argues that the client-consultant relationship is central and that a primary task for the consultant is to make the client feel comfortable, both with the consultant and with the process. Similarly, Kakabadse et al. (2006) suggest there is wide agreement that effective consultancy interventions should start with establishing the relationship. However, traditional consulting processes often do not make this stage explicit.

Order and process is typically observed with consulting processes consisting of similar stages to the five proposed by Kubr: entry; diagnosis; action-planning; implementation and termination (Kubr, 2002). Or, the four elements proposed by Kakabadse (1986): entry; intervention; evaluation; and disengagement. Whilst these models may well imply a focus on relationship in the initial stage of gaining entry to the organisation, they do not reflect the importance assigned by many commentators. In addition, they often suggest that the engagement is a single intervention with terms such as 'termination' or 'disengagement' signalling the end of the engagement. Therefore, these common process steps do not adequately reflect the focus or emphasis of an engaged relationship, either from the perspective of stressing the importance of starting with relationships, or in terms of encouraging a sustained relationship over time. An alternative view, proposed by Stumpf and Longman (2000), begins with a first phase aimed at creating enough interest to encourage a client to begin a conversation. The approach then incorporates initial conversations, which in the engagement stories were repeatedly stressed as important. This is followed by a needs analysis, again mirroring the argument made in the distinctive engagement part of the model, in which a bespoke solution is developed and, according to Stumpf and Longman, leads to the first engagement. Two more stages in the model emphasise the focus on a sustained relationship. The first is termed enrichment, where the consultant adds value to the client. This then progresses to a 'sole vendor' status, or as the senior manager in the 'greatest strength' story stated, a situation where the organisation 'become[s] the provider of choice'.

Clearly, relationship building can be understood in terms of process, from its beginnings through to a long-term relationship, but this also introduces a temporal dimension: the critical factor of time. A temporal understanding of relationship building enables a consideration of the effect of time relative to process. According to Liang and Lian, the time orientation of a relationship is both about the time already invested in the relationship, as well as the 'expected future length of the relationship' (Laing & Lian, 2005, p. 116). Laing and Lain draw upon Yorke's (cited in Laing & Lain, 2005) argument that as the relationship develops over time, the client and provider's expectations are likely to converge with a 'meeting of minds'. Laing and Lain conclude that 'a long-term perspective or time orientation is central to the formation of close inter-organisational relationships' (Laing & Lain, 2005, p. 116). This view was supported by the client from the contrasting provider story, who felt that 'if you are going to get quality at the end you have to invest the time.' The willingness to commit the time to the relationship, appears to be a central factor in developing a sustainable relationship.

The third consideration relates to the spatial aspect of relationship building, in this case spatial refers to level in the organisation. Earlier in this chapter the issue of complexity in client relationships was discussed. A helpful way to resolve such complexity was proposed, based on Schein's (1997) view of a client system with different types of client, with varying needs and expectations. This approach stresses the importance of investing time building relationships at different levels within a business. Similarly it is important for a business to ensure that the right connections are made between themselves and the business school so that differing expectations are understood. The strategy appeared to be effective, with the client from the relationship engagement story describing the relationships the business school had with key managers in their organisation as 'fantastic'. Building relationship also needs some thought to ensure that the right people are engaging with the right people to position what the business school could do, a view supported by Hughes et al. (2011). Such an approach builds on a multi-touch approach which moves away from a dependency on one relationship, and also can connect different services that a business school can provide to different parts of a business (Thorpe & Rawlinson, 2013).

Relationship can be considered from three perspectives. Firstly, relationship as process needs a focus on stages that are about listening, enriching and developing for the long-term. That means secondly that time needs to be invested to develop a mutual understanding and trust. Then, thirdly, a more sophisticated view of relationship building considers connecting the rights levels in the organisations and creating multi-touch points. Without doubt relationship building is a fundamental element of the model, but more is needed for an effective relational engagement.

### Credibility

The issue of credibility has proved to be an important factor in a client's decision to engage with a university provider. The motivation for a business to build a relationship in part emerges from a confidence in the competence of the provider and that has a lot to do with credibility. This has also been a central issue in the rigour-relevance debate. However, in the context of that debate, credibility is understood both in terms of the quality of research produced and also the implied credibility of academics amongst themselves. This is in contrast to the overall use of credibility in this engagement model, which relates more to the perceived credibility of providers from the client's perspective. The discussion will begin with an exploration of the general understanding of credibility, drawing on communication and relational marketing theory to inform the debate. These ideas will then be applied to the context of credibility in the engagement model.

The 'selection story' emphasises credibility alongside other factors, for example where the client indicated that track record, expertise and reputation were especially important. Whilst track record and previous success, especially with similar organisations was emphasised by the client, it was interesting to note the importance of individuals as factors in the establishment of credibility. It was clear that trust, expertise, reputation and credibility were all considered to be important factors for selecting and working with a provider. These factors are also prominent in relevant literature from communications research and relational marketing. For example, two factors are commonly recognised as particularly important to understanding credibility, namely: trustworthiness and expertise (Ferguson, 1999; Hilligoss & Rieh, 2008). This argument has been extended to include goodwill as a third primary factor associated with credibility. Goodwill refers to perceptions of care and genuine interest, and an ability to display an understanding of others' ideas, feelings and needs (Gass & Seiter, 2015). Interestingly, all three factors were prominent in the engagement stories. Good will is an interesting focus, where a business school can demonstrate that it really wants to help, to find out the client's needs, and shows genuine interest by spending a considerable amount of time in discussions to better understand the organisation.

The importance of relevant expertise as a credibility indicator was emphasised by one client from the engagement stories who stressed the value of trust and feeling comfortable with people. This manager expressed the very core of what it means to be credible: 'the belief that they are able to deliver on the agenda'. This is a view supported by Herbig and Milewicz who, whilst recognising there is no clear agreement on a definition of credibility, argue that at its essence credibility is about 'believability', the extent to which a client believes the intentions and the capability of the provider (Herbig & Milewicz, 1993).

Hilligoss and Rieh include the notion of benevolence in their work on credibility, which is the extent to which a client believes the provider is genuinely concerned with the client's interests (Hilligoss & Rieh, 2008). In the engagement stories confidence seemed to be established relatively quickly, for example with one client manager commenting on being 'terribly impressed' with individuals who seemed to make an impression personally and professionally with their expertise. According to Herbig and Milewicz 'to achieve credibility a provider must first build a reputation' (Herbig & Milewicz, 1993, p. 30). In their explanation, credibility represents the extent to which the client believes in the intention of the provider at that particular time, whereas reputation is based on what has built up over time. Often, reputation is referred to as 'track record' (Glasser, 2002). The interplay between credibility and reputation indicates that they are closely related. Herbig and Milewicz (1993) suggest that a good reputation produces credibility, whilst Glasser contends that credibility is 'one of the prime determinants of reputation' (Glasser, 2002). In the engagement model being developed here, reputation is seen as informing credibility (which is identified as a main theme in the model), since credibility is what the client perceives at the time of the engagement. However, the two concepts reinforce each other. Credibility builds the reputation of the provider, which in turn helps establish credibility with the next client. In this sense reputation and credibility inform each other.

In both the literature and in the engagement stories, there is a clear recognition of the importance of the credibility of the individuals involved in the engagement.

According to Glasser (2002), the distinctive factors that shape credibility-building are interpersonal skills, which he argues is not surprising given the central role of relationships in consultative engagements. In the engagement model, as already suggested, relational engagement was significantly affected by a combination of recognised experience and engaging personal qualities, in the provider personnel involved. This clearly resulted in the rapid establishment of trust and confidence between client and provider. It certainly indicates the importance of having the 'right people' involved in the relationship-building if it is to develop and succeed. Indeed, perhaps in relation to using the 'wrong people', Hughes et al. (2011) identify the credibility of individual academics as a key factor which might also *hinder* engagement. The 'right people' on the other hand, can generate credibility and can also begin the relationship-building which creates the conditions for relational engagement.

### Nurturing

The argument so far positions relational engagement as informed by relationship-building; investing time; connecting levels; progressing through stages of development; and informed secondly by credibility through reputation, expertise, building trust and confidence. However, there is another factor to consider, one which may not immediately be apparent, and that is the discipline of nurturing relationships. A first impression of the 'nurturing story' might indicate that the key message of the story is about building rapport. Yet the story describes a skilful approach to relationship building. Networking and rapport-building are of course important when connecting relationship-building with credibility in an attempt to establish sustainable engagement. However, it became apparent through what was subsequently labelled as the 'nurturing story' that the business school senior manager in the story was doing more than building a rapport. There seemed to be more depth, and a wider agenda, implicit in that narrative.

According to that senior manager, the 'nurturing story' is initially about establishing a rapport, which suggests activities to be found during the early stages of relationship-building. However, the manager also emphasised that it is crucial to maintain this focus on developing the relationship, on an on-going basis. Initially it may have seemed appropriate to think of this activity as proc-essual, a normal, early-phase part of relationship-building. And there is no doubt that rapport-building is vital during the initial stages of engagement, something evidenced by the 'breakthrough' effect described as key to convincing a potential client to enter into a contract. However, it is clear that the senior manager did not intend that this approach should be limited to the early stages of the process, and that the relationship-building approaches in the story may have much greater significance in any attempt to better understand engagement. It is for this reason that the story was not labelled the 'rapport-building' story but rather the 'nurture story', as a better reflection of the on-going nature of this activity.

Like the 'relationship story', the 'nurturing story', also demonstrated the importance of personal relationships. The senior manager clearly emphasised the need to build rapport by finding common ground and interests, in order to better connect with the client. This approach needed to be genuine and based on integrity, but it also had a clear intention: to put the provider in a better position to help the client. Similarly, the senior manager's argument resonated with Stumpf and Longman's (2000) view that, the extent to which a client will share information is dependent on the ability of the consultant to build both trust and emotional depth in the relationship.

According to a dictionary definition, nurturing is about encouraging development, caring for someone and cultivating behaviours (Manser & Thomson, 1997), which implies actions associated with supporting and sustaining. In this model the theme of nurturing helps to reflect the depth and breadth of engagement approaches, which include building both rapport and networks, both of which are crucial for establishing effective relationships. For example, according to Wilson (2012), in his review of university and business collaboration, networking is fundamental to the process of collaboration. In explaining the importance of networks, Wilson draws upon Smith's understanding of networking as 'the human process that creates and maintains relationships based on trust for the exchange of valuable knowledge and collaborative working' (Smith, 2007, p. 9). Rapport building and networking both are essential parts of the model, but the ability to nurture a relationship is what sets apart a sustained engagement.

Another useful way to explore the theme of nurturing is to relate it to collaboration. The engagement model adopts the idea of there being a collaborative sphere between a business school and a business, and as noted earlier, this is adapted from Connor and Hirsh's (2008) collaborative model. The reasons for organisations collaborating rest upon the expectation that advantage and synergy can be achieved. According to Huxham (2003) one critical factor in making collaborations work is the requirement to nurture the relationship, suggesting that 'the nurturing process must be continuous and permanent' (Huxham, 2003, p. 414). Rosabeth Moss Kanter's, earlier work on collaborative relationships came to similar conclusions. In developing her argument, Moss Kanter contends that collaborations need to do three things: generate more possibilities beyond the original reason for partnering; add value beyond the traditional customer/supplier exchange; and finally they need to be nurtured. In fact, Moss Kanter argues that relationships across organisational boundaries should be regarded as key business assets, implying that 'knowing how to nurture them is an essential managerial skill' (Kanter, 1994, p. 108).

## Sustainable Futures

### *Springboard to New Opportunities*

If a collaboration results in more being achieved than could be done apart, and adds value to both organisations, then it is important to represent this in the engagement model. The 'springboard story' provides an example of how an engagement can result in continuing benefits, and in particular can enable clients to do things they were not able to do before the collaboration. The client in this story recognised the value of working with the provider, in order to enhance the wider capabilities of their organisation.

The notion of sustainable relationships brings together strands from other inter-related themes in this section. For example, the idea of client-specific knowledge, emphasised by client managers. A long-term relationship means that the provider has begun to develop a deeper understanding of the client organisation. This increases the business schools ability to help with this deeper understanding of both the client organisation and the context in which it operates. This argument resonates with relationship-building, where the length of time invested in the relationship builds understanding of the client. It also indicates that providers need to bring more to the engagement than just general knowledge. What really seemed to count was specific knowledge of the organisation and its context.

This notion fits well with the credibility theme (in relation to expertise), but it also emphasises an important distinction: that the client values specific expertise. This argument is supported by Stumpf and Longman (2000) who advocate two ways to encourage a sustained relationship. Firstly, they make a similar point about the need to gain sufficient knowledge about the organisation in order to identify where value can be added. Secondly, they make a point that relates to the concept of benevolence, as discussed earlier in relation to credibility. They argue that a provider needs to foster the client's belief that they are committed to the organisation's interests, and to helping the client to continue to develop.

A final factor in developing sustainable relationships arises from the senior manager in the 'greatest strength story' discussion of continuing engagement between interventions. The senior manager acknowledged an inevitable aspect of client interventions is that they will always rise and fall. He called for both client and provider to identify opportunities for other activities, and to find ways of connecting in-between interventions. The traditional consultancy model would tend to suggest that the end of an intervention leads to a termination to the consultancy. However, from a sustainable future perspective, a different view needs to be adopted. Interestingly, Sieg, Fischer, and Wallin (2012), within the context of professional services, propose a continuing client dialog between projects. For this to be effective they advocate a dialog that stimulates with 'important, interesting, challenging, or even entertaining problems' (Sieg et al., 2012, p. 256). This strategy fits well with the earlier discussion of academics presenting their latest thinking to practitioners. Indeed, it is these very activities in which a business school might be seen to have a distinct advantage over other potential competitors. It also addresses part of what may be considered the wider remit of an engaged business school's mission. Such a perspective also resonates with the nurturing theme, with its emphasis on maintaining and growing relationships even when there may not be an immediate return on the activity.

## Skills and Systems

The factors discussed so far are necessary to develop a model of engagement that is distinctive, relational and sustainable, but of themselves they are not sufficient.

Good intentions and good ideas can come unstuck if they are not supported and enabled by the right skills and systems. Considerable energy and time can be spent compensating and finding ways to work around issues that fundamentally are about staff not having the skills to work effectively with businesses, and university systems which are not fit for purpose and don't recognise the different processes needed for a business customer.

The 'necessary skills story' presents a dilemma between intent and reality. It captures the tensions between the business world and the world of academia, with the main point of the story arguing for a shift of balance. The story points to an important consideration of both the skills and capabilities needed by universities to engage with businesses, and of the processes required to manage client programmes. One tension evident in this story relates to different time dimensions between academia and business, in a similar way to that which Bartunek and Rynes (2014), identify longer timespans as a tension in relation to research. According to this story, longer timespans are also a wider issue than just in the domain of research, they are also reflected in the length of education programmes, and in the time taken to validate a new programme. Then there is also a tension between more traditional academic teaching approaches and teaching and learning styles appropriate for business. The story supports the need for different teaching approaches (Thorpe & Rawlinson, 2013), and the difficulties in finding staff with the right mix of academic and business skills (Kewin et al., 2011). The story also suggests that relevance and rigour may not just be an issue related to research, but also applies to teaching. There are concerns that client programmes dumb down content, and that pushing for accelerated validation processes may potentially compromising the rigour and therefore quality of the process.

The skills and capabilities to engage with business were acknowledged in the stories as being different from traditional academic teaching. The picture emerges of teaching that broadens thinking with academic insights, informs practice with relevant research, but that also facilitates discussion to learn from the experiences and insights of the delegates on the programme. This story provided confirmation that there appear to be too few academics with the skill or the inclination to engage in this kind of executive/practitioner teaching, a view that supports findings from wider research (Kewin et al., 2011). Too often there is little development and support available to help academics gain the skills to work effectively in a business context. There are progression pathways emerging in business schools which recognise engaged scholarship, but in many cases these routes still need more clarity about the comparable scholarship criteria for progression. More importantly, they also need to be accepted as equivalent to traditional research progression. Putting in place a means to develop the academic skills for engagement and the progression pathways to reward academic achievement in these areas will be crucial to growing engagement and to enable it to be sustainable with sufficient staff with the skills to engage effectively.

An interesting perspective on the different skills required is proposed by Piercy. In a provocative article where he challenges some traditional views of the role of academics, he advocates the need for a more engaged academic able to combine high academic capability with effective engagement with businesses. An academic with an ability to be respected in both worlds (Piercy, 1999). Piercy calls this kind of academic a chameleon, and interestingly recognises that they are increasingly pulled between the tension of academic achievement and the world of business. The tension described resonates with the discussion to date, with a 'chameleon' role representing the kind of academic who might effectively reframe the tension, as opposed to continually compromising. The idea suggests someone who is comfortable in both contexts and able to adapt and perform.

A second possibility is to view the academic as a catalyst. The metaphor draws upon the idea of being able to spark thinking and change, of creating an impetus for participants to reflect and act. The idea in itself suggests the academic is engaging with participants as opposed to it being a passive experience. As a catalyst the academic seeks to bring together the conditions in which ideas can spark action. As previously discussed, this may be with vivid stories as advocated by Weick, interwoven with the skilful discussion of theory and ideas which challenge and extend current thinking. Frequently it will be to build upon the ideas and challenge provided by the other participants and the catalyst effect that peers provide to each other.

This catalyst effect can be supported by a third perspective which is to think of academics as thought leaders. According to Lorange (2005), research will always need to push boundaries and be exploratory, but alongside this more fundamental research a different emphasis will become increasingly critical. He refers to this as thought leadership, by which he means research that is closer to business, 'where the test will be whether the new insights have an impact' (Lorange, 2005, p. 785). Lorange draws two important implications from the idea of thought leadership. The first is that this kind of research needs to be 'disseminated more quickly, to ensure that it remains cutting edge' (Lorange, 2005, p. 785). Secondly, expressing a view supportive of Weick's (1996) teaching as a scholarship of integration, Lorange advocates that thought leaders should learn while teaching, and effectively research while teaching.

A fourth view, draws upon the recognition that business issues do not tend to fit within neat academic disciplines. Useful knowledge is not isolated or bound in a particular academic function (Asik-Dizdar, 2015). Consequently running management courses that are based upon functional disciplines is being challenged, since as Gosling and Mintzberg succinctly argue 'management is not business' (Gosling & Mintzberg, 2006, p. 424). From this stand point what is needed are academics who are 'deep generalists' (Thomas, Lorange, & Sheth, 2013, p. 154). This is a role that is able to combine depth and breadth so that academics can help managers make connections with related themes and disciplines. It implies a more integrated curriculum and with it the facilitation skills to encourage managers to draw their own connections, whilst bringing a breadth of knowledge to introduce related theories and ideas to extend the discussion.

Chameleon's, catalysts, thought leaders and deep generalists of course are not the sole answer to meeting the demands of engagement. There are a wider range of client engagement roles, recognising the need for client-facing skills which are not necessarily the same as academic teaching skills. These include unfamiliar roles such as project management, client management and consultancy, as well as more familiar roles such as programme management. They point to the need to manage not just the programme or course but also the client. Although problems were expressed in relation to finding academics with the right teaching skills, finding staff with the right client management skills could well be more problematic.

The final aspect of this theme relates to the supporting systems to enable engagement. The issues revolve around a tension of different time-frames between business and academia, but they also reflect that in clients, universities are dealing with a different kind of customer. University systems are set-up around the individual student, and not to cope with the needs of an employer organisation. Things become difficult if systems are not set up that are fit for purpose. One significant system issue illustrated how tensions (such as relevance and rigour) can apply to the validation of accredited, tailored, programmes. In this example, relevance means a customised programme, approved in a timely manner. Whereas rigour refers to the proper scrutiny of a new programme before being approved by the university. In the 'nurturing story' case this tension was resolved by the existence of an existing, robust framework which was already in place to enable timely accreditation which still fulfiled the university's quality criteria.

## A Dynamic Model of Purposeful Engagement

Each of the engagement themes have now been explored, using the engagement stories, their tensions and literature from relevant fields to inform the model development. What has emerged are important factors for successful engagement and their relationship with each other and their interconnectivity. The factors can now be drawn together into a dynamic model. Therefore, the model is represented as a diagram with a narrative to explain the inter-connectivity of the factors for successful engagement.

The engagement model is a way to describe the relationship between business schools and businesses. At the heart of the model is a tension between demand-led and leading demand approaches. It is a tension that resonates with the relevance-rigour tension experienced more widely within the business school context. The model represents a method for re-defining the tension, rather than reliance on pole selection, or on attempts to separate the two, or indeed on compromise. Re-definition is effected by adopting Seo et al.'s (2004) 'connecting' strategy and by viewing the two poles as mutually enhancing. This is an important relationship to capture and is positioned at the top of the diagram, with 'demand-led' emerging from the employer side and being interpreted through a consultative approach to inform the research and teaching. The 'leading demand' activity arises from the university/business school side and through a research-led approach, interacts with the consultancy and teaching activities. The connection is represented by a venn diagram at the centre of the model, depicting the inter-relationship between consultancy, research and teaching and their impact on practice.

The model captures the concept of distinctive engagement that has been argued throughout the book, one that is characterised by listening and leading. A listening approach recognises that businesses are often unclear about their needs, whilst leading with ideas introduces different thinking that can effectively shape and create demand. The model assumes a consultative process to identify needs which in turn represents an emerging skill set for academics to both diagnose needs and then apply latest thinking to those needs. Consultancy therefore combines with research and teaching to form a critical core to the model. The distinctive engagement represented in the model holds the tension between demand-led and leading demand so that both sides of the tension are enriched by the other. The specific needs of the client are informed by latest thinking and the research agenda is enhanced by those needs prompting directions for inquiry.

The second major theme that has emerged is relational engagement. The model depicts the factors that inform this theme, with 'credibility' bridging from the university/business school towards a collaborative engagement and similarly 'relationship building' connecting the employer to the business school. Research, teaching and consultancy form the critical core expertise of the business school, which together with a track record, reputation and trust begins to develop the school's credibility. Therefore, as already indicated, the interconnection between research, teaching, and consultancy is portrayed at the centre of the relational diagram, with its focus on improving practice. A 'demand-led' approach flows into the consultancy sphere, interpreting employer needs, whereas 'leading demand' informs the research domain to help shape, create and lead demand. Academic staff with the right skills and experience then establish the credibility of the business school. The new skills and roles identified in the engagement stories, and the associated responsive systems, all underpin the capacity to build credibility and relationships and are shown as enablers from the business school side of the diagram. In parallel to demonstrating credibility is the critical activity of relationship-building. It is through their credibility that academic staff can initiate exploratory conversations with clients and build a rapport with the client that then develops into a constructive relationship. These two important themes are represented on the diagram with credibility emerging from the university side of the diagram, to enable collaboration with the employer, and relationship-building with the employer is similarly shown on the employer side of the diagram. The two themes form a bridge into the central collaborative area of the diagram, signalling their crucial, dynamic role in the process.

The model so far has incorporated two factors associated with relational engagement. Firstly, relationship-building through investment of time, establishing networking connections across levels, and progression through stages of development, then enables the Business school to capitalise on its credibility. Then, secondly credibility provides an entrance to the client, developed through reputation, expertise, building trust and confidence. Staff then need to build on that start, connecting with the needs of the organisation, listening and demonstrating understanding. However, to sustain a relationship a third factor is incorporated: the idea of nurturing. An important realisation from the engagement stories was that something deeper and more encompassing was happening in the client relationships. Without doubt rapport-building and networking are essential for relationship building, but they are not sufficient. Nurturing conveys a deeper intention of continuing vigilance and care for the client. Neither is it a linear activity that happens as a stage in relationship building, it is far more pervasive than that. It is therefore represented in the model as encircling the collaborative space between a business and the university. This is intended to depict the all-embracing nature of nurturing underpinning the relationship and strengthening it for the long term.

The relational engagement process, of establishing credibility, building relationships and sustaining them through nurturing behaviours, is developed within a wider collaborative context. As a result, this ensures Kanter's (1994) three principles of effective collaborative relationships are applied: generating possibilities; creating extra value; and nurturing. This focus on relational engagement and on meeting the client's needs can then develop towards a stage of enrichment, in which value is added (Stumpf & Longman, 2000), as captured in the theme; 'sustainable future'. The idea of creating value for the employer is represented at the bottom of the diagram, emerging from the collaboration sphere but signalling movement back to the employer. Similarly, the theme relating to new possibilities emerging for the business school is indicated at the bottom of the diagram, returning to the university from those same collaborative activities.

The model captures the relationship between important themes and concepts, representing the mutual benefit of those inter-connections between the themes. The model emphasises circular, cyclical and iterative relationships which emerged from the engagement stories as being crucial to the development of an effective relationship. The multi-faceted nature of the model helps to address the limitations of more one-dimensional processual models, which may overlook or obfuscate patterns that are crucial to sustaining relationships. However, the model does indicate a progression from initiation of a relationship towards the creation of a sustained relationship, which is of mutual benefit to both client and provider. The model clearly shows how value is added to the client, with broader

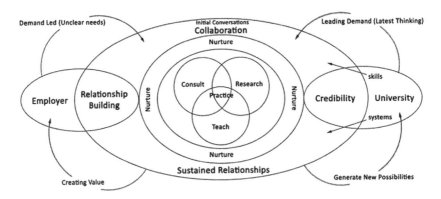

Fig. 1.    Purposeful Engagement Model.

capabilities developed, whilst at the same time business schools learn and transfer the enhanced credibility and experience towards generating new possibilities and research opportunities. Therefore, a processual element is evident down the central spine of the model, indicating progression towards achieving outcomes from the relationship. This mutually beneficial relationship has been labelled 'purposeful engagement' (Fig. 1), a title which has been adapted from a phrase used by one of the clients from the contrasting provider story.

# Chapter 6

# The Engagement Process

## The Business Need for Engagement

Up to this point a framework has been used to develop a common language, illustrating the different levels of engagement in order to more clearly understand what an engaged relationship means. Then a model has been built which brings together the factors that enable successful engagement, and which stresses the importance of the interplay between the key aspects necessary to make it work. What is now needed is a process which provides guidance about how to put engagement into practice. In this chapter stages and steps are proposed that can help businesses and business schools consider how they engage in practice.

### To 'Engage' is Not Enough

In the context of competing demands even succeeding with an initial intervention with a business can be hard enough for a business school. Alternatively if a transactional approach is adopted, then there may be no expectation or desire to extend and grow the work with a business. The intent of the engaged business school is to establish long term relationships, and that requires more than just focussing on the intervention in hand. The engagement process addresses this issue using ENGAGEMENT as a mnemonic and is divided into two phases. The first phase is represented by ENGAGE, the second by MENT, together they emphasise an important principle of the engaged business school: the need to build and sustain relationships. A simple way to illustrate the difference between the two phases is to consider the meaning of the word engage and contrast it with engagement. Engage is typically defined as: to get involved, to participate and to become interested in something. This meaning changes and gains extra significance when the suffix 'ment' is added. The suffix extends the word's meaning to express a continual state of being engaged. The change in emphasis from engage to engagement is mirrored in the process mnemonic. ENGAGE indicates the stages for a single intervention, whilst MENT represents the stages for a continuing relationship. This change in meaning from engage to engagement reinforces the principle that an engaged business school should be one that develops sustainable engagement, a continuing state. This is an important point of

The Engaged Business School, 95–116
Copyright © 2023 Anthony Sturgess
Published under exclusive licence by Emerald Publishing Limited
doi:10.1108/978-1-80382-941-820231012

difference in the process. To engage is difficult enough but can often end with only a single intervention with the employer.

### Sustainable Engagement Requires More

The ENGAGEMENT model is proposed as a way to help develop a sustainable engagement. The first six steps reflect a more processual model, progressing from initial interactions through to delivering a programme or intervention. These steps (Entry – Negotiate – Gather – Analyse – Generate – Employ) could be used to develop initial or one-off client relationships. However, the sustained growth of client relationships is dependent on addressing the final elements of the model (Manage – Evaluate – Nurture – Transfer). It should be noted that in the second phase the steps are not necessarily processual and tend to be cyclical in nature. This second phase emphasises continuity firstly by stressing that it is important to *manage* the client, not just the intervention or programme, and to *evaluate* the whole intervention with the client, not just the sessions or the individual parts. Then more holistically, there is the need to *nurture* the relationship from initial rapport building through to continually sustaining the vitality of relations. The continuing value of the relationship is generated by ensuring the *transfer* of experience and learning so it is shared in the business and importantly within the business school, using it to promote engagement within the organisation and to other potential clients.

### The 'How' of Engagement

The stages place an emphasis on 'what' is needed to be done, but importantly it also matters 'how' the activities are carried out. The process requires skills which promote a relational approach. Therefore, alongside each stage of the process there is a suggested skill and therefore an associated focus for those involved to guide how the stages can be carried out effectively in order to build relationships, credibility and trust. There are of course many skills needed at each stage of the process, so the intent here is to highlight skills which reinforce the focus on a relational engagement.

The first phase, ENGAGE, is about initiating through building confidence and commitment. Therefore the *entry* stage has a focus on *empathy* to build understanding, leading to the second stage of *negotiating* with an emphasis on *navigating* the differing client expectations. Then *gathering* information takes place with the intent to *galvanise* agreement and commitment within the organisation. *Analysing* the situation is done *appreciatively* to build on strengths which then enables the next stage which is to *generating* ideas. The focus and skill at this point is about a *generous* attitude which goes the extra mile. Finally, *employing* the interventions is done with the intention of *energising* action.

The second phase, MENT, has a broader emphasis on continuing the relationship and is more expansive, looking beyond the programme or interventions. Accordingly, the *manage* step has a focus on *maximising* the benefit and potential of the relationship. Then the *evaluation* process is about *empowering* by recognising the value and worth of what has been achieved. *Nurturing* is built upon effective *networking* and finally *transfer* of learning should seek to be *transformative*.

Before considering each stage in detail, we will return to some of the central arguments about why engagement matters, to draw out some of the implications which need to be considered in the process stages.

## What Are Businesses Looking for?

Increasingly businesses are asking for customised solutions, relevant to their needs, recognising good practice they already have in place, and fitting around the participants schedules. The content and the process, and the intended outcomes all need to come together to form a solution designed for that particular organisation. In fact, some organisations have commented that whilst specifically asking for customised solutions in bid processes they noticed that many providers were actually proposing what they already had in place. Clients are becoming increasingly discerning and can see through thinly disguised standard offers purporting to be tailored programmes. It is worth noting that any suggestion of such compromises are prevented when co-creation is adopted as part of a collaborative relationship.

In the context of the engagement process, three priorities for effective interventions will be considered, followed by three levels of delivery for interventions. To illustrate this further the ideas will be discussed in the context of learning and development interventions. Firstly, the three priorities for engaged interventions are to ensure that they are relational, distinctive and underpinned by a shared responsibility.

## The Value of a Relational Approach

The argument embedded in this book makes the case that building trusting relationships is essential for effective engagement. The idea recognises that developing effective interventions such as learning and development programmes are a shared responsibility, requiring such relationships to be in place. Underpinning this approach is the value to the organisation of a business school developing its knowledge and understanding of their business. At the same time the client is building their understanding of how to access and capitalise on the wider expertise available in the business school.

Being trusted with a client's business goals and the development of its people is a privilege and responsibility that business schools need to take seriously. Therefore, when an organisation chooses to work with a business school it has the potential to mark the beginning of a proactive partnership. Realising that potential begins by supporting the client to clarifying their needs before tailoring solutions that fit the requirements and then working responsively to build a long-term relationship based on mutual trust, shared knowledge and credibility. An engaged approach should open doors for a client to connect their organisation directly with people and processes within the business school and together inform, create, shape and lead future directions through new thinking and research.

### *Distinctive Engagement and Practice*

It is clear that many areas where business schools engage with business such as executive education or leadership and management development whilst being large markets are also crowded places with many competitors. Being able to offer a distinctive approach in this environment, and one that may be attractive to business, could place business school in an advantageous position.

Take for example the leadership development market. The choice of provider is often one made between approaching private training providers, consultancies, or executive education services within a Business School. At one end of this spectrum, there tends to be more focus on practice and skills, the other advocating a more theoretical standpoint. An Engaged Business School holds to both principles, and in doing so offers a more distinctive approach to promote both thought leadership and practice. A focus on practice can limit the potential to introduce thought leadership and evidence-based approaches garnered from a more theoretical perspective. However, to be too theoretical can feel removed from the day-to-day experience of leaders and lack relevance to practice. As discussed earlier, too often, there is the risk of being neither responsive to the needs of business, nor the source of insight, to lead and help shape demand in the future. With this position comes unsatisfactory compromise. Such risk is countered with a focus on distinctive engagement and distinctive practice, within an overarching ethos of building sustainable relationships for the longer term.

As we have argued, distinctive engagement is about being both 'demand-led' and 'leading demand'. This requires business schools to plays two roles, one responding to demand (helping clarify demand and then tailor solutions to fit), the other shaping demand, helping to inform, and create (with new thinking and research). Allied to this distinctive engagement is the need for distinctive practice. This captures the ideas discussed earlier in Chapter 4 on the tensions associated with engaged teaching. Distinctive practice adopts a 'clinical' perspective of wisdom that is embedded in the practice of management (Schoemaker, 2008) alongside the value of theory applied appropriately (Rouseau, 2012). This is helpfully illustrated by Pearce, a US Business School Dean (Pearce, 2004), who discusses two kinds of knowledge which she uses as a senior manager and as an academic. The first she characterises as 'folk knowledge' which can be seen as useful applied knowledge, whereas the second is academic knowledge, which is rigorous but of limited use in practice. She argues for the two types of knowledge to more closely overlap, which would require subjecting folk wisdom to more careful analysis, whilst at the same time directing academic scholarship towards important organisational problems.

Underpinning this approach is the notion that practice matters, but practice that is shaped and informed by an evidence base. Theory and ideas are important, but so is being able to put ideas into practice and to do them well. And working this out needs time and space and often distance from the here and now of action. The dual strategy advocated encourages participants to move between a focus on practice and a reflection on theory, and a business school can provide the safe space and time for that to happen.

## A Shared Responsibility

A relational approach becomes self-evident if the development of people and especially managers and leaders in an organisation is thought of as a shared responsibility. Such interventions are best developed in partnership, co-created with the Business School, together with the organisation and the delegates for whom it is intended. In fact, it can be seen as a four-way responsibility. First, and foremost the responsibility for development is always that of the individual. Implicitly, this is something everyone recognises, however, it is all too easy to sit back and expect others to put things in place. But individual development is too important to leave to others. Therefore, the primary driver in order to gain the most from any intervention should be each individual. Secondly, it is the organisation's responsibility, who self-evidently will benefit from improving leadership. It is an important role since for leadership development to be effective organisations need to create the conditions for the interventions to work. Thirdly, the business school as provider of the development has a responsibility to support, to challenge, to stretch thinking and encourage participants to reflect and improve their practice. Finally, comes peer responsibility. Each participant on the intervention has responsibility to support each other, to encourage and share experience and expertise, to learn from each other. It is this fourth responsibility that participants often say they have valued most.

## Three Levels of Intervention

Another way to illustrate the practice focus together with the emphasis on theory is to consider learning at three important levels or layers in development programmes. Firstly, participants typically value acquiring practical skills and tools needed for day-to-day effective working. Secondly, they benefit from a grounding in a solid evidence base that explains the rationale behind the skills and tools. This evidence based allied to the tools and techniques should support and enable a more effective workplace. But, thirdly, they also need to be challenged, stretched and encouraged to think differently, to develop their intellectual skills and insights, in order to take them and their practice to the next level.

Such an approach to interventions especially in areas such as management and leadership development connects with the idea of distinctive engagement, and presupposes three things:

- *An evidence based approach which is grounded in research.* There is a strong case made that UK organisations could improve their performance by more clearly applying and adapting ideas which already have evidence supporting their effectiveness. For example, management practices, workplace innovations and people practices are three key areas identified in a UKES commissioned report (UK Commission for Employment and Skills, 2016). London School of Economics also found that good management practice closely correlated with a range of business performance measures (Bloom, Lemos, Qi, & Van Reenan, 2011).

- *Thought leadership and insight from emerging ideas.* The intent here is to recognise the need for research to be brought closer to businesses. There is a pressing need to adopt approaches that connect with organisations, where the focus is on impact. This approach firstly implies that thought leadership should bring ideas to practitioners as they emerge as we discussed in Chapter 5. Then there is a second implication: that disseminating and communicating ideas should be balanced with listening and learning from the dialog with business to improve the thought leadership. To enable this the notion of promising practices (Delridge, Gratton, & Johnson, 2006) is helpful, where practitioners and academics actively explore practices that appear to be working to better understand and evaluate them, and then consider how to shape them to meet the specific context of a particular business.
- *Recognising the value of ideas that have stood the test of time,* but which may need adapting to current needs. These are sometimes referred to as tried and tested techniques and technologies (HM Government, 2019). They are ideas that organisations often know about, but don't consistently practice (Higson & Sturgess, 2014).

Given this context of the engagement process (see Fig. 1), each of the engagement steps will now be considered in turn, drawing upon leadership and management development examples to illustrate the steps.

## Phase 1: To ENGAGE

The first six steps of the process focus on enabling an intervention with a business. They will be considered in turn with their associated skills to consider what is involved and how each step develops the relationship. The initial reason for engagement could be due to a number of things, but behind it is a perceived need for support. The engagement model introduced in the previous chapter proposed three broad activities, that of teaching, research and consultancy. The perceived need may fall broadly into one of these areas or incorporate a combination of the three. Typically, the most common activity with which a business starts to engage with a business school would be in the teaching area, where learning is a key part of what is needed. It could be argued that part of growing and strengthening the relationship would be to develop a rounded set of interventions which bring together the three areas of teaching, consultancy and research for the benefit of the client. To illustrate the ENGAGEMENT process in the next section it will be assumed that the initial engagement is based around a set of learning and development interventions. However, it should be noted that effectively all three areas of teaching, research and consultancy come into play, with consultancy and research supporting and enabling the teaching process. As discussed earlier in the book, teaching activities constitute a significant part of business school engagement with businesses.

Fig. 1.   The ENGAGEMENT Process.

### Entry -the Initial Engagement With a Client

Entry starts with the initial contacts that are made. In practice business schools tend not to be short of potential contacts. There are often possible connections of which business schools may not be wholly aware. For example, there will be opportunities to harness existing connections or to make the most of previous affiliations with the university. It may also be the case that other businesses who work with the business school provide the word-of-mouth recommendation or the confidence by association for a potential client to engage with the business school.

If a business school is seeking to grow its engagement a good place to start is the hidden connections it already has and the potential open door to conversations that they represent. One of the hardest parts of entry is to find a way into an organisation, in this respect business schools and universities may well have an advantage that they don't recognise or appreciate.

The strength of an intervention increases significantly with the ability to first consult on the issues the client is trying to address. As discussed earlier an important part of the initial stages is to create sufficient interest so that the client begins a conversation (Stumpf & Longman, 2000). Wherever possible a consultative first phase is valuable, and almost becoming essential, especially if the client is requesting bespoke solutions. It provides the opportunity to listen more widely in the organisation and meet managers at different levels and roles. This will often start to open up other opportunities and crucially allow managers for whom the intervention is intended to contribute, as well as those who manage the target group being able to express their wishes. The skilful facilitation of these consultative discussions are both a spring board into the programme and an opportunity to understand the client better. The more the client is understood and is encouraged to contribute to the design of the interventions, then the stronger the foundations for a long-term relationship. It becomes a shared design and development, and of course that is not to forget that the clients will often have excellent ideas to contribute.

The first step is about initial conversations that will need to do a number of things. First and foremost, entry is about adopting a consultancy approach which is built upon listening and not proffering ready-made solutions. Listening is also a pre-requisite to a demand-led approach to meet needs and similarly is needed to identify possible thought leadership that could lead demand with the client. For listening to be effective it needs to be reinforced by demonstrating understanding. A key aspect of this step is to see things from the client's perspective. Investing time matters at this stage, it is easy to progress too quickly without doing this important groundwork properly.

From a business perspective, the entry stage is equally important to ensure that the business school adopts the right kind of approach. Thus, a business will want to ensure that the business school establishes credibility and trust. The three aspects of engagement introduced at the beginning of the book, namely, being distinctive, relational and sustaining by adding value, can play an important part at this entry stage. Firstly, for a business to ask questions about the distinctiveness of the approach taken by the business school and look for a partner who will adopt the dual approach of being demand-led and leading demand. Secondly, to seek out partnering and relationship building behaviours and thirdly to explore how this partnership would be sustainable and continue to grow and add value for the business. This is often demonstrated in the track record of the school, where credibility is not just about expertise, but is about the way the business school works with a business.

There are also important questions for both organisations to answer which should be considered at this early stage. Both organisations should consider the degree of fit with their overall strategies. They should also assess whether the areas of intervention are strengths for the business school. Capacity and resource to make this work should be considered from both sides. From this initial stage will also emerge some indications as to whether the relationship looks like it could work. Of course, the answers may not always be apparent so early in the relationship. Crucially, the client needs to work out if it wants to work with an engaged business school. Not all engagements and interventions will be thought of as part of a longer-term relational commitment. That may or may not be something that develops and grows. If it is likely to be a single intervention then the first phase of the engagement process, ENGAGE, is of more immediate relevance than the second.

Underpinning the ease with which initial contacts can be made, is the presumption of credibility. Establishing credibility, is based on the provider's ability to demonstrate knowledge and expertise, but not just general knowledge. Crucially, as explored in the engagement model, businesses place most value on specific knowledge about the organisation and its context. At the entry point this will mean the business school preparing properly, doing the ground-work in advance to understand the organisation and the current sector issues.

What has also emerged as significant from the engagement stories is that individual relationships seemed to be particularly important, even though in the literature, relationships are often discussed in terms of organisational relationships. The schools credibility and the initial forming of a relationship were dependent on key individuals, suggesting that the right people are critical to success, and reinforcing the importance of interpersonal, as well as inter-organisational relationships. The individuals in the engagement stories had recognised experience and engaging personal qualities which enabled the rapid establishment of trust and confidence between client and provider. It certainly indicates the importance of having the 'right people' involved in the relationship-building, if it is to develop and succeed. It also seems to be the case that the 'right' people are good at something else; the ability to network. There was striking evidence in the engagement stories of individuals forging a wide network of relationships with key managers in the business, across a range of organisational levels.

The relational focus for this stage is the need for empathy. Empathy underpins the approaches needed in this initial stage, whether it be building credibility, taking the time to listen or establishing initial relationships. Clearly taking the time to listen and build understanding requires empathy. Similarly, empathy is evident when showing care and genuine interest, which as was established in the previous chapter is an important part of building credibility. Empathy is critical in one other respect; trust building. The engagement stories indicated that the skill of individuals in the initial stages enabled the rapid establishment of confidence and trust. That trust is built when genuine care and interest is being shown.

## *Negotiate – Agreeing How to Proceed*

Gaining entry into an organisation is followed quickly by a negotiation phase. This crucially establishes the initial scope of the interventions. It is borne out of an understanding of the client's needs and an ability to replay to the client that understanding with insight. It provides an assessment of the client's initial needs and a proposal for how they can be addressed. At this stage there is much that is still not known, so it is important to indicate that seeking to understand is an ongoing process. It should be noted that a client may well have identified a need for the interventions but may not be clear about what is needed. There should also be an early conversation about the tension between customised and standardised solutions to clarify the position. Businesses tend to prefer organisation-specific solutions to address their needs, but that may not always be the case, and some interventions or part of the range of interventions may draw upon existing provision within the business school.

It is also at this stage that there is a need to navigate between differing client expectations. A client's position is not necessarily represented by one person or group within the organisation. As Schein (1997) suggested it is more helpful to recognise that there is a 'client system'. In many cases the initial contact may well be with a learning and development team, but other parts of the client system need to be considered such as the senior team, the managers to whom the target group report, and of course those who will be delegates on the interventions. At this negotiation stage it is valuable to try to identify who the decision makers will be, their relative power and influence and if they have differing expectations that need to be addressed. This stage may well include a formal tender process and presentation.

Presentations offer the opportunity to convey a distinctive approach and to communicate the ethos and principles of the business school. An engaged approach begins to explain not just what is proposed to be done, but also how the business school will work with the organisation and the value to be gained from working with the school. This is important because it emphasises the shared responsibility for the interventions being a success. The three strands of an engaged business school provide a helpful framework:

- Distinctive – why should a business work with the business school
- Relational – how will the business school work with the business.
- Sustainable – how will the business school continue to add value

Alongside negotiations with the client, internal negotiations also need to happen within the university. The right resources and approach will need to be brought to the interventions and that may not be straight forward. There is nothing worse than promising certain things, and then having to deliver with a compromise of resource.

One frustration that businesses highlight is when those involved in building initial relationships then disappear when a contract is signed. One of the engagement stories made just this point, recounting a university who offered a very persuasive and dynamic person to lead the negotiations, who then disappeared as soon as the contract was signed. There is good reason for introducing at the negotiation stage some of the team who will be working with the client, this helps build credibility and trust discussed in the entry stage.

An important skill at this stage is the ability to navigate the complexities of an organisation and understand the needs of different groupings of internal stakeholders. This will involve understanding where there are differing expectations and sometimes competing demands. Navigating differing perspectives from various groups is not an easy task, and draws upon listening carefully to those voices in the organisation. In turn, it is helpful to reflect concerns and expectations in any proposal at this negotiating stage. In parallel to this, there is also a need to navigate internal systems in the university in order to respond in a timely manner to clients.

### Gather Information to Understanding the Need

The third stage is about gathering information in order to design interventions which address the business needs. At this stage organisations have agreed a contract and often want to move quickly and directly to delivery. They may have taken some time to get to this point, but frequently once they have reach it they want to see action. Holding back delivery however is important to ensure the interventions are appropriate.

The business may also have good evidence to inform the design and often has conducted some needs analysis of their own. This existing work will need to be recognised and built upon. There also may have been previous similar interventions in the organisation, which will mean that it is important to understand the impact that they have had in the organisation. The information gathering activities also allow the business school to get to know more about the organisation, with strategy, vision and culture all providing valuable insights. Some aspects of culture for example often will form part of any leadership intervention. Usually this stage involves interviews and focus groups and preferably will take place with all the client groups referred to in the negotiation stage. This ensures that the right people are engaged in helping to design the programme.

A helpful way to determine who needs to inform this information gathering stage is put forward by Revans (1998), the founder of action learning. He suggests asking the straight forward question: who needs to be involved? In his view three types of people are needed, those who know, those who can, and those who care. The first group comprises those who actually know about the situation and context, they usually know how things are currently done, and are likely to have good ideas about what needs to change. Secondly, look for the people who can make things happen. They are people who are in a position to enable the changes to happen. This is not just about those in key senior roles, it is also about the gate keepers or influencers who may be needed to ensure the interventions can be supported in order to have the intended impact in the organisation. These are the people who have the power to get things done, whether that be due to their position, expertise or influence. Finally, Revan's advocates finding those who really care about making the changes, they are crucial because they are motivated to support the interventions. Most important of all is the need to talk to the intended participants, and of course they are likely to be in one of Revan's groups. Their involvement ensures that they have a sense of ownership of the programme and that their specific views about their needs are part of the design.

The relational focus at this stage is to galvanise support by engaging key groups in the organisation. Gathering information is not a dry exercise, but rather is about galvanising a desire to find solutions. There are likely to be differing views regarding the underlying causes and the viable solutions. So developing an accurate picture of what is needed also requires skills to bring together a consensus in the organisation of what is needed. This will involve galvanising opinions and commitment, alongside clarifying the organisations responsibilities to ensuring the success of the programme.

### *Analysis – Making Sense of the Situation*

Analysis is inextricably connected to the information gathering stage. Much of the information gathered will be qualitative, although the organisation may have some performance data to inform the process. This stage is about finding focus by analysing the various information sources. In many ways this step of the process involves academics adopting research investigative skills. The analysis phase can involve identifying themes and coding, alongside identifying factors that might limit success and the wider organisational issues that need to be considered. The skills for carrying out a needs analysis lie somewhere between consulting and research, nevertheless these skills are very similar and a research rigour is actually something very helpful and distinctive that academics can bring to this phase. Implicit in the approach is the need to balance coming to the information without pre-conceived ideas and the fact that experienced academics in this field bring insight and interpretative skills based on their own knowledge. This stage is a process of discovery asking questions to clarify the problem, and what isn't the problem. In a similar manner discovery questions are asked about the opportunities presented by addressing the issues.

Analysis therefore, can be enriched by the discipline of research practices. To illustrate this, we will turn to what has become an important means of exploring issues with engagement: the value of holding tensions. One of the tensions in research analysis leads to helpful ideas about how to develop insightful ideas through analysis. The tension is expressed by on the one hand some who argue that there is considerable value in attempting to consider the data without pre-conceived ideas (Gioia, Corley, & Hamilton, 2012). Yet, in reality, a researcher always comes to a situation with some level of understanding, and often may be well informed, wherein lies the tension. Having a pre-understanding of the situation is, in one sense, inevitable, especially if the researcher has a professional background in the field. Indeed, this can also be advantageous to the research process. For example, Gummesson (2000) argues that a pre-understanding can prevent a lot of unnecessary work. A view counter-balanced by Gioia et al. (2012) who advocates a conscious attempt by the researcher to distance themselves from theory, and focus on the data of the research. This is both a dilemma and a tension which Sigglekow captures when arguing that 'an open mind is good; an empty mind is not' (Siggelkow, 2007, p. 21). Acknowledging this tension between knowing and not knowing offers a useful approach to analysis, one that recognises the 'fine balancing act that allows for discovery without reinventing the well-ridden wheel' (Gioia, Corley, & Hamilton, 2012, p. 21). The benefit of trying to hold the tension of knowing and not knowing when analysing information is helpful to arrive at insightful and productive ideas to shape the next step in the process, the design stage which generates interventions.

The relational focus for this stage is to adopt an appreciative attitude. This involves considering where the organisation has strengths that can contribute to the solution. An appreciative approach draws upon what works well in the organisation. This can have a number of benefits, firstly it affirms good practice in the organisation, and secondly it seeks to identify areas of strengths that can be incorporated into the design and delivery.

### Generate – Interventions to Meet a Client's Needs

This stage begins with presenting the analysis to the client and sense checking the findings. This conversation with the client also starts to provide suggestions from the client that can inform the design stage. Having met with the client it is then helpful to bring the academic team together to provide cross-discipline insight and encourage a whole team ethos. It is easy and often expedient to adopt a silo-based approach of asking academics to work alone on ideas related to their own discipline area. However that can be limiting. A better approach is to gather a panel of academics together who provisionally will be delivering the programme to discuss ideas and approaches, together with the analysis team presenting their findings. This opens up cross-discipline conversations to generate ideas. Too often design of workshops or specific interventions are the sole preserve of an individual academic, and consequently suggestions from their colleagues and also discussions about the connections between themes and workshops can be missed. Bringing different perspectives and disciplines together develops an interconnectedness to the programme, and a narrative about the learning that is required. It also provides a context for cross-fertilisation of ideas. This stage needs academics to draw upon theories which can inform and shape the development required, based on the needs identified. It requires staff to identify theory and ideas which can help and to explore more widely the literature and thinking that could inform the delivery. This is a scholarship process at the interaction between theory, emerging ideas and the context and needs expressed in the organisation.

Design is not only about the content it is about the learning process too. It may be that some of these requirements have already been indicated in a tender process, but an important part of the design will be to determine the learning processes that can be effective for the client.

If the client is intent on progressing to delivery quickly, then adopting a rapid development and delivery process can help. Typically this works as follows, the generate phase focuses on the first event co-design so that the content and delivery approach meets the client's needs and is ready to deliver before the other interventions. Then in a rapid development process the programme can start whilst the second intervention is still being developed. Lessons from the first delivery can be fed forward to improve the delivery of the second. Any broader lessons are incorporated into the design of other events. This method ensures that the programme is rapidly designed in parallel with delivery, incorporates feedback, and can also be responsive to any organisational development as the programme rolls out. If the activities are learning interventions the design team may want to consider learning that addresses the three levels or layers discussed earlier. At the first level to build in skills and techniques which focus on how to do things to address needs. Then secondly, to incorporate evidence-based practices which underpin being more effective in the organisation. Third and crucially, ensure that the design provides intellectual challenge and insight to step up to the next level, and take their organisation forward.

The relational focus of this stage is generosity. It is not a word you expect to find in a step process such as this. However, it captures the desire to 'go the extra mile'. This stage is exemplified by the intellectual generosity demonstrated by a willingness to give time and insight. Generosity at this stage sets a tone for the interventions. It is a generosity that is not just with the client, but extends to colleagues providing insight across discipline areas.

### Employ – Delivering the Interventions

Putting the design into action is the culmination of the ENGAGE process. It is also the critical stage where the planning and design come together. It is an important stage to adopting an engaged approach to delivery, it is where engaged scholarship in particular comes into play. As discussed earlier there is an argument that conventional approaches to teaching practitioners and professionals which tend to be didactic in nature are inappropriate. Instead, a more facilitative approach is needed to work together with the participants and with their experience, to explore the theories and ideas in the context of practice. This approach builds an environment where ideas can be extended, adapted and explored in the light of experience.

Creating the space for ideas to be explored by participants, so that they draw upon their experience and context suggests that participants should come to the workshop/session prepared. One way of doing this is through a 'flipped learning' approach which provides a curated combination of focussed theory, ideas and activity prior to a workshop or event. This then enables the event to have maximum benefit for the participants concentrating on exploring ideas in depth, reflecting on practice, sharing experiences and stretching thinking.

Flipped learning is where theory and ideas that would normally be taught in the classroom are provided before the session usually using a virtual learning environment (VLE). This then creates the space for the session to focus on exploring the ideas, and their application to practice (Carrie A. Bredow, Roehling, Knorp, & Sweet, 2021). Flipped learning though requires participants to be engaged and committed to carrying out the pre-work. It also places a responsibility on the engaged scholar to effectively curate content and to guide the participant through the learning using the VLE.

There is often pressure from a client to reduce the time that participants are away from the workplace engaged in a learning activity, and therefore when they are at a workshop there is an expectation that the time is particularly productive. Flipped learning can be a way to minimise this concern, but it needs to be coupled with an experience that has impact and value to justify the time away from work. However, underlying this concern about taking participants away from their job is an assumption about the separation of learning and working. It may be time to begin to change this narrative. When workshops have a strong application, building shared experience and fostering ideas for impact, then the argument begins to be made that such sessions can be and perhaps should be an integral part of work. Blurring the boundary between work and learning expands into a wider conversation about how workplaces can become more like places of learning, and perhaps learning spaces should become more like workplaces?

Creating a learning environment where application, shared experience and ideas for impact are emphasised raises an important question about how to encourage learning to be applied. There are helpful practices which can increase that likelihood that ideas gain traction and learning 'sticks'. For example when:

- They are memorable. People remember things that are surprising or striking or that they recognise as significant. Salience matters, people are drawn to the novel. Remember Weick's approach of using vivid stories to take practitioners out of their comfort zone. Challenging convention and different thinking can also have this effect. There is also a suggestion that to make a workshop memorable, or a programme for that matter, beginning and endings matter. In general, when people are asked to recall experiences they tend to remember beginning, peaks and ends. In fact, beginning well matters, but ending well matters more (Voss & Zomerdijk, 2007).
- They resonate with individuals when their relevance and potential to help the learner can be seen. Sometimes ideas can connect with experience to offer an explanation or they can indicate a promising practice to apply.
- They are applied and have an impact. There is no better way for learning to stick than for it to be put into practice and have an impact. Therefore application activities should be built into delivery. Interestingly, people are more likely to commit to do something if they do so publicly. Finding ways for participants to agree together what ideas they will take away and apply to practice may therefore be helpful.

- They are shared experiences. When peers on a programme or respected role models from within the organisation making contributions and share their experiences at the workshops it reinforces what is possible and builds a willingness to change. This kind of learning is likely to stick because we are strongly influenced by what others do.

One of the important elements of an engaged relationship is the potential for co-delivery. This will involve key members of the organisation contributing to the programme. The business specific knowledge that someone inside the organisation can bring can be invaluable, as can a senior leader joining for part of a session to participate in a discussion and answer and ask questions.

Finally, the academic team should be learning from the experience of delivering the programme. Firstly, they should be improving the programme by sharing ideas about effective delivery based on what is working, but secondly and more importantly they should be building knowledge about the organisation, and sharing that understanding so that the depth of knowledge of the client increases and is used productively to help the client.

The relational focus for this stage is about energising action. At the heart of this phase is the need to bring ideas to life and energise participants to apply ideas, to make an impact and to feel valued.

## Phase 2 – From Engage to Engagement

It is at this point that the largely sequential steps to effective deployment of interventions turns to steps which are aimed at sustaining and building the relationship. These steps by their very nature are more integrated, continuous, and cyclical rather than sequential, and reflect the premise of this second phase, which is to build for the long term.

### *Manage – The Relationship and Not Just the Intervention*

The first thing to note is that managing the programme and interventions is crucial and well run interventions are essential to an engaged relationship, but they of themselves are insufficient. Managing should be broader than the programme, it needs to be about managing the client. However, even managing the programme needs to have a strong relational focus as well as ensuring the essentials are in place. We will consider programme management first.

Managing the programme can be thought of as comprising five responsibilities which surround the primary responsibility of the participant experience. This first responsibility is about how participants experience the programme and their engagement with it. Their experience is managed by ensuring that the various elements of the programme connect to create a whole journey experience for participants. Then, a sense of engagement is developed as the delivery builds relationships with participants so that they feel listened to, supported and challenged. The second responsibility is to ensure that the learning environment, physical and virtual, is in place so that participants and academics are free to focus on the content, process and the participant experience of the programme. Then the third responsibility focuses on leading the academic team to collaboratively work together, blending the different strengths of the team, feeding forward ideas and insight from their respective sessions. The next two responsibilities turn towards managing the processes associated with a client programme. The Fourth responsibility is the administration, logistics and communications that underpins the participants experience. This too has a strong relationship focus, ensuring that administration works closely with the academic team and with the participants. A client programme is different from a conventional programme and this is particularly the case with respect to the participants. They are often experienced professionals and managers within an organisation. They are busy people, so the connections and replies to queries need to be responsive and professional. This needs close interaction between academic and administrative staff, and it needs administrative staff with the skills to work well with this kind of participant. Then finally the fifth responsibility is the management reporting, progress monitoring and evaluation. At one level this is about establishing the team meetings to manage the programme and to monitor progress and continually improve, liaising with internal university processes, and addressing issues. However, it is also about listening to the participants view of their experience and evaluating at both the session level and then the overall programme.

However, whilst good programme management is essential, more is needed. An important distinction about working with a business is the need to manage the client and not just the programme. It is not just participants on the programme that need to be considered. This is especially so when adopting a co-design and delivery approach with a genuine partnership in place. Learning from the programme as it develops means gathering information and sharing with the client to agree how things can be improved. But it also means there will be ideas and insight that emerge from participants which are about improving the organisation which, with permission from participants, can be fed back to the organisation as the programme progresses. A partnership recognises a shared responsibility for the success of the interventions, which needs both parties to be clear about their responsibilities and to support each other to achieve them. The wider client management responsibilities include setting up project meetings with the client, providing reports and updates, and most importantly building the client relationship.

As a consequence, business schools engaged in this kind of work often set up different roles to manage the client. These may vary based on the size of the interventions, but they represent the need to not just manage the programme but to manage the client. To illustrate this roles often are set up to engage at different levels of the organisation. At a strategic level a Client Director works collaboratively with senior client equivalents on the strategic direction of the programme and relationship. A client manager acts as the main point of contact, providing regular updates, schedule planning, and project/contract meetings. In addition to the client manager, a programme leader has responsibility for the delivery and

Table 1. Client Management Roles and Responsibilities.

| Client Director | Client Manager | Programme Leader |
|---|---|---|
| Collaborative working with client strategic lead on the strategic direction of the interventions, and broader relationship themes | Day-to-day operational management of the programme, and evaluation. Single point of contact for the client | Leadership of the programme content and delivery team, and delegate support |
| Establish and agree overall evaluation criteria for the success of the programme | Maintaining and enhancing consistent quality standards | Regular communication and support for delegates as they progress |
| Identify and assess improvements and wider innovative services with the client | Cohort scheduling and feedback | Administer programme |
| Generate opportunities to capitalise on the programme to enhance the clients credibility through awards and extend thinking through research | Interact with internal academic processes and the client to ensure seamless programme management | Provide academic support to learners |
| Ensure that the business school exceeds expectations and delivers in keeping with client vision and values | Regular meetings with client to fit the programme needs | Evaluation |

performance of the programme team. Table 1 sets out typical responsibilities for the respective roles.

The relational focus of this stage is to explore ways to maximise impact. This is impact that goes beyond just the programme or intervention to effect the wider organisation. Managing the client encourages a focus on maximising the benefits of the relationship.

### Evaluate – Appreciating Value, Recognising Worth and Demonstrating Significance

Evaluation is widely acknowledged as an activity that is not done well, and too often it is done at no more than a superficial level. A Chartered Institute of

Personnel and Development's (CIPD) survey found that one in four organisations did not carry out any form of evaluation of learning and development. If they did, it was at best superficial and only inquired of user satisfaction. Learning transfer and wider impact were conspicuous by their absence, only evident with a small minority of cases (Chartered Institute of Personnel and Development, 2021). According to the CIPD, evaluation typically covers three areas, engagement, which provides an indication of how learners are energised and involved, followed by learning transfer which looks to how individuals apply what they are learning to their practices and workplace. Third is impact, which asks questions about how the learning is changing and improving performance (Chartered Institute of Personnel and Development, 2022).

The evidence would suggest that evaluation isn't particularly valued by businesses, so it might be helpful to step back and think about the intention behind evaluation. The roots of the word are from its Latin origin meaning 'to strengthen' or 'to empower'. Its meaning is to form an idea or judgement about the worth of something. Evaluation is therefore an estimate of value or worth, to determining merit, worth and significance. Consequently, it is helpful to remember that whatever evaluation is being adopted, what is being sought out is the worth and the value of what has been gained from the experience. In practice it would appear that much of that has been lost in an instrumental interpretation which focuses on a superficial counting of user satisfaction.

Effective evaluation should be built into the processes of the programme at the design stage. It should take into account what the organisation is hoping to achieve through the interventions and needs to be a shared responsibility between the business school and the client. A first step is to clarify the purpose of the evaluation, and to explore what is hoped to be gained through the process. Evaluation often only focuses on the participants in the programme and rarely has a wider remit. However, from an engagement perspective evaluation should assess the whole intervention and relationship with the client, not just at session or programme level. Expanding evaluation to consider the whole intervention involves a different perspective. Invariably this level of evaluation has the intention of recognising a wider impact. Building on Moss Kanter's view of collaboration then an evaluation of an effective relationship could look for three things: generating more possibilities beyond the original reason for partnering; adding value beyond the traditional customer/supplier exchange; and evidence that the relationship is being built for the longer term (Kanter, 1994). These aspects of evaluation assess the effectiveness of the relationship with a focus on how more is being achieved by the way the partners work together.

The relational focus of this stage is about enabling new possibilities through recognising the impact on individuals, their team and the organisation. The wider focus of evaluating the relationship and not just the programme enables new possibilities by seeking out the value and worth being created by the relationship as a whole.

### *Nurture – To Build a Sustainable Relationship*

Nurturing may not be the term or the idea that would first spring to mind when thinking about maintaining an engaged relationship. A phrase such as building rapport more readily comes to mind, and rapport is indeed a vital part, but it doesn't capture the depth, sense of purpose and continuity that nurturing conveys. Similarly, networking is also closely associated with building relationships, and has an important place in forming relationships, but doesn't capture the whole.

Nurturing suggests a persistent determination to add value, to prioritise the interest of the one being nurtured. Continuity is important because the trust that is essential for an effective relationship can be fragile. Nurturing evokes notions of caring and cultivating and of growing a relationship.

Nurturing is more encompassing than rapport building or networking, reflecting a depth and breadth to engagement. Without doubt building rapport and networking are important elements, crucial for establishing effective relationships, but it is the idea of nurturing that can make the difference. In terms of building a relationship, initial activity does focus on rapport building and on making connections in the organisation to establish a network of relationships. This is the ground work which forms the basis for a nurturing relationship. Sustained relationships are demanding and whilst nurturing behaviours are crucial to achieving long term relationships they are not an easy option. For example, in the previous chapter we explored the idea of maintaining a relationship during periods when there may not be contracted interventions in place. Whilst this may suggest a demanding requirement, for a business school it also is an opportunity. A business school's wider remit to bring businesses together through networks, and to disseminate research fits well with keeping in touch with businesses.

The relational focus for this stage is to network. That is because networking is a key building block for nurturing to then take place. Networking seeks and establishes the mutually beneficial connections which then enable nurturing activity to develop and grow the relationship.

### *Transfer -Learning Into Practice and Learning for the Partnership*

Transfer of learning happens primarily with participants developing their own practice, but it also happens at the relationship and partnership level too. Transfer of learning is usually thought of in terms of those directly participating in the interventions and it is core to the idea of engaged interventions. The point has already been introduced earlier, that the more that learning is considered part of the workplace, then the less learning transfer is thought of as a separate activity. Transfer in effect becomes embedded as the interventions create space for new theories and ideas to be thought through, conversations to gain shared understanding, sharing of expertise and good practice, problem solving, idea generation and questioning of different possibilities and current practice take place. The workplace becomes more like a learning place.

Continuing and building the relationship requires more than this. Good relationships result in both partners, the business and the business school, developing new capabilities, which are mutually beneficial. With this intention, the purpose of the interventions will be to develop new capability of some sort in the organisation, but it should not be forgotten that the same should happen with the business school. Business schools should always be learning as they encourage others to learn. This idea closely reflects the benefits that Moss Kanter (1994) argues should be evident in a collaboration: the generation of possibilities and the creation of extra value. In good relationships, value is added to the client along with the development of broader capabilities, whilst learning is shared and transferred in the organisation. Similarly, the business school benefits by itself learning and using the enhanced credibility and experience it gains from the relationship (an important aspect for reputation-building) for the generation of new possibilities. These possibilities can be with new clients or in the extension of the existing relationship.

The business can reflect on the new capabilities it has developed through the interventions and recognise that as a consequence it may now be able to do things that previously were difficult to do, or indeed not possible. This opens up opportunities for the organisation. It also may present areas where it might want to extend activity with the business school as the business becomes more aware of the different possibilities of working with the business school. Both organisations gain knowledge about each other which means the business schools is more able to help and support, whilst the business is more aware of the wider expertise that it can draw upon.

The potential to increase credibility and reputation is important. The positive support and testimonial from an organisation is far more valuable than anything a business school my try to say about itself. In addition, there may be mutually beneficial opportunities such as research and case studies from which both partners would gain.

To achieve these wider benefits requires looking beyond the normal understanding of learning transfer, and intentionally seeking a much broader notion of learning transfer. For this to happen takes a proactive and reflective approach to step back and see what is emerging from the relationship. In many ways transfer of knowledge and experience is like the springboard effect characterised in the stories of engagement. It is therefore worth thinking about how the springboard idea is made an intentional part of the ending of a phase of an intervention. Specifically considering a springboard event at the end of a phase of interventions can ask questions of the participants about how they will take their learning forward, and crucially it can also ask questions of the partnership about the opportunities open to them. A springboard event constitutes a memorable end, but an end that is really the end of the beginning.

Finally, transfer of learning, like the other stages in this model, is more than just an activity at a participant level, it needs to happen more broadly at an organisation level. This final step requires outcomes to be transformed into new possibilities.

## Summary

The ENGAGEMENT process begins with a first phase that combines a more recognisable sequential set of steps with elements that are common to developing training solutions and to consultancy. The second phase of the process crucially has activities which do not follow a linear, start and finish model. They are more encompassing and continual. Viewing the engagement from this broader and more strategic perspective raises the potential for both partners to gain more by working together. For a business school this approach should offer the possibility of working with clients towards providing a full service across teaching, consultancy and research expertise. For a business they can capitalise on the breadth of capability within a business school. With respect to teaching related activity a business can gain from micro-credentials, and development support to stretch and extend capability in the organisation, through upskilling and reskilling. Consultancy can investigate issues and opportunities in a collaborative manner making the most of the knowledge the business school has gained of the organisation, to act as a critical friend. Then research capability presents an organisation with the options to pursue ideas, with a virtuous circle of applying research to practice, and developing research from practice.

The ENGAGEMENT process has explored practical stages to implement an engaged approach which is distinctive, relational and sustainable and conveniently leads into a broader consideration of the engaged business school in practice.

# Chapter 7

# The Engaged Business School in Practice

The intent of this book is not to prescribe but to describe, and therefore, it is hoped that business schools will utilise the ideas to make their own assessment of their engagement and develop strategies which bring together their strengths and aspirations to chart their own way forward. Similarly for businesses, they can also assess their needs and aspirations to be better placed to know how to connect more effectively.

This chapter draws the strands of the framework, model and process together to visualise the engaged business school in practice. Firstly, the engagement framework will be used to illustrate three practical applications: to explore how mission might be developed, to understand stakeholders and their expectations and to map activity and connections. There is much that is already in place within business schools that can shape mission. Here some possible influences of mission are suggested. The second use of the framework is to identify and understand stakeholders and their relative needs, which in turn will begin to suggest areas of potential conflict and where synergies might be possible. It allows stakeholders to be assessed in terms of how they relate to the mission and purpose of the business school and then to think through how the relationships should then be built with stakeholders. Thirdly, the use of the framework as a mapping process will be illustrated. This is a vital exercise which often surfaces hidden connections and opportunities that are not realised. However, whilst there is a logic to this order of progression from mission to stakeholder and finally to consider how the different aspects, initiatives and activity might be mapped, it is not the only way to sequence the applications. When starting in a new situation beginning with mission makes sense where there isn't much existing practice, or where the intent is to come at engagement from a fresh and new perspective. The reality though for most business schools is that there is much already in place, especially at the activity level, but as was pointed out in the discussion in Chapter 2 it is disconnected, sometimes hidden and very often does not take into consideration the other levels of the engagement framework. The point was illustrated by the story of the non-executive director commenting that the business school in question was a 'well-kept secret'. The premise behind the story is that business schools are more engaged than is often recognised, but much of that is latent potential that it is not being realised; they are not as engaged as they could be. In this situation, the mapping exercise is about surfacing where engagement is already happening and

**The Engaged Business School**, 117–141
Copyright © 2023 Anthony Sturgess
Published under exclusive licence by Emerald Publishing Limited
doi:10.1108/978-1-80382-941-820231014

identifying isolated practice and potential connections. Thus, starting with the mapping exercise indicates where there are already stakeholders, and also provides a basis for mission to emerge from some of the current strengths of the business school, even if they may be undervalued or not clearly recognised as strengths until seen from this perspective.

The three ways to apply the framework help explain and 'frame' engagement which then naturally progresses from this sense of mission to consider the purpose of an engaged business school. Purpose, in turn, prompts a debate about how business schools differentiate themselves. There have been a number of calls for business schools to consider what makes them distinctive, and there are several frameworks which attempt to capture the possibilities. They represent the tensions inherent in the identity and purpose of a business school. It is therefore instructive to explore how these tensions are expressed in the respective frameworks. Differentiation begins to clarify the big picture of the shape of a business school, but as significant is what that means to the key stakeholders of a business school; businesses, managers, students, academics and the wider university. These are relationships that are central to an engaged business school, so it is important to pay attention to what difference it makes for them. Therefore, the engaged business school will be considered from their different perspectives to think through how each group can make the most of their relationship. Finally, in Chapter 8, the discussion will return to a bigger picture to consider the ways in which an engaged business school might contribute and seek to play an important role in supporting recovery and growth especially in response to crisis.

## Framing a Mission

In Chapter 3, the engagement framework was introduced and the theme of mission was explained in the context of the strategic drivers of mission at national and institutional levels. It illustrated the renewed emphasis on ideas of engagement as mission. What the discussion did not do was explore what mission means for an individual business school. That is the intent of this next section.

Developing a clear sense of mission galvanises the other levels of engagement. There are, of course, many ways that a sense of mission could be developed. This section will consider mission in terms of its breadth and depth, as outlined in the discussion of the ladder of engagement framework in Chapter 3. The understanding of breadth in this context is a broader view of stakeholders beyond an economic and business focus to a wider societal perspective. Alongside this, a complementary approach of being locally sensitive, where depth refers to being rooted in a particular place and its communities. Both perspectives encourage a focus on contribution to society. Many business schools already have commitments which would contribute to a broader mission of engagement. For example, the Principles for Responsible Management Education (PRME) agenda provides a clear focus and many business schools already have made a statement of intent in this area. PRME is based upon the UN sustainable development goals, and together, particularly around sustainable futures would help to shape a sense of engagement as mission. Other areas that may inform an approach to developing an engaged mission could be the notion of fair work, responses to grand challenges and consideration of public value. Fair and good work could be developed from the findings emerging from, for example, the Taylor review of modern working practices (Taylor, 2017). It is a broad and encompassing theme, and one that is being debated with a renewed interest as businesses and employees consider how working practices should change post-pandemic. Good work correlates with a wide range of health measures and according to the future of work commission: 'the ultimate purpose of work is to support health, wellbeing and to enable individuals to flourish' (Institute for the Future of Work, 2022). Themes such as good work which have a broader societal impact inevitably are addressing a complex set of problems. Tackling more complex themes leads to the second area that can inform mission, namely grand challenges, which represent difficult but important problems, often intractable, but significant. Grand challenges ask some different questions of business schools. In scale they are significant, and they are not discipline specific, cutting across boundaries and needing a multi-disciplinary approach. The pandemic did see society turn to universities for solutions, and it did also highlight bigger questions about many areas including health, fairness, and how our businesses and systems operate when under extreme pressure. Therefore, in the next chapter the idea of grand challenges informing a business schools mission will be explored in more detail.

The third area that can inform an engaged mission is the notion of public value and public good, they are areas which have also gained an increasing place in business school strategic intent. A local sensitivity could draw upon the ideas associated with civic engagement discussed earlier. Such a focus is also likely to connect with local strategies and priorities. Frequently, this will involve considering how small business in an area can be supported. Initiatives such as the Small Business Charter for example, emphasise the role that business schools can play supporting small businesses, local economies and student entrepreneurs. There are clearly a wide range of themes which can inform an engaged mission, and not all will necessarily fit with one particular business school. However, they all suggest a commitment to engagement with the business community and wider society as a means to shaping different futures.

## A Framework for Stakeholders

Clarity of mission will begin to identify the areas and themes where a business school seeks to excel, and it will give an indication of the kind of stakeholders who will be important to the mission. As discussed earlier gaining a clear sense of the breadth of stakeholders and their differing expectations is crucial to ensuring synergies and areas of potential conflict are identified. This is particularly important when resources are stretched. It ensures that there is more transparency in the way resources are invested, identifying where they are misaligned and particularly where complementary expectations can help with resourcing. The four levels of the framework provide a means for clarifying the position with a stakeholder. Table 1 indicates the kind of questions which can

Table 1. Stakeholder Engagement Framework.

| | |
|---|---|
| Engagement as mission | How does each stakeholder inform your engaged mission? Who is the engaged mission trying to serve? |
| Engagement as vocation | How can you connect engaged scholars to this stakeholder? What are the knowledge needs? What scholarship and thought leadership relates to the stakeholder? Are there engaged scholars with the knowledge and expertise to support the stakeholder? |
| Engagement as relationship | How do you engage with stakeholders? What kind of relationships need to be developed and nurtured? What is the stakeholder needs and expectations? How can stakeholder expectations be met? |
| Engagement as activity | Think about the activities that support and relate to each stakeholder. How can activities complement different stakeholders? |

provide an assessment of stakeholders and of the engaged provision in the school. The framework allows stakeholders to be considered from the mission perspective, suggesting on the one hand the kind of groups that fit the mission, and on the other hand considering how existing stakeholders may inform the mission. The vocation level probes the areas of knowledge and the kind of scholarship that would support the stakeholder. In part this stage asks questions about their knowledge needs, but it also encourages a broader view of the areas of knowledge and scholarship that may be informative for the stakeholder but are not something they immediately recognise, this is about identifying possible areas of thought leadership. Crucially, there also needs to be an assessment of whether the business school has the expertise to engage with the stakeholder. The relationship level explores how engagement is established and the nature of that relationship. An important aspect of this level is to develop an under-standing of the stakeholder's expectations. Then the final area is to consider what kind of activities might be appropriate for this stakeholder. It should be noted that the process that has been described is in reverse to what typically happens, which is to begin with activity. The framework encourages a proactive approach where an assessment of the kind of activities needed happens after the relationship and the scholarship that addresses expectations have been determined and the associated knowledge needs and possible thought leadership for the stakeholder have been identified.

## Framework Mapping Exercise

The third application, as mentioned earlier, can take place after considering mission and stakeholders as the logical next step to map what needs to be put in place to connect mission and stakeholder. But it can also be used as a helpful way to map current provision, initiatives and activity. This is particularly useful since most business schools already have activity and connections, often at the level of individual academics which may be isolated and not well recognised.

When exploring mission a number of possible areas were introduced as possible ways to inform that mission. They themselves can be utilised to illustrate areas to explore when mapping. The mapping exercise can both look for what is already there and/or map themes, initiatives and activities which could be incorporated to build the ladder of engagement. Table 2 provides an example of the kind of things that may already exist, or that could be mapped to fill gaps, and

Table 2. The Engagement Ladder.

| Mission | Purpose, values and strategy | An engaged business school. Taylor review of modern work practices – good work. PRME – principles of responsible management education. UN sustainable development goals. Build back better, as a civic business School apply the values/principles into action |
| --- | --- | --- |
| Vocation | Research and scholarship | Applied research, scholarship of engagement. Research informed practice/practice informing research |
| Activities | Knowledge exchange, advice, consultancy | Evidenced-based leadership/management/business practices to improve productivity and performance |
| | CPD/teaching/enterprise | CPD short courses, hybrid programmes. In-company programmes |
| | Employer support | This is a two-way relationship. Employers involved in programmes, providing support. Business schools providing students via placements and then graduates to employers |
| Relationship | Networks and business engagement | Relationship building with the business community rooted in a sense of place, and then expanding nationally and internationally |

connect isolated initiatives or activity. In the table mission is connected to purpose, values and strategy and vocation to research and scholarship.

In practice, the mapping exercise often involves a business school assessing where its contribution is at the moment, and surfacing the various good practice that it may already have in place. It is important to recognise existing strengths as well as where the gaps may be.

The engagement ladder is a useful means of illustrating examples of engagement that could fit within the wider framework of different futures for business schools. It also enables a business school to assess elements of their engagement activity, and how they could be integrated with the four levels of engagement to improve impact.

Engagement as vocation prompts a business school to explore what scholarship and research should look like if it is to enable an engaged mission. Underpinning mission and vocation is relational engagement. Identifying existing relationships, and mapping potential and important relationships and their interconnections, is essential in order to appreciate the strength, breadth, interdependency and degree of influence possible. Finally, engagement as activity provides tangible elements which will differ across business schools but which can be organised in such a way that in combination they have a greater impact on engagement.

The diagram in Fig. 1 utilises the descriptions in Table 2 to indicate what to look for in each of the four levels of engagement. Each level of the ladder of engagement is expanded to suggest the elements a business school could bring together to form a more integrated approach and in doing so provides an illustrative example of engagement in practice.

The diagram has the relationship theme at the base of the framework to attempt to represent the idea that it is relationships that are foundational, not activities. In the engagement framework relationships are positioned above activities, in order to indicate a greater depth and a critical lynchpin role they hold between activity and vocation. For the purpose of this diagram they are represented at the base to convey the notion that they uphold and form the groundwork for what appears above. What will be immediately obvious is the busyness of the diagram, that is because it is illustrative and has numerous possibilities indicated, many of which may not be relevant to any one business school. On the other hand, it does indicate the level of interventions that may be taking place in a business school, often not connected, happening in different parts of the business school and without a clear mission or strategy. A broad engagement of staff across the business school is needed to carry out the mapping exercise if what is currently happening is to be recorded.

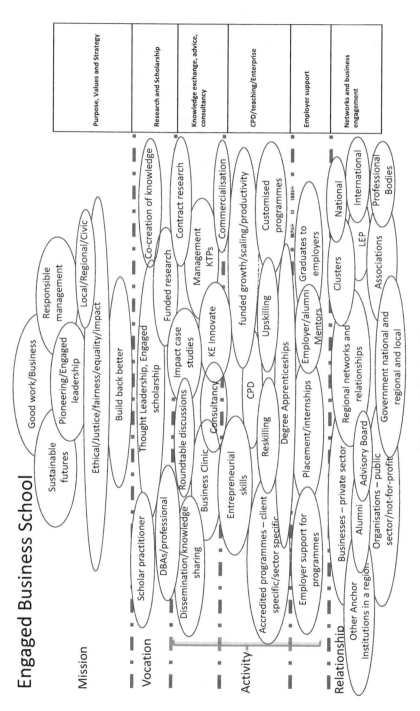

Fig. 1. Mapping Framework.

## A Differentiated Business School

Throughout this book, the argument has been made for a distinctive approach to engagement. The emphasis has been to think firstly about what distinctive might mean from the point of view of businesses. In this next section, we will turn to some helpful ways to think about the future of business schools. To do this we will first explore some frameworks which have been developed to try and characterise differing types or models of a business school. Secondly, we will return to the past to see how the early forms of business schools might provide some insight about their futures.

It is inevitable that any discussion about how business schools differentiate themselves needs to begin with the underlying tensions of the identity and legitimacy debate. These tensions have been widely recognised as problematic for business schools. Previously in Chapter 4, the legitimacy debate was positioned as being about whether business schools research and teach 'about' or 'for' businesses which then informs its place in a university to the extent it is perceived as a social science or a professional school. Addressing tensions has been a central focus throughout our discussions of an engaged business school. So it is no surprise that with these tensions too, the challenge is to resist the tendency to adopt a binary approach and seek different thinking to meet both sides of an apparent tension in ways that transcend the dilemma.

That is what Starkey, Hatchuel, and Tempest (2004) have suggested and in so doing resisted the pull to one position or the other. They argue that not only should knowledge produced by business schools be both 'for' and 'about' management, but it should also be both 'for' and 'about' society. To envisage how a business school might achieve this they suggest thinking about business schools occupying a space where knowledge is co-created, drawing upon different parts of society, it is a place where ideas are discussed and emerge from businesses and from communities. A place where different stakeholders come together to engage in a meeting of minds. They used the image of the Greek Agora to illustrate the idea, where different parts of society came together from the political, commercial, judicial and social communities in an open space for debate (Thomas, Lee, Thomas, & Wilson, 2014). With this more embracing view of a business school in mind some of the different ways of positioning business schools will now be considered to inform thinking about how business schools differentiate themselves.

A starting point is to recognise what business schools currently do and where they currently place their focus. Osbaldeston (2006), then director of Cranfield School of Management, positioned the debate around the strategic issue of the type of business school being developed. He contrasted a research oriented academic institution where education funds research, with a practice-oriented teaching institution where research enriches education. Other similar continuums can be identified between a specialised school with a full service school, a local/regional focus with an international/global outlook, and an undergraduate/post graduate emphasis as against a post experience provision. At a basic level continuums provide a means for business schools to clarify their positioning.

A second group of approaches build on the idea of continuums to develop a matrix to frame different ways a business school may be positioned. What is notable is that they often are based around continuums which reflect tensions within business schools. Typically they contrast a teaching versus research focus on one continuum with an organisational focus versus an academic or scholarship focus on the other (Ivory et al., 2006; Wedgwood, 2007). For Ivory et al. four profiles emerge, two located more towards the scholarly continuum characterised by a social science and a liberal arts approach. Whereas the other two, which are associated with organisational impact are represented by a knowledge economy approach and a professional school. For Wedgwood the organisational focus is expressed in a 'relevant to business' approach and a 'knowledge application' approach.

Both frameworks recognise that business schools typically exhibit a mix of the activities with variations in the relative influence of approaches resulting in different profiles. The frameworks extend the earlier discussion where the contrast between a professional school and a social science school was used to express the question of where a business school looks for legitimacy. The questions that arise here are about whether a school adopts a strategy which fits one of the quadrants, or develops a distinctive profile which blends a mix of the quadrants. Ivory et al., echoing the approach to tensions advocated in this book, suggest that schools should consider an 'and' rather an 'or' approach, but to do so they stress that business schools need to think through how they intentionally organise to do that and be clear about the strategy behind the particular mix and balance being advocated.

The two frameworks discussed so far provided continuums across the tension of internal and external focus. More recently, Kitchener et al. (2022) proposed a matrix with an underlying assumption that all business schools engage in some way. The earlier frameworks also effectively assumed this by indicating that business schools would include a mix of activities, some of which would be outward facing and engaged. Interestingly, the premise of Kitchener et al.'s paper is to deepen and broaden engagement, which resonates with the argument made earlier in this book in relations to stakeholders. They suggest that the dominant business school strategy is an instrumental one focussed on outcomes, resulting in restrictive engagement that privileges a few stakeholders, again connecting with the discussion earlier in the book. This framework is relevant to the discussion not just because it focuses on engagement, but because it also posits a broader view of engagement. They propose a purposeful strategy as an alternative to an instrumental strategy, by which they mean a wider public good view of engagement. The two views of strategy (instrumental to purposeful) form one continuum, with the other continuum describing how engagement is managed, from an emergent through to a coordinated position. Here too there are similarities with the discussion in Chapter 2, the emergent end of the spectrum is characterised as being initiated by enthusiastic and purpose driven individuals, which was a factor identified earlier in both the literature and the engagement stories. At the other end of the engagement spectrum the coordinated pole represent business schools that are intentionally setting up to engage. The model argues that a purposeful strategy and a coordinated engagement results in the purpose-led business school.

The framework perspectives have been built around issues such as the place of a business school in the university and providing a challenge to the suggested dominant strategy of instrumentalism. They have contrasted a teaching versus research focus and the tension between a narrow emphasis on business and academia versus a broader societal engagement. They suggest alternatives that business schools can consider within the current tensions and contentions. A different lens is offered by thinking about the future of business schools by returning to their roots and learning from the past. One call to reflect on returning to roots draws upon a similar view to Ivory et al. where professional schools and more traditional academic schools are compared. Pfeffer and Fong (2002) propose that Business Schools might usefully rediscover their roots as university-based professional schools and become more like other professional schools. However, Pfeffer and Fong (2002) attempt to hold two views together; being relevant to the management profession they serve whilst behaving less like the businesses they teach and more like university academic departments. Returning to roots will now be considered from a broader historical perspective. In the UK, there is a diverse and rich history to how business education and thus business schools have emerged. In an informative and timely article, Spicer, Jaser, and Wiert (2021) draw upon some early forms or traditions which they term 'Schools' to illustrate the potential to learn from the past. The Mechanics Institutes in the 1800s are thought of as the Workers' School with a local focus on broadening access to education and skills for work. They are a reminder of a social mobility tradition that is just as relevant today. Then the Civic Schools formed with close links to local business and communities embody a tradition which resonates with the renewed debate about civic engagement today. They connect with a sense of public value and suggest that business schools could have an important convening role of bringing together differing groups representing diverse stakeholders.

Movement Schools, represented by Quaker-run companies such as Rowntree and Cadbury's brought together management thinking and a sense of the wider responsibilities and the contribution of management to areas such as well-being. In this tradition there are echoes of responsible management and of current calls to embrace grand challenges. More recently Collegiate Schools developed from a desire to educate and develop senior managers, of which Henley and Ashridge are examples, have emerged. They employed social learning, often in safe spaces coupled with reflective practice. The Collegiate School encouraged a more interdisciplinary view of general management. Many of these practices are still influential in management development. The reflective practice emphasis and the value of stepping away from the workplace to spaces where there is time to reflect on practice are worth rethinking in the context of different futures for business schools (Spicer, Jaser, & Wiert, 2021).

Connecting with rich traditions from the past can be a powerful way to create new narratives. What is striking from the formation of each of these schools is the motivation and sense of purpose expressed in the endeavours. Central to their purpose is a close connection to the context they are in and a desire to change and improve lives, business and society through education. What is clear is that they all demonstrate purposeful engagement in their different ways. They provide an opportunity to reflect on engagement that increases social mobility and enhances workplace skills, an engagement that connects and leads in the communities that are served with a strong sense of civic duty. Importantly, they also point to a broader responsibility to tackle grand challenges in society and not just a focus on business. More specifically for the field of management, there is scope to emphasise the responsibilities of management and business beyond a narrow focus on profitability. This view mirrors what Mayer refers to as the purpose of business which is 'to produce profitable solutions to the problems of people and planet' (Mayer, 2021). Reflecting on the past is also a timely reminder of the value of spaces where there is time to reflect. The workplace without doubt has merits as a place to learn, but it is also a very busy and messy place. As Charles Handy argued 'learning is experience understood in tranquility' (1998, p. 225). Business schools can create that kind of space.

It is possible, and perhaps understandable, to look at the options and possibilities presented by the frameworks and by learning from the past and to only see complexity. But, it is also possible to view them and to see choices that are based on a richness that difference and diversity within a business school can bring. Differentiation through developing a diverse profile is not necessarily an easy task and without doubt appropriate structures are needed. Whilst engagement doesn't presume only one type or structure, as evidenced by the frameworks, structure does matter. The way business schools are structured and organised of course can either help or hinder, so finding the right structure is important. However, two other factors are critical, one that is associated with pressure to conform with a dominant paradigm and the other is the inability to change due to a dominant academic culture.

What is perhaps striking, given the range of possibilities that have just been discussed is that there is an argument that they do not seem to have resulted in increased diversity in the way business schools organise themselves. Instead, there is an 'apparent convergence and isomorphism' (Irwin, 2019, p. 67). According to Kitchener et al. an explanation for this is that an instrumental strategy dominates business schools. This results in a tendency to conform towards narrow discipline based teaching which is more shareholder than stakeholder in focus. There is an environment where student number and revenues dominate. Research is too market driven not cross-discipline, or produced for the benefit of individual career enhancement rather than advancing knowledge and public value. This pattern is fostered by systems that prioritise accreditation and ranking as measures of success, leading to more conformity rather than diversity (Kitchener & Delbridge, 2020; Kitchener, Levitt, & Thomas, 2022; Thomas, Chian, & Cornuel, 2012; Thomas, Lorange, & Sheth, 2013).

A second challenge to overcome is that of a dominant academic culture which privileges working in 'silos' as opposed to working in collaboration (Thomas, Lorange, & Sheth, 2013). There is a necessity for internal engagement of faculty colleagues across the spectrum of business disciplines and research approaches. Whether academics identify with a rigour and dispassionate viewpoint of research or a relevance of applied research there is a need to rise 'above the politics of identity and recognise the benefits of collaboration' (Gulati, 2007, p. 781). Blending diverse perspectives within a school requires mutual respect from colleagues for the differing value they bring. Collaboration challenges those who see engagement as separation, distinct and distanced, where value is generated by being separated from practice, to work together with those who advocate proximity and co-production of knowledge by being close to those engaged in practice. Together they may be able to realise Heifetz and Linsky's (2002) memorable rejoinder to be both on the balcony and the dance floor. Underpinning this principle of colleagues valuing each other is an obvious need for incentives and recognition systems to do the same, demonstrating equal value for the differing strengths from colleagues. That means traditional recognition associated with publications in star rated journals needs to be balanced with valuing of engaged and impact evidence. Not forgetting that alongside a willingness to collaborate and the incentives to do so, there is the obvious need for resources to be invested, which brings the discussion back to having clarity in what is being done when resource constraints are apparent with so many competing demands on staff time.

Commentators when considering the future of business schools, stress the risk that a likely outcome will be that they muddle through to a decline (Thomas, Chian, & Wilson, 2014). Such an unsatisfactory outcome emphasises the need for clarity. One lens that can be used to provide clarity is that of the engaged business school. The engagement framework discussed earlier in this chapter can help to frame an engaged mission that then aligns and better meets the expectations of stakeholders. In addition, the various frameworks and profiles, and the lessons from the past suggest there is no lack of possibilities for differentiation. Yet, this is not an easy task, with prominent barriers in play creating pressure to conform with instrumental demands to 'deliver the goods' and a dominant academic culture that suggest a resistance to change. However, there is also another scenario which assumes that business schools do find some clarity about how to take more of a lead in determining their own future. In this view of the future, creating more value for stakeholders is an important factor (Thomas, Chian, & Wilson, 2014). Therefore, the discussion now turns to how different groups with a vested interest can make the most of their relationship with an engaged business school.

## Making the Most of Engagement

The central theme of this book is to investigate the relationship between business schools and businesses. That is where this section will begin, with the benefits to and for business. But business is not the only group that has much to gain from an engaged relationship with a business school. Those who are already in the workplace such as managers, leaders and working professionals[1] also have a stake. Then the current students of a business school and the academic staff are clearly important stakeholders. Finally, the university within which the business school is situated has a vested interest in an engaged business school. This section will consider what the potential benefits are for each of the these stakeholders.

---

[1]In this section, I will use the term manager to be interchangeable with leader and working professional.

## The Benefits to Business

Many businesses do not see the benefit of engaging with business schools. Sometimes this is because their previous experience of working with Universities and business schools has been frustrating. They may be unaware of the support available, or feel that they cannot access the right people or services, or indeed they remain unconvinced of the merits of doing so. However, by way of contrast there are also many in business who do see the potential and who also have previous positive connections with academia. With such businesses there is a suggestion of latent goodwill towards working with Universities and business schools. It is therefore vital to harness latent support and equally to convince doubters by understanding why some engagements work better than others.

A business takes a risk when it places the responsibility for the development of it staff, especially senior staff, into the hands of a provider and therefore needs to be confident it is making the right decision. The same is true if a business invites a provider to develop other interventions within its business. The argument of the engaged business school has been that businesses value engagement that is distinctive, relational and sustainable. Therefore it is these three themes that should be the primary areas that a business looks for in a business school. In Chapter 1, we suggested that there were three questions a business should ask about a business school. They are relevant questions to return to here when discussing the benefit for business of working with an engaged business school.

The first question is about why a business would choose to work with a business school, and relates to being distinctive. It is about a dual priority: focusing on meeting business needs, and providing thought leadership and latest thinking. The second question seeks to understand how the business school will work with the business and concerns the relational theme. This emphasises that businesses value the quality and depth of the relationship with a business. Then, the third question explores how the business school continues to add value. Engagement needs to be sustained if it is to be purposeful. A mutually beneficial relationship should lead to an ongoing connectedness.

In addition to the three themes above, there are some specific areas where a business can benefit from its relationships with a business school. We will explore four areas and their potential benefits. The first area to be discussed is about making more of some of the existent, latent or hidden connections. Secondly, there are opportunities to gain from the wider networking connections a business school offers. Thirdly, to consider accessing some of the other services a business school can provide. Finally, and importantly, ideas about how a business can get involved in developing the next generation of young people entering business.

Businesses often already have connections or contacts with business schools. There are plenty of examples where businesses have existing relationships, often at an individual level, which are built on mutual trust (Abreu, Grinevich, & Hughes, 2008), but which tend to be isolated and disconnected. Similarly, they may have staff who have attended courses at the business school. Indeed some may have studied applied masters programmes where they have applied their learning in the organisation. If a business is looking to build a more purposeful relationship with a business school, then these constitutes a good starting point, but too often their potential has not been realised.

Secondly, there is a broader role that business schools play which captures the idea of the 'agora' as a place where ideas are discussed using the convening power of a business school. This creates the potential for businesses to be involved in broader conversations related to themes of significance with other stakeholders, allowing ideas to be shared and new opportunities considered. This networking forum creates space for updates, and roundtable sessions which bring together sector and cross-sector representation to explore key areas. It is a place where academics share latest research related to relevant areas to start a debate about the ideas and their relevance to practice.

Thirdly, there are also opportunities for a business to benefit from consultancy and research. Businesses who are engaged with a business school can be a part of shaping the research landscape. They can inform conversations about what should be researched and contribute to knowledge co-creation, with obvious benefits to the business. Knowledge is of course also produced in businesses, and such a focus can help a business to further develop ideas through working with academics.

Finally, businesses have a crucial role to play in the development of the next generation of business leaders. Businesses can inform and help shape the development of young people for work. In collaboration with business schools, there is much that can be done. Businesses can contribute to the curriculum, and act as a sounding board for the academic team. They can provide guest speakers and facilitate question and answer sessions or pose business problems for student teams to solve. Closer links with business could also involve the mentoring of students, placements and setting live projects for students to work on.

There is a further equally important area, which relates to how businesses ensure they are attractive places for the next generation to join. What does a business need to think about and change to be attractive for next generation managers and business leaders? This is a question that together with a business school could be explored. There is a further crucial area where businesses can engaged. They can be part of a conversation with business schools about the future knowledge and skills needs. The skills of the future are no easy area to anticipate, but are vital. They integrate with technology advancements and with working practices, along with changes to the services or products and markets of the business. Understanding the future skills of a business will need reflection from within the business, boundary scanning from without and more forward thinking research with a business school. Both businesses and business schools have a vested interest in this area of future skills.

### For Managers and Professionals

There are good reasons for leaders, managers and professionals to seek out an engaged business school, whether they are MBA or executive education students/ delegates or perhaps not yet connected in any way. A well-connected business school will bring together managers from a wide range of businesses enabling those managers to gain a rich connection with their peers, and allowing them to gain from the relationships a business school has across a wide range of organisations. There is often an energy associated with the networks created by managers on MBA and executive education programmes as they come together from differing businesses, share together and explore how they are tackling issues and applying ideas to practice. An engaged business school should be creating the conditions to nurture and foster such relationships. For this to happen there needs to be an engaged approach which recognises the voice of business and the experience of managers. And for managers the relationships they develop with fellow participants from different organisations can be transforming not just for the programme duration but beyond.

Another kind of relationship also matters. Managers are also able to learn with academic staff who see engaged scholarship as integral to their practice. Such relationships offer the rich potential for manager and tutor to engage in applied research, relating concepts to practice, developing different thinking to make good practice more consistent. The relationships here too can often form for the long term. Managers and professionals then begin to develop as scholar practitioners valuing research and its application to practice and able to bring an academic perspective to practice. They gain skills in conducting research and investigations in their organisations, skills that continue to be useful for them and their organisation. They occupy a potentially influential position to enable business and business school engagement to be more effective. In effect they are often acting as internal consultants.

There is also a growing evidence base of the benefits managers and leaders gain from their connection with a business school and particularly from having taken a management development course. Firstly, not only do managers gain themselves from their own development, but as a consequence there is evidence that they then impact their organisation. For example policies to improve skills generally are found to be more effective when management practice is improved at the same time (Valero & Feng, 2019), they are complementary. In addition, qualified managers are more likely to implement strategies to introduce new or improved products and to improve efficiency (Bosworth, Davies, & Wilson, 2002). This matters more given that UK businesses are slow to adopt modern management practices and that this failing is attributed to being a significant weakness to UK business productivity (Homkes, 2014). Indeed, there is evidence that in many cases businesses are not managed well, yet when they are, good management practice correlates with better performance. It would seem that good managers do make a difference, and perhaps just as interesting (and not surprisingly) it isn't easy to do. Good management resembles what resource based management thinking refers to as a sustainable advantage, when something is hard to do, not easy to imitate but at the same time can deliver significant benefits to productivity, growth and profitability (Sadun, Bloom, & Van Reenan, 2017).

Researchers also found, what they considered to be robust evidence, that when the level of education of both managers and workforce are high better management practices are evident (Feng & Valero, 2019). In addition, and perhaps not unexpectedly, they found that what matters with new skills is how they are utilised and that depends on improving leadership and management, improving working practices in the organisation to do this (Payne & Keep, 2011; Warhurst & Findlay, 2012). All very much the responsibility of good managers.

In summary, skills and management skills matter but in an interesting twist Feng and Valero also found that businesses located closer to universities have a higher skilled workforce and better management practices (Feng & Valero, 2020). Proximity to a university brings benefits to a business and their managers. Secondly, and provocatively there is the suggestion that outstanding leadership and great strategy count for little without operational excellence (Sadun, Bloom, & Van Reenan, 2017), and that needs good management. There are of course caveats to the findings and it should be noted that much of this work identifies correlations and not causality. For example, although the authors consider that proximity to a university correlates with better management performance, they can't discount that businesses with better management performance choose to locate near to a university. Caveats do signal some caution, but perhaps the greater risk comes from a very big question that remains unanswered.

Why is something that seems so obviously beneficial apparently not more recognised by organisations? Partly, it could be that it isn't easy to do. If improved management practice does have a significant impact on business performance, one might expect all businesses to make it a priority, but evidence suggests they don't (Bloom, Sadun, & Van Reenan, 2012; Sadun, Bloom, & Van Reenan, 2017). So why don't more businesses capitalise on ideas that are essentially free and widely accessible. According to Bloom, Dorgan, Dowdy, and Van Reenan (2007) whilst the lack of take-up might be because implementation is too difficult or perhaps not prioritised, it may also be for another reason. In their interviews, Bloom et al. (2007) were surprised to discover that managers were unaware of the overall performance of the organisation (Bloom, Dorgan, Dowdy, & Van Reenan, 2007, p. 3). They conclude with a striking statement that in their view 'many organisations are probably missing out on an opportunity for significant improvement because they simply do not recognise that their own management practices are poor' (Bloom, Dorgan, Dowdy, & Van Reenan, 2007, p. 8). Managers stand to benefit both with their own performance and it would seem with encouraging and enabling those around them to put their talents to use.

Crucially, a manager's connection with the business school should not just be for the duration of a programme, but for the longer term. Ideally managers and professionals should seek business schools where such relationships are encouraged. Managers should gain from a lifelong relationship via alumni and relationship networks with peers and business school staff. The focus of the relationship is therefore a long term collaboration which is mutually beneficial, and not limited to a discrete programme. The engagement of a manager naturally develops into an alumni relationship. In this context there is a means for managers and professionals to keep up to date, which is an aspect of development that is recognised to be of increasing importance. Some knowledge may stand the test of time, other knowledge may need to be renewed, or indeed unlearned and new knowledge and skills developed. Then there is the contribution that alumni can make to the business school in their support of undergraduate students, and next generation managers and leaders. Such activity is a benefit for both managers and for students.

## Students: Engaging the Next Generation of Leaders and Managers

Arguably the most important responsibility of a business school is the education and preparation of the next generation of leaders and managers. At the beginning of the book the question was asked as to whether the relationships a business school develops with business can have an impact on undergraduate students. An education with a business school should be rich in experiences, consequently it is worthwhile for students to seek engaged business schools, where their education and experience is integrated with supporting and engaging with the business community. In such business schools students will find academic staff who are pursuing research which impacts on the communities they serve, and that points to a future which such students will be shaping. The business school would be a place where learning and practice come together, and young people make early contributions to organisations while studying.

An example of this is the growing interest in business clinics where local businesses, especially small businesses, not-for-profits and social enterprises engage with students on consultancy projects which tackle real issues or opportunities in their organisation (Kitchener, Levitt, & Thomas, 2022). Academic staff provide support to the students and to the process to ensure that the project delivers both for the student and the organisation. The context provides engagement with businesses, who are usually already connected to the business school, with students learning through working with the business on a specific project. Many of the businesses have broader purposes associated with social enterprises which gives students direct experience of social purposes providing a value led service (Chartered Association of Business Schools, 2021). Business clinics are characterised by learning and knowledge being sought based upon the need of the project. They are a facilitated process with students leading their own development. This kind of learning calls upon different spaces in business schools which look less and less like a classroom and more and more like collaborative working spaces. A second example is the Finnish team academy model. Developed in the 1990s, it now has a number of UK versions and variants in place. Its premise is that participants form a team and then set up a business through the course of the programme. The approach focuses on team learning in collaborative spaces with academics taking the role of coaches, adopting action learning principles applied in real business settings (Tosey, Dhaliwal, & Hassinen, 2013).

There is scope to develop more initiatives which challenge traditional approaches to teaching and the typical teaching spaces within which they take place. There are a number of possibilities which can be drawn from the business clinic and team academy examples. Firstly, there is the opportunity to explore how more emphasis on students learning through experience can be achieved across undergraduate programmes. Are there opportunities for more projects that connect to business and organisations, and for connections with business networks and wider communities to be incorporated in undergraduate provision? In many ways the practices described in business clinic and the team academy models are not new, they build on similar approaches which are common in executive education where projects and experiential learning are important mainstays of the provision. This raises a further opportunity to considered practices used in executive education which might be helpful in undergraduate teaching.

Second, the engagement with social enterprises and not-for-profit organisations also provides further opportunities. For example, the British Academy encourages a cross-discipline approach to teaching using a focus on 'solving problems for people and planet' (British Academy, 2022). They argue that this brings together a movement of businesses towards more of a focus on purpose which connects with a similar trend with students. Third, there is also the potential to look at ways to develop team learning in other programmes and adopt collaborative approaches that are cross-discipline, where knowledge is drawn down based on relevance and the needs of a project. Fourthly, the teaching in these examples incorporates coaching and acting as a guide alongside allowing students to lead their own development. Here too, the practice indicates a very different role for the academic, and raises the question about whether it has potential to be more widely applied. Fifth, there is an opportunity to consider the changing needs of learning spaces to facilitate this kind of group and collaborative learning. There may be options to co-locate similar activities providing a context where cross-fertilisation of ideas and shared experience can happen, and where students experience being closer to organisations as they too use the space.

Apprenticeships and placements have a long tradition of engagement, with degree apprenticeships providing a renewed interest in this area. In principle they represent a possible way to see business and business schools sharing responsibility for the education and development of students in ways that are more integrative. The extent to which this is happening is uncertain. There is opportunity to rethink how business and business schools work together so that the shared responsibility is evident. Shared responsibility recognises that employers have an important role in developing students whilst studying a degree and similarly that studying a degree whilst working might be a powerful way for businesses to benefit from being involved with a business school. One challenge is to make the workplace a dynamic place for learning and the business school an environment where exploring ideas, reflecting on practice happen with space to do so collaboratively. An important part of the relationship and engagement with organisations should be with the leaders and managers in the organisation who play such a significant and critical role in releasing the talent in others. Whilst the apprenticeship initiative has the potential to act as a springboard for skills development across a wider range of skills, it is managers and leaders who need to identify talent, develop and encourage the development of talent, and it is their skills that can help organisations make the most of the emerging talent. As already discussed, there is consistent research evidence to point out that skills development alone will not raise productivity and growth in employment. In fact, it is skills utilisation (how skills are brought together in an organisation) that matters, and not skills per se, that is the significant indicator of whether productivity will be improved, and that depends to a greater extent on the quality of management. Utilising the skills of a workforce, especially a highly skilled workforce, 'requires skilful management' (Bloom et al., 2004, p. 22).

Building rich experiences for students with business are not easy options to pursue and in some ways the examples discussed offer ways to experiment with ideas that could be adopted more widely across programmes. To do so will be challenging when business education copes with large student numbers in a mass education system.

It is a system where size can create difficulties with maintaining learning that is personal and engaging. As intimated earlier in the book, the relationship with business where the education of business students is seen as a shared responsibility could point towards a way where complementary resource from business could share the load.

A number of different forms of learning could create a distinctive employment-focussed business school, where traditional boundaries between learning and working are broken down. Charles Handy makes the argument that learning often happens by reflecting on practice, yet so much of what is called education focuses on teaching that is separated from practice which then only happens much later on. How to manage is taught before the experience of managing (Handy, 1998). An engaged business school could create the possibility for places of learning to be more like work places, and encourage the workplace to become more like a place of learning. Students should look for business schools that explore interesting ways in which they can gain experience and knowledge together. Too often the teaching spaces available limit the possibilities, but a challenge for all is to think through what learning and working places might look like in the future.

An engaged business school often has connections with networks and clusters where students can participate and be involved in network events. There are of course examples in some of the professional schools in a university where very close relationships with the sector indicates a dual responsibility for the development of students. Health and education are two prime examples. Are there ways that the business community can take a more proactive responsibility in the development of the next generation? As discussed earlier placements have long been an important feature of business qualifications, and now degree apprenticeships provide another means in which business and education can combine. Business schools often have the connections and the influence to bring business together to benefit students, and much of this does happen often at the level of individual staff using their contacts. The challenge is to build on this and explore how a more widespread and consistent impact can be achieved.

Undergraduates never come into contact with much of the broader activity in a business school, and that is not just a pity it is a lost opportunity. Business schools should find ways to introduce their undergraduate students to how they can make the most of their services. That benefits the students immediately with a richer education, but it does more. Today's students are the next generation of managers and people in business. It makes sense for students too to be aware of the various contributions that a business school makes. The business school should be the natural place to which their undergraduates return, because they know the benefit it can bring.

Business schools are not necessarily good at connecting what they do with business with what they do with undergraduates. The engagement framework could be instrumental in mapping out where those connections could make sense. The map potentially indicates different relationships that a business school has and the areas where such relationships could benefit students. There is a promising opportunity for business schools to not only seek to improve how they engage with businesses, but to then look for where that involvement can be connected with their students.

### *Engaged Academics*

For academics the engaged business school offers the opportunity to pursue engaged scholarship. The possible roles for academics in an engaged business school were explored earlier. In this section those roles related to research, teaching and consulting will be highlighted to indicate the opportunities for academics.

Firstly, engaged scholarship provokes a challenge to re-think the tendency to separate relevant applied research from more dispassionate and fundamental research. Engagement with business calls for academics to collaborate across their strengths and value their different perspectives in order to gain from both distance and proximity with businesses. Impact has become an increasingly important marker for academic endeavour. This requirement can leave some academics struggling to seek out a context and find ways to demonstrate impact because connections to practice are not obvious or have not been intentionally sought. An engaged business school offers the potential to create a context where impact is a natural and an integral part of engaged scholarship. Central to this debate is the sense of vocation and the motivation to engage with businesses and seek a wider impact in society. Engagement can provide a rich context to pursue research that relates directly to businesses, working alongside practitioners co-producing knowledge. At the same time engagement with society and grand challenges of the day broadens the perspective to be engaged with the issues of the day that affect society.

Alongside familiar research processes, will be an emphasis on exploring ideas in a collaborative manner with thought leadership used as a way to share ideas more quickly with business than the traditional research publication cycle, and to do so with a spirit of listening and further developing the ideas. It involves adopting approaches which explore practices that look like they hold promise, testing ideas, adapting them and assessing their impact (Delridge, Gratton, & Johnson, 2006; Lorange, 2005). Academics should look for business schools which value engagement on an equal footing with traditional research routes.

That will mean that there are clear progression routes which encourage an engaged scholarship track. It also means that impact and engagement has parity with being published in a three or four star rated journal. Many universities do have differing pathways for progression which begin to encapsulate the aspirations of engaged scholarship. However, these routes are still emerging and often in need of more clarity both in what is stated and in how it is then interpreted, in order to recognise, differentiate and celebrate scholarship through engagement. This is an area that business schools can help their university to develop and is also an area where cross sector discussion can inform consistency.

Secondly, there is the potential to re-invigorate the nature of scholarly teaching and engaged learning. Together engaged research and teaching opens different prospects for career development and academic fulfilment. In the context of teaching, the classroom becomes a place of mutual learning, where ideas are critiqued, extended and re-imagined by educator and by student. Thinking differently about the context of teaching resonates with the earlier discussion of Weick's extension of Boyer's engaged scholarship. The classroom forms a bridge to working with the organisations and businesses represented by the participants. The nature of working with experienced professionals demands bringing together research that can inform and challenge practice. This places a requirement for academics to be up to date not just with research but also with issues in the business context they are working with. It involves making sense of research, contributing to new research and sharing emerging ideas. The classroom becomes a legitimate context for dissemination, a two way process with the opportunity for co-creation of knowledge. This description of engaged teaching conjures up the image of teaching as curating. It has always been the responsibility of a scholar to critique, evaluate and synthesise research in order to make sense of a field of study. These skills resonate with the image of an academic as curator. The Latin roots of the word curate is to care. There is the sense that care is taken in bringing together the research and ideas. In the engaged business school that care involves listening to the needs of business to curate ideas that will inform, challenge and spark different thinking. Similarly, curation involves exploring and searching for ideas to then critically evaluate, filter and categorise in order to build a mean-ingful narrative that connects the ideas (AACSB, 2022; Deschaine & Sharma, 2015; Lund, 2020). With the emerging use of flipped learning, curation is becoming an ever more important and distinct part of academic scholarship. Academics in this context occupy a position of trust with the responsibility of bringing what is appropriate and salient to the participants (AACSB, 2022).

An engaged business school should also open up the potential for consultancy-led activities. If relationships with business and with the wider regional community are strong, then there will be opportunities to help business and provide wider support in the region through consultative interventions. Impact of scholarship can happen in diverse settings that may not always be recognised, a prime example is where the classroom with experienced managers and leaders becomes a place where different thinking is encouraged and student participants are encouraged to apply, adapt and experiment.

Consultative approaches can actually be far more widespread than is often recognised. They are evident when beginning an engagement with a client where, as has been argued, the client expects a tailored approach involving listening to their needs, but which often requires the needs to be identified. Other areas discussed earlier also presume that consulting skills are adopted. The business clinic and the team academy initiatives imply that academics both adopt and model consultancy behaviours and that they then develop those skills and behaviours in their students. Interestingly, that is also often the case in masters programmes where experienced professionals are conducting research/consultancy projects in their organisations. This area of work has considerable potential for mutual benefit with experienced participants on executive education and masters programmes acting as internal consultants and in partnership with an academic creating opportunities for consultancy and applied research. Then there are management knowledge transfer partnerships, where similar skills and behaviours are also implicit in the relationships and processes. The breadth of possibilities is illustrated with the evidence discussed earlier in Chapter 3 that businesses engage with business schools across a wider range of business operational areas offering scope for consultancy (Hughes, Kitson, Salter, Angenendt, & Hughes, 2022). It is also evident from the earlier discussion of skills utilisation where developing skills through CPD and programmes of learning, which is a common request from businesses, would benefit from a consultative relationship. For new skills to improve performance there is a need for consultative support to ensure an organisation has in place the wider practices to utilise those new skills effectively.

Together the above examples indicate that consulting behaviours and skills are widespread, but their value and importance may not be explicitly recognised. There is an argument for recognising them more explicitly with staff, and as importantly recognising the value of developing consultative skills for students.

### Engagement With the University

Business schools occupy an important position within universities as a major revenue stream, often cross-subsidising other activities and departments. They have the most students in the UK HE system with close to one in six of all undergraduate students on a business and management course (British Academy, 2021; Thomas, Lee, Thomas, & Wilson, 2014). Yet they also occupy a difficult position, with uncertainty about their relationship to the wider university. Research funding is lower than other social science subjects, prompted by the challenge of recruiting high student numbers and the resulting teaching demands which put pressure on research activities (British Academy, 2021). Its position in a university can also be isolated, separated from other departments (British Academy, 2021) with a tension about whether they are considered as a professional school, or a social science school.

Whilst there are differences that may separate a business school from other parts of a university, there are also many similarities. For example, they have many things in common with professional schools, and much to learn from social science roots. The potential to gain by improving collaboration is summed up by a call to lower the walls between other departments and faculties, encouraging interdisciplinary cooperation (Currie, Davies, & Ferlie, 2016). In effect, it is a call for business schools to engage with the university, just as it seeks to engage externally with business. A low walled business school assumes that engagement happens internally across faculties and disciplines. For that to happen encouragement from the institution is needed. Initiatives that focus on themes such as social value and grand challenges are good ways to do that, giving purpose and validity to collaborations, since by their nature the themes are cross-disciplinary. But it will also need individual relationships to be valued and supported as colleagues collaborate. The British Academy's call for business teaching to be more cross-disciplined within a business school by placing more focus on problem solving 'for people and planet' (British Academy, 2022, p. 11) can equally be applied across faculties.

Time constraints and an already over stretched agenda within business schools can so easily get in the way of good intentions to collaborate. Therefore building upon common areas that have the potential to overlap and similarly connecting the things that are already happening make sense. The engagement framework applied to other faculties can indicate possible areas of overlap and show where collaboration is already happening even though it may be on a small scale. It is too easy to label collaboration as too difficult and whilst complexity may be a risk, a more involved call to collaborate can also be seen as opening up a richness of shared learning. Engaged scholarship is not the preserve of business, and neither are the engaged pathways for progression within a university. Connecting the wider community of like-minded engaged scholars across the university can build trust and explore ways in which collaborative engagement makes sense.

Of course, the position of a business school in a university will always depend on the culture, intentions and strategy of the institute. And it may actually be strategy and intention which offers the best opportunity for a business school to find its place. Many universities are engaging, or reengaging with civic and public value strategic initiatives. These areas are where the business school can contribute. This is especially the case for an engaged business school with its established relationships, its wider connections and crucially its approach to building relationships. Civic and public engagement agendas are where business schools can and should play a full role offering leadership, support and collaboration in many aspects, particularly where there is common cause. Then there is the potential for lifelong learning that many universities are exploring. Business schools with their strong tradition of executive education, CPD and their relationships with businesses can also inform and help to shape the response of their parent universities as they explore how life-long learning might be incorporated into its portfolio.

An area where there is immediate potential is for business schools to act as a gateway to other services and parts of the university. That is because businesses don't just want to access services that a business school can provide, they may well value being able to access other parts of the university. The effectiveness of a business schools ability to act as a gateway depends on the engagement and relationships between faculties, and thus engagement becomes important within and across a university for it to work more widely externally. It is also the case that parts of a university may well be working with the same organisations or groups of organisations without knowing it. The engagement framework is one mechanism that can be used to map activities across faculties and identify areas of mutual benefit.

Earlier in Chapter 4, the position of a business school in a university was characterised as an uncomfortable one, expressed in two tensions. The first about its relationship with business and the extent to which it is relevant, and the second in relation to other faculties and the extent to which it is considered a proper university 'school'. Making sense of tensions has been an important part of the development of the engaged business school, particularly the challenge to hold tensions, as suggested by Anderson as a way to value the differences of what appear to be opposing or conflicting positions which often have merit in their own right. It is a more nuanced position, but offers the potential to view things more creatively and apply paradoxical thinking which seeks to hold both perspectives at the same time and resist a tendency towards binary views. It is at this intersection of managing dilemma and paradox where business schools may be able to be at their most effective.

Therefore, as discussed in Chapter 4, a level of discomfort might actually be an indicator that a business school is in its rightful place. A position that holds the tension between proximity to and separation from business, being close but not too close, and separated yet not distant, able to challenge and encourage, and both to critique and relate. In a similar way its position within a university straddles that of offering a professional education with a more liberal intellectual education, which contrasts a vocational emphasis with a critical theory stance. In turn these contrasting positions result in questions about the extent to which a business school should be considered as a professional school or a social science school. Holding the tensions, refuses to reduce the debate to binary perspectives. Perhaps a business school that is able to hold the tensions offers a distinctive position which is valuable to a university. It might provide strengths which enable other faculties of the university to better connect and engage with their constituent stakeholders and encourage and support a more engaged focus for the parent university.

### When Work Places Are Learning Places

We will conclude our discussion of the benefits of an engaged business school with a provocative question. Earlier, the idea of work places becoming more like learning places and spaces was introduced, but what if businesses were to be more like universities? That is a question that Charles Handy (1995) posed to a conference, with one reply from the conference floor of 'God help us'! The point he was making was that for a knowledge economy the importance of learning and putting that learning to use are crucial and one of the places to look for ideas about how to do that is where knowledge has always been key. For example, there is an argument for those who lead in areas of importance for the organisation should also be teachers, with their knowledge valued and shared. In a related point Peter Drucker suggests that knowledge workers learn most when they teach. He argues that in a knowledge economy enterprises not only need to become learning organisations, they must become a teaching institution (Drucker, 1999).

So how would a business which behaved more like a university act? Perhaps it would have knowledge faculty's with thought leaders leading groups of knowledge that have been identified as giving a competitive advantage. A proportion of everybody's time would be allocated to knowledge activities, with staff learning to be better at what they are already good at, and finding out what new knowledge needs to be learnt. This would reflect the academics time for scholarly activity, to learn, research and keep up to date. Teaching would be a more significant part of the activities of the organisation, since sharing knowledge will be valued. The connections with universities and business schools would also become critical and strategic. The intent would be to bring together the internal strengths of an organisation with the complementary expertise of a business school. The capability of the organisation to partner in shared delivery, consultancy and research would be increased. There might be joint roles between the business school and a business, with thought leaders in the organisation studying for professional doctorates to become leaders in their field. Many of the areas discussed earlier in the chapter could support this focus on learning, and not least the idea of blurring the work place with a learning place.

# Chapter 8

# An Engaged Response to Recovery and Growth

Previously we have made the argument that the idea of an engaged business school is timely for a number of reasons, none of which are more pressing than recovery from a global crisis. The need to engage is more compelling when combined with an urgency that recovery from a crisis brings. Crises have always been double edged in the sense that there are dangers to avoid as well as opportunities to embrace. They can often magnify issues and problems, whilst the necessity to act quickly can, in contrast, be the crucible of change and improvement. During crises, change can and does happen much more quickly, whether it be for the better or for the worse. It is a context where business schools could and should be well placed to respond to this dual challenge, of addressing the problems and realizing some of the possibilities. A willingness to contribute is not in question, neither is there doubt about the expertise upon which business schools can draw, but there are questions about how business schools bring these elements together. This then raises questions about the part that business schools can play in supporting recovery. This chapter will consider some ideas about how this could be done and where contributions could be made, drawing upon elements of the engaged business school to inform the discussion. What is certain is that there is no shortage of areas where business schools could engage.

Firstly, the idea of distinctive engagement can inform how a business school might respond. This approach advocates both listening and leading and is a helpful way to initiate and frame the contribution that can be made. The dual priorities of listening to the needs of organisations, their experience and the lessons they have learned, alongside leading through new ideas can come together in working out ways to address some of the issues emerging from the pandemic. Adopting the two perspectives prompts business schools to consider options across a breadth of possibilities, from those ideas that may emerge from practice, to ideas that can be drawn from new thinking and research taking place in other areas.

Stakeholder relationships provide a second way a business school might connect with need. Existing relationships and connections can often provide an immediate context where a business school could contribute as part of recovery and growth. Existing stakeholder connections can be built upon using the convening power of a business school to draw together other businesses around

**The Engaged Business School, 143–148**
Copyright © 2023 Anthony Sturgess
**Published under exclusive licence by Emerald Publishing Limited**
**doi:10.1108/978-1-80382-941-820231016**

common themes that are emerging from the pandemic and to gain a collective sense of the possibilities. This is especially valuable in a local and regional context. Business schools can have an important influence in their regions and engage in scoping some of the grand challenges and their relative tensions as they impact a particular region. Being able to influence in such ways without doubt is made easier if a business school has already built trust through its stakeholder relationships and with the wider communities it serves. But offering help in this way also becomes an opportunity for business schools to quickly establish relationships and as a result provides a means to accelerate development of an engaged business school.

The processes of listening, convening and sense making imply a dialogue between practitioners and academics, and point to a third way forward: through engaged scholarship. There is a crucial role that engaged scholars can play, drawing on the experience of practitioners, to determine the lessons that can be learned and the questions that remain unanswered. As discussed in Chapter 7, engaged scholarship should not only be about connecting with external partners but also about engaging across academic discipline areas. The need for collaborative working is particularly apparent with many of the themes emerging from the pandemic which cross traditional academic discipline boundaries. This issue too presents an opportunity to quickly build more collaborative approaches which otherwise may have proved more challenging given the embedded traditional approaches of academics focusing on their own discipline areas. Responding to the pandemic should also challenge another aspect of scholarship. Earlier in the book we noted the tendency for academics to focus on new research at the expense of making sense of what is already known to then inform teaching. As a consequence, the potential of identifying where existing knowledge might resonate and have impact on practice has been undervalued, but could be particularly helpful with the array of issues now presenting as businesses recover from the pandemic. An important part of the engaged scholar role should be to explore and assess the insights from existing research that can inform and help. Given the profound effect that the pandemic is having upon organisations there is significant potential for business academics to begin to help and to do so quickly by drawing upon what is already known that could impact recovery (Bailey & Breslin, 2021). Such an approach has several advantages. Firstly, as suggested, it can be a rapid response since it calls upon knowledge that is already known. Second, there is particular relevance where existing issues have been amplified or accelerated due to the pandemic, and these existing issues are often areas where research is already taking place. Third, this approach can be combined with an engaged teaching/facilitation, where the ideas are developed with practitioners to assess their potential, extend and adapt the ideas and then implement as promising practices.

So what kind of issues are emerging and what are the differing knowledge areas where business schools could provide support? As the recovery and reaction to a global pandemic are taking shape, there are strong indications of a desire for more fundamental change, to rethink what businesses are for, alongside reinterpreting our relationship to the planet, to each other, and to work. There are also significant questions about the quality of leadership in a crisis and concerns expressed where responses have been poorly managed. Moreover, notions of building back better, and in ways that are fairer and sustainable are emerging. These are wide ranging possibilities, but they are also all areas where engaged business schools can and should inform and help shape thinking to explore ways forward.

The pandemic has revealed several themes which hold the potential to be significant changes for business and society. The following section is intended to illustrate some of the significant areas, and is by no means exhaustive, but it does indicate the breadth of possibilities for business schools to consider. Firstly, we will start with how businesses themselves might be changing both in terms of their shape and purpose. Business models and operations had to adapt and shift with unprecedented speed towards online models during the pandemic. Some of those changes have remained, and now prompt questions about how to shape businesses post pandemic. Other changes may have reverted back, but nevertheless still pose questions about whether business can or should go back to how things were before the pandemic. Not least there is value in better understanding the ability and agility of businesses to pivot their business model so rapidly, as many did. For these organisations the changing business models represent important points of departure with which they are still grappling as they try to determine the right shape for their organisation going forward.

Closely associated with the changing views of business models is the broadening of a business's sense of purpose. This is an area that was already gaining traction before the pandemic and may well be accelerated post pandemic (Chartered Association of Business Schools, 2021). There appears to be a growing recognition of the profit with purpose argument put forward by the British Academy (British Academy, 2022). Nowhere is the profit/purpose narrative more apparent than in calls for a sustainable future. Concerns about the planet and the shared responsibilities with business for its preservation have been prominent. These concerns have only intensified since the pandemic with international conflict emphasising the vulnerability of energy supplies. This in turn reinforces a focus on green issues again prompted by the awareness of our interconnectedness and interdependences which were so clearly exposed during the pandemic. Concerns about the environment were of course already prominent before the pandemic, but as plans are being formed to grow economies post-pandemic the priority and focus may have shifted. The government's build back better plan (HM Treasury, 2021) and the CBI's recovery plan (CBI, 2021) both emphasise sustainable futures, which promote a green economy with net zero targets. The plans prompt thinking about the kind of businesses that can lead a green industry and the requisite skills that will be needed. More broadly the challenge is to think about what is needed for all businesses to flourish in their respective sectors with sustainability as an essential part of what they do, and not just an add-on.

Most notably, a lack of resilience in systems was exposed during the pandemic. Nowhere was this starker than in supply chains across all sectors. Business approaches to supply chains were suddenly laid bare along with some of the principles underpinning them. Similarly, food production and the sometimes complex supply chains were highlighted during the pandemic. The fragility of food systems has continued to be an issue with ongoing international conflict, as indeed has the supply of energy.

Further questions of resilience were raised in health as hospitals struggled to cope, prompting a recognition that a system that was already running 'hot' in terms of staffing levels, beds per capita and critical beds, had little capacity to cope. Of course since the pandemic was above all else a health crisis, health and well-being and tackling how to deliver this well is a theme all recognise as important. This is especially so for an older population and is a primary challenge for the future.

It is not just the old who fared badly through the pandemic, young people appear to have also been particularly affected by the pandemic. This is evident in terms of education where there are questions about how to address what was 'lost' during the pandemic. However, there are not just educational concerns, the Resolution Foundation found that young people have been disproportionately negatively affected by the pandemic both in terms of economic security and mental health (Sehmi & Slaughter, 2021). There may be implications for business schools and businesses as this generation progresses to university and into the workplace, particularly when nearly one in three 18–24-year-olds are in some form of education (Sehmi & Slaughter, 2021). This generation may also have differing views and expectations about work informed by their experiences through the pandemic.

Education is an issue not just for the young. As economies emerge from the pandemic there are new skills needed to create different possibilities and there are skill gaps due to the implications of the so called 'great resignation' (Cable & Gratton, 2022). These needs together suggest a demand for reskilling and ups-killing in order to create the new possibilities of a future economy. Such thoughts return appropriately to a consideration of what and how business schools teach both for an upcoming generation and for those already in the workplace or at the margins needing to reskill and upskill.

In the workplace change happened immediately, as working practices were rapidly adapted out of necessity towards hybrid and remote working and in many cases functioned surprisingly well, raising questions about the future workplace and workspaces. As a result, the relationship of people to work highlights important areas to explore from workforce planning, fair work, future skills gaps, hybrid working, well-being and health at work, to name a few. Subsequently, in the UK there have been interesting pilots carried out to evaluate 4-day weeks (Schor et al., 2022), perhaps signalling an appetite for exploring changes to the future of work. Good work and the future of work have gained importance with the pressures created by the great resignation. Similarly, connections between work and health, which have been known for some time, are now gaining more significance in the debate.

As well as questions about the effect of work practices on people, there are concerns about productivity and performance. These concerns were evident following the financial crisis but are now gaining even more significance in a post pandemic recession. The UK when compared to its international competitor countries has some world class businesses, but it also has a long tail of poor performers, longer than its competitors. Productivity has been a concern in the UK economy for over a decade with little evidence that it is improving (Haldane, 2018; Resolution Foundation & Centre for Economic Performance, LSE, 2022).

Then of course leadership has continued to be highlighted as vital through the pandemic with issues of integrity and honesty, alongside timely decisions and the ability to adapt and change quickly, each testing leaders across all parts of society. The difficulties faced by leaders from politics, the academy through to business, emphasise a recognition of the unpredictable and complex global environment.

These areas are by no means exhaustive, but they are extensive, ranging from health, education, sustainability and a green economy, to business recovery, resilience, supply chains, working practices and the nature of work. Then there are issues of productivity, the purpose of businesses with social responsibility and recurring questions about leadership. These are all big issues which cut across business and society, for which business can only be part of helping to solve, but nevertheless business can have an important part to play. They are also areas where business schools have expertise to contribute.

To address these wide ranging issues two approaches will be proposed to frame an engaged response to recovery. Firstly, given the scale and complexity of some of the issues introduced above, grand challenges will be considered to recognise issues of significance and importance to aid and shape recovery. Secondly, a complementary route of building upon the use of tension and paradox as a means of responding to conflicting and competing demands for businesses. Both grand challenges and tensions have intensified due to the crisis, and are indicators of areas of firstly significance with grand challenges and secondly of potential for different thinking with tensions. There has been an ongoing concern that both research and teaching has not satisfactorily addressed issues of significance. Grand challenges provide a means for this to happen and at the same time connect with some of the themes emerging from the pandemic. Tackling significant issues, which are often complex, cross discipline boundaries and are represented by conflicting demands by implication requires different thinking.

## Grand Challenges in a Crisis

Grand challenges are problems of significance to society, which if they can be resolved would have wide ranging impact and benefit. They address economic, social, environmental and sustainability complexities. They are about the health and wellbeing of people and planet, and 'behind them lie the difficulties of generating sustainable and inclusive growth' (Mazzucato & Willetts, 2019). In many ways, these challenges have now been amplified by the crisis. They provide possibilities for impact at a macro level, and they also indicate issues of global importance. Grand challenges have been gaining prominence as an area of interest and possible focus within business schools (Smith & Tracey, 2016). Prior to the pandemic crisis there have already been calls for academics to join efforts to resolve grand challenges in order to 'turn research into actionable insights to frame and tackle some of the biggest challenges that we face in our global community' (George, Howard-Grenville, Joshi, & Thianyi, 2016, p. 1880). Such calls are now timely and reinforced with some urgency. Grand challenges are an opportunity to bring together impact with work that matters 'and what can have more impact in a world turned upside down?' (Howard-Grenville, 2021).

Grand challenges of themselves highlight conflicts and competing demands, in effect they are characterised by tensions and paradoxes. This is clearly demonstrated by the United Nations acknowledgement of conflicting priorities in their ambitious plans for sustainable development. They recognise that implicit in the UN goals are 'co-benefits, trade-offs and tough choices' (United Nations, 2019). In their 2019 report they signal a need to address these tensions differently. Rather than the tendency for economic and short term benefit to be prioritised over social and sustainable environment goals they intend to seek a focus on co-benefits and move away from trade-offs. In so doing they are describing an intent to use tensions as a means of finding different thinking to unlock ways forward that are synergistic, they are seeking 'and', not 'either/or' solutions. If grand challenges indicate important and worthwhile area to focus, then tensions signify where the opportunity for different thinking may lie.

## The Role of Tensions as Business and Society Seek to Recover From a Crisis

Earlier in this book the idea of tensions as an indicator of the need for different thinking was explored. We will now consider these ideas in the context of business recovery. Tensions can be utilised to consider the dilemmas evident as business and society seek to recover from a crisis. This can be considered at a macro level, with big themes as we have just discovered with grand challenges, and equally as important at an individual business level. Tensions can be a helpful approach to framing promising ways forward and point towards possibilities for different thinking.

The pandemic has highlighted tensions which represent significant challenges, many of which are already recognised, such as tensions between short-term versus long term, economic versus social goals, economic needs versus health, competing versus collaborating and profits versus purpose, to name a few (Carmine et al., 2021) (Smith & Tracey, 2016). In addition, the crisis has highlighted tensions between local versus global supply, and supply chain agility and fragility, and many management areas about the way we work together and how businesses survive and grow (Howard-Grenville, 2021). These tensions have been amplified by the pandemic, not least where leadership and management has really mattered, raising questions about the quality of leadership in a crisis and of management where responses to the crisis have been poorly managed. These are all areas where business school academics have a voice and expertise that could help to make a difference. Consequently, a critical role for business schools is to be an enabler and catalyst of engagement with businesses and society to build back better and fairer and support economic recovery.

Chapter 9

# Conclusion: Answering the Call With Action

The book started with a call to action, and now ends with a challenge to answer the call. There have been many calls to action for business schools to variously rethink their purpose, identity, legitimacy and business models. There is frustration with the tendency towards homogeneity and conformity rather than diversity and differentiation (Ivory et al., 2006; Kitchener, Levitt, & Thomas, 2022; Thomas, Lorange, & Sheth, 2013). To date, there have not been many answers to those calls with suggestions of how this may be done (Peter, Smith, & Howard, 2018). The engaged business school proposes one way forward. It is a roadmap for change, one with scope for individual business school to determine their own path.

The arguments for change are not new, over 20 years ago a report by the Work Foundation argued that change needed to happen in UK business schools and needed to happen whilst in a position of relative strength (Keep & Westwood, 2002). It is a call which Mintzberg (2004) has subsequently picked up, arguing that change should happen while business schools are doing well, before a decline in success forces change. They point to the old adage that nothing fails like success. There has also been concern expressed that the most likely scenario for business schools going forward will be an unsatisfactory muddling through (Thomas, Chian, & Wilson, 2014). Sadly, it appears that little has changed despite the continuing concerns and for some, the sense that the sector may be on the brink of significant disruption (Peter et al., 2018). Why has it been so difficult to change? There are of course strong forces to preserve the status quo and to stand still, along with the usual inertia within large institutions (Thomas, Lee, Thomas, & Wilson, 2014). There are always vested interests, with the prevailing argument that if something appears to be working why change. And business schools are working, in the sense that they still generate significant income and accordingly have popular courses. Then the reward and recognition at both organisation level and for the individual tend towards conservatism and maintaining how things stand. If academics find reward with rules that they know how to play by, then what is the incentive to change?

The Engaged Business School, 149–150
Copyright © 2023 Anthony Sturgess
Published under exclusive licence by Emerald Publishing Limited
doi:10.1108/978-1-80382-941-820231019

So why change now? The book is a call to the academic and business communities to come together and release the promise of engagement between businesses and business schools. Business schools in many respects are a success story. They have experienced significant growth with some of the largest numbers of undergraduate students in the UK. Yet there is a persistent frustration about their relationship to business. As understandable as this may be, given the competing demands of juggling mass-education and the resultant resource constraints, this is not an inevitable outcome. There is a deeper sense that more could and should be done. Business need, policy direction and responding to crisis raise expectations and pressure for change with a motivation to do so, and an urgency to do so now.

The engagement of business with a business school is an opportunity, and the two worlds do have distinctive things they can offer each other. What makes them different is what makes engagement so valuable. Grey's (2001) argument about universities being different and distinctive is important, yet difference does not have to mean separation. As I have argued, a business school can be distinctive but can still maintain a mutually beneficial focus on being responsive to demand, whilst creating and disseminating the latest thinking that leads demand.

That said, the promise of a distinctive, mutually beneficial relationship between business schools and business is unlikely to be realised without effective relational engagement or, as one client manager concluded, 'it's all about the relationship'.

In 2010, Sir Michael Marmot produced a seminal report reviewing health inequalities in England. As the impact of the pandemic has revealed the stark consequences of what happens when inequality gaps are not addressed, so Sir Michael's words gain renewed significance. He argued that 'we have in our heads the knowledge, we have in our hands the means, to close the gap in a generation. The question is: what do we have in our hearts? Do we have the political will?' (Marmot, 2010). In a similar manner, Marmot's challenge can be directed to the topic of this book. So much of what is needed to build engaged business schools is known, and we have the means, the question becomes do we have it in our hearts?

Sir Michael Marmot's challenge asks whether there is a will to change. To this question, Edgar Schein suggests something more is needed in order to motivate the will to change. He describes frustration as often being the agent of change, implying that 'all forms of learning and change start with some form of dissatisfaction or frustration' (Schein, 1996). A frustration with the current reality and a recognition that we know how things could be different are a good starting place. However, Schein persuasively argues that frustration is not of itself enough. He proposes that to motivate change you need to 'connect with something you care about' (Schein, 1996). Frustration is more than apparent with so much of what passes for engagement between business and business schools. And the knowledge and the means to change are demonstrated in the engagement model, framework and process. So that leaves us with just two questions to answer; do we have the will to change and do we care enough to make it happen?

# Chapter 10

# The Engagement Story – The Study Behind the Story

The monograph is based upon my doctoral research of the engagement of one business school with several clients. I have subsequently applied the findings in a second business school and used that experience to further develop the model, framework and process.

The original study was inspired by my desire to reflect on a significant period of time invested developing a client provision within a business school. The motivation to explore the relationship between an employer and a business school is there partly because of the evident potential in such relationships, but equally because of the frustration that so much of that potential seems unfulfilled. The study provided the opportunity to reflect on a nine-year period spent developing approaches for working closely with employers in a university context. During that time I experienced first-hand the potential and frustration inherent in university/employer relationships.

Having established and developed the Business School's client provision (from almost nothing to the establishment of a client-specific department within the school), my research was aimed at developing a better understanding of the client/provider engagement process. In particular, I was interested in the factors that contributed to the development of those relationships. However, of equal importance was my intention to clarify my own thinking in terms of these relationships, and in so doing to add to the understanding of others involved in this kind of work. It is my hope that this research might help them avoid some of the frustrations I experienced, whilst also helping them to realise some of the opportunities which were evident from the cases.

The original study is the start point, but it then has been reinforced and extended with a six year period of application of the principles and practices in developing an engaged provision at another business school, where previously there had been none. Two areas of the study will be highlighted because of their significance to the approach taken in the book. The first area provides an explanation of how the importance and significance of the engagement stories emerged from the study. The second extends the application of tensions, a central theme for understanding some of the complex issues surrounding engaged business schools, to be used as part of the research analysis.

The Engaged Business School, 151–155
Copyright © 2023 Anthony Sturgess
Published under exclusive licence by Emerald Publishing Limited
doi:10.1108/978-1-80382-941-820231022

The original study applied a direct interpretative stance, supported by coding techniques to identify themes. This is in line with Stake's (2005) view that qualitative research often utilises both approaches, but with one or the other being used as the primary analysis, in this case that being direct interpretation. The holistic approach of a direct interpretive study was achieved by analysing stories to keep intact the views of those telling the stories. This approach countered the concerns that coding can result in the fragmentation of qualitative data (Saunders, Lewis, & Thornhill, 2003).

This may sound like a logical progression of an argument, however in reality the realisation of the importance and significance of stories to this study was something I stumbled upon. The contribution of stories to this study was almost missed, only becoming apparent during one of the later interviews. This interviewee told a story that strongly influenced the emerging code of 'building a rapport'. I had some doubts about this code, sensing that there was something more that I was missing. The story told was so powerful that it encouraged me to extend the scope of the theme, leading to the development of a code which was much more broad and significant: 'nurturing'. This expansion of the code would have been unlikely had the story not been read as a whole, enabling me to see the emergence of a much bigger picture. This then led me to re-read the findings section and the transcripts, in order to search for other stories which may also have inferred salient themes resonant with the findings so far reported. My intention here was to deliberately seek stories which were striking and thus helped to convey and reveal the broader 'story' of this study: how a business school develops a relationship with an employer organisation. I found that the interviews were full of stories, and it became clear that the use of stories may be a vehicle to keep participants' thoughts and ideas intact, in a way that would also more easily enable a direct interpretive stance.

I then turned to relevant literature to explore how to take the analysis of stories forward. What became apparent is that what I had discovered by accident did make sense and resonates with wider evidence, and it was also evident that I didn't seem to be the only one to nearly miss the potential of stories. This is a perspective supported by Maynard-Moody and Musheno (2014), who argue that 'stories should have an intactness, a wholeness, that should not be fractured during analysis' (2014, p. 349). What was also noticeable was that stories emerged naturally as a part of the conversation/semi-structured interview. This tendency is actually widely recognised in the literature as interviewees, often without prompting, tell a story to make their point, rather than simply answering questions asked of them (Elliot, 2005) (March 2010) (Maynard-Moody & Musheno, 2014). Yet despite this implied prominence in interviews, researchers have often suppressed stories or seen their analysis as problematic, and in so doing 'have not recognized the persuasiveness of stories' (Mishler, 1986, p. 69). Moreover, there is a view that such stories can be potentially advantageous for the qualitative researcher, because the interviewee uses the story in '"making sense" out of experience' (Elliot, 2005, p. 24). Since 'stories are told to make a point' (Elliot, 2005, p. 24), as a consequence, the narrator assumes responsibility for making their points clear, allowing a better understanding of their perspective to be gained (Elliot, 2005).

That is why the book uses the engagement stories of those who have been directly involved in an engaged business school relationships. The book then draws upon several differing sources to build the argument. Significant debates on contested issues are framed, and a wider evidence base from academic research, national reports and government reports are reviewed. Together they affirm and shape the themes that emerged from the practice captured in the stories. Then the continuing experience of applying these principles and the model in practice served to confirm, affirm and extend the ideas.

The recognition of the importance of tensions and exploring ways to understand them has been an important and recurring theme throughout the book. It therefore may not come as a surprise that there are arguments that indicate tensions are also important in the context of research.

Eisenhardt argues that the interplay between analysis, data and theory provides a particularly helpful context for theory building, asserting that 'creative insights often arise from the juxtaposition of contradictory or paradoxical evidence' (Eisenhardt, 1989, p. 546). Similarly, Klag and Langley use the phrase 'conceptual leap', to explain the process of 'bridging the gap between empirical data and theory' (Klag & Langley, 2013). This, they argue, can be achieved by exploring conflicting tensions that emerge in a study. This bridging process, avoids a tendency to move towards one extreme or the other of a tension, and instead encourages a progression to synthesis. It therefore seems pertinent to explore the application of the concept of tension as part of the analysis process. There is a clear suggestion, in the engagement stories, that competing tensions play a significant part in the debate about business school engagement with organisations. This recognition of the importance of tensions became a continuing theme as the data from the engagement stories emerged, prompting this discussion about how tensions can be incorporated into the analysis. In this respect Eisenhardt's (1989) contradictions and paradoxes, and Klag and Langley's (2013) conceptual leap to bridge a gap, both suggest that there is potential for tensions to inform theory building.

There is also a second way in which the concept of tension can be applied to analysis. As they reviewed the literature relating to conceptual leaps, Klag and Langley 'were struck by the frequency of elements of opposition or contradiction' (Klag & Langley, 2013, p. 152). This led them to identify four tensions which they considered helpful in creating the conditions for conceptual leaps. For example, the contrast between a deliberate, structured research method, and the results derived from the happy co-incidence of serendipity. There is also a tension between engaging with, and becoming immersed in the research data, and stepping back, becoming detached, and allowing thoughts to incubate. Not surprisingly, there is a key tension to be balanced between prior knowledge and pre-understanding, and the state of 'not knowing' (Klag & Langley, 2013). It is argued that holding these tensions, which are about how analysis is conducted, can provide a means for 'navigating among and around a series of dialectic tensions' (Klag & Langley, 2013, p. 161), in order to achieve a conceptual leap.

Klag and Langley particularly suggest that there is a common pattern to these tensions. Each of the tensions has one pole which seems grounded in structure and discipline, whilst the other pole reflects 'a liberating influence, offering openness to chance, to imagination, to surprise' (Klag & Langley, 2013, p. 161). They stress that an over emphasis on one or the other can be detrimental, instead arguing for a healthy recognition of the value of the different poles of the tensions. This perspective is not that dissimilar to Weick's (1989) call for disciplined imagination in the theorising process, which is another way of framing the pattern Klag and Langley suggest is evident in the tensions they identified.

What has emerged is that just as with the tensions evident in the discussion of engaged business schools, tensions in the research process indicate similar opportunities to seek different thinking.

## Making Sense of Research

One primary purpose of the study was to enable understanding of a particular case and to share that new understanding more widely. That said, I do hope that such understanding can offer opportunities for wider impact as suggested by Tsoukas's strategy of focussing on the particular, to refine and draw distinction with the general (Tsoukas, 2009). Consequently, a level of detail was presented in the study which allows readers to make connections and consider the extent to which the findings resonate with their own experience. In that respect, presenting some of the key stories told by participants can help readers to gain a rounded picture of interviewees who were '"making sense" out of experience' (Elliot, 2005, p. 24). The overall approach is based on a 'common sense' view of generalisability, as argued by Campbell (1975) and by Stake (1994), who contend that readers of case research will find value if the material resonates with their experience. Readers are therefore left to make up their own minds (Elliot, 2005), an approach which Tsoukas implies may be particularly relevant for a practitioner audience. As Tsoukas concludes, 'practitioners are invited to reformulate distinctions relevant to reported cases to take account of their own experience and thus make even more refined distinctions' (Tsoukas, 2009, p. 299).

## Research as Storytelling

Given the central place that stories play in understanding the engaged business school, it is interesting to note a view of researchers as story tellers. This is a perspective developed by Stake (1994) as a means to emphasise the value of studying the 'particular' in case studies. Stake echoes Campbell's sense of discovering what might be a messy and incomplete reality of the social world, whilst also recognising and accepting the competence of human beings to make sense of things (Campbell, 1975). Stake (1994) argues that readers of case research will find value if it resonates with their experience. In order for this to happen, Stake appeals to researchers to ensure that the case story is well told (Stake, 1994). According to Stake, such an approach recognises that the case should faithfully present the findings, but it also implies the need for the researcher to tell the story well. In doing so, the researcher, if not deciding what story to tell, to some extent certainly shapes which parts of the story is being told.

In that respect, I hope that I have been able to faithfully tell the stories of those engaged in business and business school relationships. Their stories are worth telling and I hope that the ideas we have explored and the concept of the engaged business school spurs us all to develop our own stories of engagement.

# References

AACSB. (2020). *2020 guiding principles and standards for business accreditation.* Tampa: AACSB.

AACSB. (2020, November 24). *How COVID reconfigured the business school enrollment funnel.* AACSB. Retrieved from https://www.aacsb.edu/insights/articles/2020/11/how-covid-reconfigured-the-business-school-enrollment-funnel

AACSB, I. U. (2022). *Lifelong learning and university-based business schools.* Tampa: AACSB.

Abreu, M., Grinevich, V., & Hughes, A. (2008). *Universities, business and knowledge exchange.* London: Council for Industry and Higher Education, and Centre for Business Research.

Aguinis, H., Shapiro, D., Antonacopoulougnosis, E., & Cummings, T. (2014). Scholarly impact: A pluralist conceptualization. *The Academy of Management Learning and Education, 13*(4), 623–639.

Alajoutsijarvi, K., Juusola, K., & Siltaoja, M. (2015). The legitimacy paradox of business schools: Losing by gaining? *The Academy of Management Learning and Education, 14*(2), 277–291.

Alimo-Metcalfe, B., & Alban-Metcalfe, J. (2005). Leadership: Time for a new direction. *Leadership, 1*(1), 5–143.

Alvesson, M., Karreman, D., Sturdy, A., & Handley, K. (2009). Unpacking the client(s): Constructions, positions and client—Consultant dynamics. *Scandinavian Journal of Management, 25*, 253–263.

Ancona, D. (2012). Sensemaking. Framing and acting in the unknown. In S. Snook, N. Nohria, & R. Khurana (Eds.), *The handbook of teaching leadership: Knowing, doing and being* (pp. 3–19). London: Sage Publications.

Anderson, R. (2009). The idea of a university. In K. Wither (Ed.), *First class? Challenges and opportunities for the UK's university sector.* London: Insitute for Public Policy Research.

Asik-Dizdar, O. (2015). To be or not to be... a profession: Management education and its discontents. *The Journal of Education for Business, 90*(8), 443–450.

Atta-Owusu, K., & Fitjar, R. D. (2022). What motivates academics for external engagement? Exploring the effects of motivational drivers and organizational fairness. *Science and Public Policy, 49*, 201–218.

Augier, M., & March, J. (2007). The pursuit of relevance in management education. *California Management Review, 49*(3), 129–146.

Bailey, K., & Breslin, D. (2021). The COVID-19 pandemic: What can we learn from past research in organizations and management. *International Journal of Management Reviews, 23*, 3–6.

Baldridge, D., Floyd, S., & Markoczy, V. (2004). Are managers from Mars and academicians from Venus? Towards and understanding of the relationship between academic quality and practical relevance. *Strategic Management Journal, 25*, 1063–1074.

Banks, G., Barnes, C., & Jiang, K. (2021). Changing the conversation on the science–practice gap: An adherence-based approach. *Journal of Management, 47*(6), 1347–1356.

Banks, G., Pollack, J., Bochantin, J., Kirkman, B., Whelpley, C., & O'Boyle, E. (2016). Management science-practice gap: A grand challenge for all stakeholders. *Academy of Management Journal, 59*(6), 2205–2231.

Bartunek, J., & Rynes, S. (2014). Academics and practitioners are alike and unlike: The paradoxes of academic-practitioner relationships. *Journal of Management, 40*(5), 1181–1201.

Bloom, N., Conway, N., Mole, K., Moslein, K., Neely, A., & Frost, C. (2004). *Solving the skill gap*. London: Advanced Institute of Management Research.

Bloom, N., Dorgan, S., Dowdy, J., & Van Reenan, J. (2007). *Management practice and productivity: Why they matter*. London: Centre for Economic Performance LSE.

Bloom, N., Lemos, R., Qi, M., & Van Reenan, J. (2011). *Constraints on developing UK management practices*. London: Department for Business Innovation and Skills.

Bloom, N., Sadun, R., & Van Reenan, J. (2012). Does management actually work? *Harvard Business Review*, 76–82.

Bolden, R., Connor, H., Duquemin, A., Hirsh, W., & Petrov, G. (2009). *Employer engagement with higher education: Defining, sustaining and supporting higher skills provision*. Exeter: HERDA South West and HEFCE.

Bolden, R., Hirsh, W., Connor, H., Petrov, G., & Duquemin, A. (2010). *Strategies for effective HE-employer engagement*. London: Council for Industry and Higher Education.

Bosworth, D., Davies, R., & Wilson, R. (2002). *Managerial qualifications and organisational performance: An analysis of ESS (Employers Skill Survey) 1999*. Research brief no RBX 05-02. Nottingham: Department for Education and Skills.

Bourner, T., Bowden, R., & Laing, S. (2001). Professional doctorates in England. *Studies in Higher Education, 26*(1), 65–83.

Bouwmeester, O., Heusinkveld, S., & Tjemkes, B. (2022). Intermediaries in the relevance-gap debate: A systematic review of consulting roles. *International Journal of Management Reviews, 24*(1), 51–77.

Bouwmeester, O., & Stiekema. (2015). The paradoxical image of consultant expertise: A rhetorical deconstruction. *Management Decision, 53*(10), 2433–2456.

Box, G. (1976). Science and statistics. *Journal of the American Statistical Association, 71*(356), 791–799.

Boyer, E. (1990). *Scholarship reconsidered*. New York, NY: The Carnegie Foundation for the Advancement of Teaching.

Boyer, E. (1996). The scholarship of engagement. *Journal of Public Service and Outreach, 1*(1), 11–20.

Brannick, T., & Coghlan, D. (2007). Defense of being "native". The case for insider academic research. *Organizational Research Methods, 10*(1), 59–74.

Brennan, J., & Little, B. (2006). *Towards a strategy for workplace learning*. Bristol: Higher Education Funding Council.

British Academy. (2021). *Health of disciplines report – Business and management*. London: British Academy.

British Academy. (2022). *Teaching purposeful business in UK business schools*. London: British Academy.

Broschak, D. (2015). Characterizing client relationships. In L. Empson, L. Muzio, D. Broschak, & B. Hinings (Eds.), *The Oxford handbook of professional service firms* (pp. 302–312). Oxford: Oxford University Press.

Browne, J. (2010). *Securing a sustainable future for higher education: An independent review of higher education funding and student finance*. London: Department for Business, Innovation and Skills.

Burke-Smalley, L., Rau, B., Neely, A., & Evans, W. R. (2017). Factors perpetuating the research-teaching gap in management: A review and propositions. *International Journal of Management in Education, 15*, 501–512.

Burke, L., & Rau, B. (2010). The research–teaching gap in management. *The Academy of Management Learning and Education, 9*(1), 132–143.

Cable, D., & Gratton, L. (2022, June 13). *What's driving the great resignation?* London Business School. Retrieved from https://www.london.edu/think/whats-driving-the-great-resignation

Campbell, D. (1975). III. "Degrees of freedom" and the case study. *Comparative Political Studies, 8*, 178–193.

Carmine, S., Andriopoulos, C., Gotsi, M., Härtel, C., Krzeminska, A., Mafico, N., ... Keller, J. (2021). A paradox approach to organizational tensions during the pandemic crisis. *Journal of Management Inquiry*, 1–16.

Carrie, A., Bredow, C., Roehling, P., Knorp, A., & Sweet, A. (2021). To flip or not to flip? A meta-analysis of the efficacy of flipped learning in higher education. *Review of Educational Research, 91*(6), 878–918.

Carrington Crisp. (2021). *The future of lifelong and executive education*. London: Carrington Crisp.

Carton, G., & Ungureanu, P. (2018). Bridging the research–practice divide: A study of scholar-practitioners' multiple role management strategies and knowledge spillovers across roles. *Journal of Management Inquiry, 27*(4), 436–453.

CBI. (2008). *Stepping higher: Workforce development through employer-higher education partnership*. Literature Review. London: Confederation of British Industry.

CBI. (2015). *Best of both worlds – Guide to business-university collaboration*. London: CBI.

CBI. (2021). *Seize the moment: How can business transform the UK economy?* London: CBI.

Chambers, L., Drysdale, J., & Hughes, J. (2010). The future of leadership: A practitioner view. *European Management Journal, 28*, 260–268.

Chartered Association of Business Schools. (2016). *Business schools delivering value to local and regional economies*. London: Chartered Association of Business Schools.

Chartered Association of Business Schools. (2017). *The Impact of Executive Education*. London: Chartered Association of Business Schools.

Chartered Association of Business Schools. (2021). *Business Schools and The Public Good*. London: Chartered Association of Business Schools.

Chartered Institute of Personnel and Development. (2021). *Learning and skills at work survey.* London: Chartered Institute of Personnel and Development.

Chartered Institute of Personnel and Development. (2022, December 9). *Evaluating learning and development.* Chartered Institute of Personnel and Development. Retrieved from https://www.cipd.co.uk/knowledge/fundamentals/people/development/evaluating-learning-factsheet#gref

Clark, C., Gioia, D., Ketchen, J., & Thomas, J. (2010). Tranistional idnetity as a faciitator of organizational identity change during a merger. *Administrative Science Quarterly, 55,* 397–438.

Cockerill, T. (1994). Custom-designed programmes: The strategic response and implementation issues faced by business schools. *Executive Development,* 28–32.

Coghlan, D. (2007). Insider action research doctorates: Generating actionable. *Higher Education, 54,* 293–306.

Collini, S. (2012). *What are universities for?* London: Penguin Books.

Connor, H. (2007). *Workforce development. What works and why.* London: The Council for Industry and Higher Education.

Connor, H., & Hirsh, W. (2008). *Influence through collaboration: Employer demand for higher learning and engagement with higher education.* London: Council for Industry and Higher Education (CIHE).

Currie, G., Davies, J., & Ferlie, E. (2016). A call for university-based business schools to "lower their walls:" collaborating with other academic departments in pursuit of social value. *The Academy of Management Learning and Education, 15*(4), 742–755.

Delridge, R., Gratton, L., & Johnson, G. (2006). *The exceptional manager: Making the difference.* Oxford: Oxford University Press.

Department for Business Innovation and Skills. (2011). *Higher education: Students at the heart of the system.* Norwich: The Stationery Office.

Department for Business, Innovation and Skills. (2016). *Success as a knowledge economy: Teaching excellence, social mobility and student choice.* London: Crown.

Department for Education. (2021). *Skills for jobs: Lifelong learning for opportunity and growth.* London: Crown.

Deschaine, M., & Sharma, S. (2015). The five Cs of digital curation: Supporting twenty-first century teaching and learning the five Cs of digital curation: Supporting twenty-first. *Insight: A Journal of Scholarly Teaching.*

Dowling, A. (2015). *The Dowling review of business-university research collaborations.* London: Department for Business, Innovation and Skills.

Drucker, P. (1999). Knowledge-worker productivity: The biggest challenge. *California Management Review,* 78–94.

Dyllick, T. (2015). Responsible management education for a sustainable world. The challenges for business schools. *The Journal of Management Development, 34*(1), 16–33.

Eisenhardt, K. (1989). Building theories from case study research. *Academy of Management Review, 14*(4), 532–550.

Elliot, J. (2005). *Using narrative in social research: Qualitative and quantitative approaches.* London: Sage Publications.

Emerald Publishing. (2021). Impact Pathways – A new type of article in IJOPM *International Journal of Operations & Production Management.* Retrieved from https://www.emeraldgrouppublishing.com/journal/ijopm/impact-pathways-a-new-type-article-ijopm. Accessed on January 2023.

Evered, R., & Louis, M. (1981). Alternative perspectives in the organizational sciences: "Inquiry from the inside". *Academy of Management Review, 6*(3), 385–395.

Feng, A., & Valero, A. (2019). *Business benefits of local universities: More skills and better management.* London: Centrepiece London School of Economics.

Feng, A., & Valero, A. (2020). Skilled-biased management: Evidence from manufacturing firms. *The Economic Journal, 130,* 1057–1080.

Ferguson, S. (1999). *Communication planning: An integrated approach.* London: Sage Publications Ltd.

Finlay, I. (2008). What's learning for? Interrogating the scholarship of teaching and learning. In R. Murray (Ed.), *The scholarship of teaching and learning in higher education* (pp. 16–25). Maidenhead: McGraw-Hill.

Fish, S. (2008). *Save the world in your own time.* New York, NY: Oxford University Press.

Fudickar, R., Hottenrott, H., & Lawson, C. (2018). What's the price of academic consulting? Effects of public and private sector consulting on academic research. *Industrial and Corporate Change, 27*(4), 699–722.

Gabriel, Y., & Griffiths, D. (2004). Stories in organizational research. In C. Cassell & G. Symon (Eds.), *Essential guide to qualitative methods in Organizational research* (pp. 114–126). London: Sage Publications Ltd.

Gass, R., & Seiter, J. (2015). *Persuasion: Social influence and compliance gaining.* Abingdon: Routledge.

George, G., Howard-Grenville, J., Joshi, A., & Thianyi, L. (2016). Understanding and tackling societal grand challenges through management research. *Academy of Management Journal, 59*(6), 1880–1895.

Giacalone, R., & Wargo, D. (2009). The roots of the global financial crisis are in our business schools. *Journal of Business Ethics Education, 6,* 2–24.

Gilbert, S. (2021, November 30). The story behind the Oxford-AstraZeneca COVID-19 vaccine success. UK Research and Innovation. Retrieved from https://www.ukri.org/news-and-events/tackling-the-impact-of-covid-19/vaccines-and-treatments/the-story-behind-the-oxford-astrazeneca-covid-19-vaccine-success/

Gioia, D., & Chittipeddi, K. (1991). Sensemaking and sensegiving in strategic change initiatives. *Strategic Management Journal, 12*(6), 433–446.

Gioia, D. A., Corley, K. G., & Hamilton, A. L. (2012). Seeking qualitative rigor in inductive research: Notes on the Gioia methodology. *Organizational Research Methods, 16*(1), 15–31.

Glasser, J. (2002). Factors related to consultant credibility. *Consulting Psychology Journal: Practice and Research, 54*(1), 28–42.

Globenewswire. (2020, November 10). *Demand for B-schools increases amidst global pandemic.* Globenewswire. Retrieved from https://www.globenewswire.com/news-release/2020/11/10/2123705/0/en/Demand-for-B-schools-Increases-Amidst-Global-Pandemic.html

Goddard, J., & Kempton, L. (2016). *The Civic University: Universities in the leadership and management of place.* Newcastle: Centre for Urban and Regional Development Studies Newcastle University.

Gosling, J., & Mintzberg, H. (2006). Management education as if both matter. *Management Learning*, 419–428.

Gourley, B. (2004). What is a 'public good' and how could it be decided? In *Higher Education and the public good* (pp. 5–6). London: Society for Reserach into Higher Education.

Grey, C. (2001). Re-imagining relevance: A response to Starkey and Madan. *British Journal of Management*, *12*, S27–S32.

Grey, C., & French, R. (1996). Rethinking management education: An introduction. In C. Grey & R. French (Eds.), *Rethinking management education* (pp. 1–16). London: Sage Publications.

Gronroos, C. (1991). The marketing strategy continuum: Towards a marketing concept for the 1990s. *Management*, *29*(1), 7–13.

Gronroos, C., & Helle, P. (2012). Return on relationships: Conceptual understanding and measurement of mutual gains. *Journal of Business & Industrial Marketing*, *27*(5), 344–359.

Gulati, R. (2007). Tent poles, tribalism, and boundary spanning: The rigor-relevance debate in management research. *Academy of Management Journal*, *50*(4), 775–782.

Gummesson, E. (2000). *Qualitative methods in management research*. London: Sage Publicatons.

Haldane, A. (2018, June 28). *The UK's productivity problem: Hub No Spokes. Bank of England Academy of Social Sciences Annual Lecture*. Bank of England. Retrieved from https://www.bankofengland.co.uk/-/media/boe/files/speech/2018/the-uks-productivity-problem-hub-no-spokes-speech-by-andy-haldane

Handy, C. (1995). *The age of unreason*. London: Arrow Books Ltd.

Handy, C. (1998). *The hungry spirit: Beyond capitalism: A quest for purpose in the modern world*. London: Arrow Books.

Hawawini, G. (2005). The future of business schools. *The Journal of Management Development*, *24*(9), 770–782.

Haynes, M. (2010). Business schools and economic crisis – A need for a rethink? *International Journal of Management Concepts and Philosophy*, *4*(1), 2–6.

HEFCE. (2011a). *Higher Education and Business Community Interaction Survey 2009–10*. Bristol: Higher Education Funding Council for England.

HEFCE. (2011b). *Opportunity, choice and excellence in higher education*. Bristol: Higher Education Funding Council for England.

Heifetz, R., & Linsky, M. (2002). *Leadership on the line: Staying alive through the dangers of leading*. Boston, MA: Harvard Business School Publishing.

Herbig, P., & Milewicz, J. (1993). The relationship of reputation and credibility to brand success. *Journal of Consumer*, *10*(3), 18–24.

Higson, P., & Sturgess, A. (2014). *Uncommon leadership. How to build competitive advantage by thinking differently*. London: Kogan Page.

Hilligoss, B., & Rieh, S. (2008). Developing a unifying framework of credibility assessment: Construct, heuristics, and interaction in context. *Information Processing & Management*, *44*, 1467–1484.

HM Government. (2019). *Business productivity review*. London: HM Government.

HM Treasury. (2021). *Build back better: Our plan for growth*. London: Crown.

Hoare, S. (2010, July 20). Good lessons in bad times. *The Guardian*. Retrieved from https://www.theguardian.com/education/2010/jul/20/mba-courses-career-business

Hogarth, T., & Wilson, R. (2003). *Tackling the low skills equilibrium: A review of the issues and some new evidence.* DTI Final Report, Coventry.

Hogarth, T., Winterbotham, C., Hasluck, K., Daniel, W., Green, A., & Morrison, J. (2007). *Employer and university engagement.* Nottingham: DfES Publications.

Homkes, R. (2014). *What role will leadership play in driving the future of UK manufacturing.* London: Foresight, Government Office for Science.

Hordósy, R., & McLean, M. (2022). The future of the research and teaching nexus in a post-pandemic world. *Educational Review, 73*(4), 378–401.

Housing and Communities. (2022). *Levelling up the United Kingdom.* London: Crown.

Howard-Grenville, J. (2021). Grand challenges, Covid-19 and the future of organizational scholarship. *Journal of Management Studies,* 254–258.

Howard, T., Lorange, P., & Sheth, J. (2013). *The business school in the twenty-first century: Emergent challenges and new business models.* Cambridge: Cambridge University Press.

Hughes, T., Bence, D., Grisoni, L., O'Regan, N., & Wornham, D. (2011). Scholarship that matters: Academic–practitioner engagement in business and management. *The Academy of Management Learning and Education, 10*(1), 40–57.

Hughes, A., & Kitson, M. (2012). Pathways to impact and the strategic role of universities: New evidence on the breadth and depth of university knowledge exchange in the UK and the factors constraining its development. *Cambridge Journal of Economics, 36,* 723–750.

Hughes, A., Kitson, A., Salter, A., Angenendt, D., & Hughes, R. (2022). *The changing state of business-university interactions in the UK 2005 to 2021.* London: National Centre for Universities and Business.

Hughes, T., Porter, A., Jones, S., & Sheen, J. (2013). *Privately funded providers of higher educations in the UK.* London: Department for Business, Innovation and skills.

Huxham, C. (2003). Theorizing collaboration practice. *Public Management Review, 5*(3), 401–423.

Industrial Strategy Council. (2019). *UK skills mismatch in 2030.* London: Industrial Strategy Council.

Institute for the Future of Work. (2022). *Introducing the Pissarides review into the future of work and wellbeing.* London: Institute for the Future of Work.

Irwin, A. (2019). Re-making 'quality' within the social sciences: The debate over rigour and relevance in the modern business school. *The Sociological Review, 67*(1), 194–209.

Irwin, A. (2022). Open up the business school! From rigour and relevance to purpose, responsibility and quality. *Global Focus: Annual Research, 1,* 39–43.

Ivory, C., Miskell, P., Shipton, H., White, A., Moeslein, K., & Neely, A. (2006). *UK business schools: Historical contexts and future scenarios.* London: Advanced Institute of Management Research.

Kakabadse, A. (1986). Consultant and the consulting process. *Journal of Mangerial Psychology, 1*(2), 28–36.

Kakabadse, N., Louchart, E., & Kakabadse, A. (2006). Consultant's role: A qualitative inquiry from the consultant's perspective. *The Journal of Management Development, 25*(5), 416–500.

Kanter, R. (1994). Collaborative advantage: The art of alliances. *Harvard Business Review,* 96–108.

Kaplan, R. (1989). Connecting the research-teaching-practice triangle. *Accounting Horizons, 3*(1), 129–132.

Keep, E. (2022). *What is the role of skills and the skills system in promoting productivity growth in areas of the country that are poorer performing economically?* London: Skills and Productivity Board.

Keep, E., & Westwood, A. (2002). *Can the UK learn to manage?* London: The Work Foundation.

Kewin, J., Nixon, I., Diamond, A., Haywood, M., Connor, H., & Michael, A. (2011). *Evaluation of the higher education transforming workforce development programme.* Bristol: Higher Education Funding Council for England.

Kieser, A., & Leiner, L. (2009). Why the rigour-relevance gap in management research is unbridgeable. *Journal of Management Studies, 46*(3), 516–533.

Kildruff, M., & Kelemen, M. (2001). The consolations of organization theory. *British journal of Management, 12*, S55–S59.

King, M. (2007). *Workforce development: How much engagement do employers have with higher education?* London: The Council for Industry and Higher education.

Kinnunen, H., Holm, E., Nordman, A. Å., & Roschier, S. (2018). Academic consulting – Income stream, impact and brand building. *International Journal of Innovation Science, 10*(2), 143–159.

Kitchener, M., & Delbridge, R. (2020). Lessons from creating a business school for public good: Obliquity, way setting and wayfinding in substantively rational change. *The Academy of Management Learning and Education, 19*(3), 307–322.

Kitchener, M., Levitt, T., & Thomas, L. (2022). Towards purposeful business schools: Deepening and broadening external engagement. *Futures, 144*, 1–13.

Kittler, M. (2018). Do we understand each other? Discussing academic exchange from a cross-cultural communication perspective. *International Studies of Management & Organization, 48*(3), 333–351.

Klag, M., & Langley, A. (2013). Approaching the conceptual leap in qualitative research. *International Journal of Management Reviews, 15*, 149–166.

Kriz, A., Nailer, C., Jansen, K., & Potocnjak-Oxman, C. (2021). Teaching-practice as a critical bridge for narrowing the research-practice gap. *Industrial Marketing Management, 92*, 254–266.

Kubr, M. (2002). *Management consulting: A guide to the profession.* Geneva: International Labour Organization.

Laing, P., & Lian, C. (2005). Inter-organizational relationships in professional services: Towards a typology of service relationships. *Journal of Services Marketing, 19*(2), 114–128.

Lambert, R. (2003). *Lambert review of business-university collaboration.* Norwich: Her Majesty's Stationery Office.

Learmouth, M., Lockett, A., & Dowd, K. (2012). Promoting scholarship that matters: The uselessness of useful research and the usefulness of useless research. *British Journal of Management, 23*, 35–44.

Lejeune, C., Starkey, K., Kalika, M., & Tempest, S. (2018). The impact of business schools: Increasing the range of strategic choices. *Management International*, 1–11.

Lewis, J., & Bolton, P. (2022). *The post-18 education and funding review: Government conclusion.* London: House of Commons Library.

Lewis, M., Andriopoulos, C., & Smith, W. (2014). Paradoxical leadership to enable strategic agility. *California Management Review, 56*(3), 58–77.

Li, L. (2022). Reskilling and upskilling the future-ready workforce for Industry 4.0. *Information Systems Frontiers*, 1–16.

Lock, D., & Hinxman, L. (2018). *Building an executive education team: Leadership, infrastructure and culture*. London: Chartered Association of Business Schools.

Lorange, P. (2005). Strategy means choice: Also for today's business school. *The Journal of Management Development*, 783–790.

Lorange, P. (2019). *The business school of the future*. Cambridge: Cambridge University Press.

Lund, K. F. (2020). Educators as curators: Displaying the caring art of teaching in management education. *Journal of Management Education*, 44(5), 527–532.

Machold, S., & Huse, M. (2010). Provocation: Business schools and economic crisis – The emperor's new clothes: Learning from crises? *International Journal of Management Concepts and Philosophy*, 4(1), 13–20.

Manser, M., & Thomson, M. (1997). *Chambers combined dictionary thesaurus*. Edinburgh: Chambers.

March, J. (2010). *The ambiguities of experience*. London: Cornell University Press.

Marmot, M. (2010). *Fair society, healthy lives: The Marmot review: Strategic review of health inequalities in England post-2010*. London: The Marmot Review.

Martin, J., Feldman, M., Hatch, M., & Sitkim, S. (1983). The uniqueness paradox in orgainzational stories. *Administrative Science Quarterly*, 28(3), 438–453.

Mayer, C. (2019, February 21). *The purpose and future of the corporation*. Seminer series. Cambridge: Center for Business and Government Harvard Kennedy School.

Mayer, C. (2021). The future of the corporation and the economics of purpose. *Journal of Management Studies*, 58(3), 887–901.

Maynard-Moody, S., & Musheno, S. (2014). Stories for research. In D. Yanow & P. Schwartz-Shea (Eds.), *Interpretation and method: Empirical research methods and the interpretive turn* (pp. 338–352). London: Routledge.

Mazzucato, M., & Willetts, D. (2019). *A mission-oriented UK industrial strategy. UCL commission on mission-oriented innovation and industrial strategy*. UCL Institute for Innovation and Public Purpose, London.

Mintzberg, H. (2004). *Managers not MBAs. A hard look at the soft practice of managing and management development*. Harlow: Pearson Education limited.

Mishler, E. (1986). *Research interviewing. Context and narrative*. Cambridge, MA: Harvard University Press.

Mitchell, V., & Harvey, W. (2018). How preferable and possible is management research-led teaching impact. *Management Learning*, 49(3), 363–373.

National Audit Office. (2022). *Investigation into the management of PPE contracts. Department of Health & Social Care*. National Audit Office, London.

National Centre for Universities and Business. (2022). *Modes and motivations for business-university interaction*. National Centre for Universities and Business, London.

National Co-ordinating Centre for Public Engagement. (2010). *The engaged university. A Manifesto for public engagement*. National Co-ordinating Centre for Public Engagement, Bristol.

National Co-ordinating Centre for Public Engagement. (2013). *Public engagement: What?* Public Engagement. Retrieved from http://www.publicengagement.ac.uk/what. Accessed on January 3, 2013.

Newman, J. H. (1907). Newmanreader – The idea of a university. In *The idea of a university defined and illustrated: In nine discourses delivered to the Catholics of Dublin*. London: Longmans, Green and Co. Retrieved from http://www.new manreader.org/works/idea/index.html. Accessed on 2015.

Nixon, I., Smith, K., Stafford, R., & Camm, S. (2006). *Work-based learning. Illuminating the higher education landscape*. York: The Higher Education Academy.

Nonaka, I., & Teece, D. (2001). *Managing industrial knowledge*. London: Sage Publishing Ltd.

O'Mahoney, J., & Adams, R. (2011). Critically exploring business engagement in academia the case of the U.K consulting industry. In A. Buono, R. Grossmann, H. Lobnig, & K. Mayer (Eds.), *The changing paradigm of consulting: Adjusting to the fast-paced world* (pp. 259–277). Charlotte: IAP - Information Age Publishing, Inc.

Osbaldeston, M. (2006). *Workshop: Executive education as an add-on or core business?* EFMD. Retrieved from www.efmd.org/attachments//tmpl_1_art_060131 ecwh_att_060131qojs.pdf. Accessed on July 2, 2007.

Parliament, U. (2021). *Upskilling and retraining the adult workforce*. London: The Parliamentary Office of Science and Technology.

Parry, K., & Hansen, H. (2007). The organizational story as leadership. *Leadership*, *3*(3), 281–300.

Payne, J., & Keep, E. (2011). *One step forward, two steps back? Skills policy in England under the coalition government*. Oxford: Centre on Skills, Knowledge and Organisational Performance.

Pearce, J. (2004). What do we know and how do we really know it? *Academy of Management Review*, *29*(2), 175–179.

Pearce, J., & Huang, L. (2012). The decreasing value of our research to management education. *The Academy of Management Learning and Education*, *11*(2), 247–262.

Pellegrinelli, S. (2002). Managing the interplay and tensions of consulting interventions. *The Journal of Management Development*, *21*(5), 343–365.

Perkmann, M., & Walsh, K. (2008). Engaging the scholar: Three types of academic consulting and their impact on universities and industry. *Research Policy*, *37*, 1884–1891.

Peters, K., & Howard, T. (2020). The triumph of nonsense in management studies: A commentary. *The Academy of Management Learning and Education*, *19*(2), 236–239.

Peter, K., Smith, R., & Howard, T. (2018). *Rethinking the business models of business schools*. Bingley: Emerald Publishing Limited.

Pettigrew, A. (2001). Management research after modernism. *British Journal of Management*, *12*(1), S61–S70.

Pettigrew, A., & Starkey, K. (2016). The legitimacy and impact of business schools—Key issues and a research agenda. *The Academy of Management Learning and Education*, *15*(4), 649–664.

Pfeffer, J., & Fong, C. (2002). The end of business schools? Less success than meets the eye. *Academy of Management Learning and Education*, *1*(1), 78–95.

Piercy, N. (1999). A polemic in search of excellence amongst business school professors: Cowboys, chameleons, question-marks and quislings. *European Journal of Marketing*, 698–706.

Pike, H. (2021). The Oxford miracle: Making enough COVID-19 vaccine. *The Pharmaceutical Journal*, 1–12.

Polkinghorne, D. (1995). Narrative confirguration in qualitative analysis. *International Journal of Qualitative Studies in Education, 8*(1), 5–23.

Poole, M., & van de Ven, A. (1989). Using paradox to build management and organization theories. *Academy of Management Review, 14*(4), 562–578.

Porter, M. E., & Ketels, C. (2003). *UK competitiveness: Moving to the next stage.* London: Department of Trade and Industry.

Research Councils UK. (2011). *Concordat for engaging teh public with research.* Swindon: Research Councils UK.

Research England. (2020). *HEIF policies and priorities accountability statements 2020–21 and 2021–22 to 2024–25.* Swindon: Research England.

Resolution Foundation Centre for Economic Performance, LSE. (2022). *Stagnation nation: Navigating a route to a fairer and more prosperous Britain.* London: Resolution Foundation.

Revans, R. (1998). *ABC of action learning.* London: Lemon and Crane.

Rouseau, D. (2012). Designing a better business school: Channelling Herbert Simon, addressing the critics, and developing actionable knowledge for professionalizing managers. *Journal of Management Studies, 49*(3), 600–618.

RSM PACEC. (2017). *The state of the English university knowledge exchange landscape.* Belfast: RSM PACEC.

Sadun, R., Bloom, N., & Van Reenan, J. (2017). Why do we undervalue competent management? *Harvard Business Review*, 120–127.

Saunders, M., Lewis, P., & Thornhill, A. (2003). *Research methods for business students.* Harlow: Pearson Education.

Schegelmilch, B. (2020). Why business schools need radical innovations: Drivers and development trajectories. *Journal of Marketing Education, 42*(2), 93–107.

Schein. (1990). A general philosophy of helping: Process consultation. *Sloan Management Review, 31*(3), 57–64.

Schein, E. (1996). Kurt Lewin's change theory in the field and in the classroom: Notes toward a model of managed learning. *Systems Practice.*

Schein, E. (1997). The concept of "client" from a process consultation perspective. *Journal of Organisational Change Management, 10*(3), 202–218.

Schoemaker, P. (2008). The future challenges of business: Rethinking management education and research. *California Management Review, 50*(3), 119–139.

Schor, J., Wen, F., Orla, K., Guolin, G., Bezdenezhnykh, T., & Bridson-Hubbard, N. (2022). *The four day week: Assessing global trials of reduced work time with no reduction in pay.* Auckland: Four Day Week Global.

Sehmi, R., & Slaughter, H. (2021). *Double trouble: Exploring the labour market and mental health impact of Covid-19 on young people.* London: Resolution Foundation.

Seo, M., Putnam, L., & Bartunek, J. (2004). Dualities and tensions of planned change. In S. Pool & A. Van de Ven (Eds.), *Handbook of organizational change and innovation* (pp. 73–107). London: Oxford University Press.

Shaprio, D., Kirkman, B., & Courtney, H. (2007). Perceived causes and solutions of the translation problem in management research. *Academy of Management Journal, 50*(2), 249–266.

Sieg, J., Fischer, A., & Wallin, M. (2012). Proactive diagnosis: How professional service firms sustains client dialogue. *Journal of Service Management, 23*(2), 253–278.

Siggelkow, N. (2007). Persuasion with case studies. *Academy of Management Journal,* 20–24.

Smith, R. (2007). Innovaton by networking: Why this critical capability must no longer be misunderstood or undervalued. *The View Journal Xplor European Edition,* (2), 9–12.

Smith, W., & Tracey, P. (2016). Institutional complexity and paradox theory: Complementarities of competing demands. *Strategic Organization, 14*(4), 455–466.

Smith, L., & Wilkins, N. (2018). Mind the gap: Approaches to addressing the research-to-practice, practice-to-research chasm. *Journal of Public Health Management and Practice, 24*(1), 1–11.

Spicer, A., Jaser, Z., & Wiert, C. (2021). The future of the business school: Finding hope in alternative pasts. *The Academy of Management Learning and Education, 20*(3), 459–466.

Stake, R. (1994). Case studies. In N. K. Denzin & Y. S. Lincoln (Eds.), *Handbook of qualitative research* (pp. 236–247). London: Sage Publications.

Stake, R. (2005). Qualitative case studies. In N. Denzin, & Y. S. Lincoln (Eds.), *The Sage handbook of qualitative research* (3rd ed., pp. 443–466). London: Sage Publications.

Starkey, K. (2006). *Dynamics of knowledge production in the business school.* Swindon: Economic and Social Research Council.

Starkey, K., Hatchuel, A., & Tempest, S. (2004). Rethinking the business school. *Journal of Management Studies, 41*(8), 1521–1531.

Starkey, K , & Madan, P. (2001). Bridging the relevance gap: Aligning stakeholders in the future of management research. *British Journal of Management, 12,* S3 S26.

Starkey, K., & Tempest, S. (2005). The future of the business school: Knowledge challenges and opportunities. *Human Relations, 58*(1), 61–82.

Starkey, K., & Tiratsoo, N. (2007). *The business school and the bottom line.* Cambridge: Cambridge University Press.

Stumpf, S., & Longman, R. (2000). The ultimate consultant: Building long-term relationships. *Career Development International,* 124–134.

Taylor, M. (2017). *Good work: The Taylor review of modern working practices.* London: Department for Business, Energy & Industrial Strategy.

Tenkasi, R., & Hay, G. (2004). Actionable knowledge and scholar-practitioners. *Systemic Practice and Action Research, 17*(3), 177–206.

The Royal Society. (2008). *A higher degree of concern.* The Royal Society, London.

Thomas, H. (2022). Perspectives on the impact, mission and purpose of the business school. *Global Focus: Annual Research, 1,* 2–8.

Thomas, H., Chian, L., & Cornuel, E. (2012). Business schools in transition? Issues of impact, legitimacy, capabilities and re-invention. *The Journal of Management Development, 31*(4), 329–335.

Thomas, H., Chian, L., Thomas, L., & Wilson, A. (2013). The unfulfilled promise of management education (ME): The role, value and purposes of ME. *The Journal of Management Development, 32*(5), 460–476.

Thomas, H., Chian, M., & Wilson, A. (2014). Future scenarios for management education. *The Journal of Management Development, 33*(5), 503–519.

Thomas, H., Lee, M., Thomas, L., & Wilson, A. (2014). *Securing the future of management education. Competitive destruction or constructive innovation?* Bingley: Emerald Publishing Limited.

Thomas, H., Lorange, P., & Sheth, J. (2013). *The business school in the twenty-first century: Emergent challenges and new business models.* Cambridge: Cambridge University Press.

Thomas, H., & Wilson, A. (2011). 'Physics envy', cognitive legitimacy or practical relevance: Dilemmas in the evolution of management research in the UK. *British Journal of Management, 22,* 443–456.

Thorpe, R. (2011). Positioning current UK management research. In B. Lee & C. Cassell (Eds.), *Challenges and controversies in management research* (pp. 17–29). London: Routledge.

Thorpe, R., & Rawlinson, R. (2013). *The role of UK business schools in driving innovation and growth in the domestic economy.* London: The Association of Business Schools.

Thorpe, R., & Rawlinson, R. (2014). Engaging with engagement: How UK business schools could meet the innovation challenge. *The Journal of Management Development, 33*(5), 470–486.

Toffler, A. (1970). *Future Shock: A study of mass bewilderment in the face of accelerating change.* London: Bodley Head Ltd.

Tosey, P., Dhaliwal, S., & Hassinen, D. (2013). The Finnish Team Academy model: Implications for management education. *Management Learning, 46*(2), 175–194.

Tranfield, D., & Starkey, K. (1998). The nature, social organisation and promotion of management research. *British Journal of Management, 9,* 341–353.

Tsoukas, H. (2009). Craving for generality and small-N studies: A Wittgensteinian approach towards the epistemology of the particular in organization and management studies. In D. Buchanan & A. Bryman (Eds.), *The Sage handbook of organizational research methods* (pp. 285–301). London: Sage Publications.

Tushman, M., O'Reilly, C., Feollosa, A., Kleinbaum, A., & McGrath, D. (2007). Relevance and rigor: Executive education as a lever in shaping practice and research. *The Academy of Management Learning and Education, 6*(3), 345–362.

UK Commission for Employment and Skills. (2010). *Developing leadership and management skills through employer networks.* London: UK Commission for Employment and Skills.

UK Commission for Employment and Skills. (2016). *The relationship between UK management and leadership and productivity.* London: UK Commission for Employment and Skills.

UK Research and Innovation. (2021). *Knowledge exchange and place: A review of literature.* Swindon: UKRI.

UKCES. (2009). *Ambition 2020: World class skills and jobs for the UK.* London: UK Commission for Employment and skills (UKCES).

Ulrichsen, T. (2019). *Examining the requirement for public funding for university knowledge exchange to deliver the 2.4% R&D target.* London: Research England.

United Nations. (2019). *The future is now: Science for achieving sustainable development.* UN Global Sustainable Development Report. New York, NY: United Nations.

Universities UK. (2020). *Concordat for the advancement of knowledge exchange in higher education.* London: Universities UK.

University Alliance. (2015). *Mind the gap: Engaging employers to secure the future of STEM in higher education.* London: University Alliance.

UPP Foundation. (2019). *Truly Civic: Strengthening the connection between universities and their place.* London: UPP Foundation.

Valero, & Feng. (2019). *Business benefits of local universities: More skills and better management evidence.* London: Centre for Economic Performance LSE.

Van de Ven, A., & Johnson, P. (2006). Knowledge for theory and practice. *Academy of Management, 31*(4), 802–821.

Vermeulen, F. (2005). On rigor and relevance: Fostering dialectic progress in management research. *Academy of Management Research, 48*(6), 978–982.

Vermeulen, F. (2007). "I shall not remain insignificant": Adding a second loop to matter more. *Academy of Management Journal, 50*(4), 745–761.

Voss, C., & Zomerdijk, L. (2007). Innovation in experiential services – An empirical view. In DTI (Ed.), *Innovation in services* (pp. 97–134). London: DTI.

Warhurst, C., & Findlay, P. (2012). *More effective skills utilisation: Shifting the terrain of skills policy in Scotland.* Oxford: SKOPE.

Warhurst, C., & Luchinskaya, D. (2019). *Labour market change skills utilisation: Definition, theories, approaches and measures.* Background paper for the European Company Survey 2019. The Warwick Research Archive Portal, Warwick.

Wedgwood, M. (2007). *Employer engagement. Higher education for the workforce: Barriers and facilitators.* Department for Education Services.

Weick, K. (1989). Theory construction as disciplined imagination. *The Academy of Manaegment Review, 14*(4), 516–531.

Weick, K. (1996). Speaking to practice: The scholarship of integration. *Journal of Management Inquiry, 5*(3), 251–258.

Weick, K. (2001). Gapping the relevance bridge: Fashions meet fundamentals in management research. *British Journal of Management, 12*, S71–S75.

Weick, K., Sutcliffe, K., & Obstfeld, D. (2005). Organizing and the process of sensemaking. *Organization Science, 16*(4), 409–421.

Whittle, A. (2006). The paradoxical repertoires of management consultancy. *Journal of Organizational Change, 19*(4), 424–436.

Wilson, R. (2012). *A review of business-university collaboration.* London: Department for Business, Innovation and Skills.

Wilson, D., & Thomas, H. (2012). Challenges and criticisms. The legitimacy of the business of business schools: what's the future. *The Journal of Management Development, 31*(4), 368–376.

Witty, A. (2013). *Encouraging a British invention revolution: Sir Andrew Witty's review of universities and growth.* London: Department of Business, Innovation and skills.

Worrall, L. (2010). Business schools and economic crisis – The only true wealth is the wealth of the mind. *International Journal of Management Concepts and Philosophy, 4*(1), 7–12.

# Index

Printed and bound by CPI Group (UK) Ltd, Croydon, CR0 4YY

25/02/2024

08394313-0001